# OVERCOMING LIFE

## ON A SMALL PLANET

*(HEAVEN-STYLE LIVING FOR EARTHLINGS)*

*Published by*
BASILEIA PUBLISHING
107 W. Independence Blvd.
Mt. Airy, NC 27030

http://www.basileiapublishing.com

Printed in the United States by
Morris Publishing
3212 East Highway 30
Kearney, NE  68847
1-800-650-7888

# OVERCOMING LIFE
# ON A SMALL PLANET

*(HEAVEN-STYLE LIVING FOR EARTHLINGS)*

*by*

Ron McGatlin

# DEDICATION

I lovingly dedicate this work to my children and my twenty six grandchildren
who are here now and all those yet to come.  May they always continue to be,
as they are now, real life examples of "kingdom living".

# ACKNOWLEDGMENTS

To all of my family and friends who have contributed so much to my life
and subsequently to this work:  Thank you from the depth of my heart!

Special acknowledgment and thanks:
to  Johnny McGatlin for his generous contribution of many hours of computer work;
to Lynne McGatlin for her delightful work on the illustrations;
and to Joe Hammond for his invaluable inputs on content.

# CONTENTS

## OVERCOMING LIFE ON A SMALL PLANET

*(HEAVEN-STYLE LIVING FOR EARTHLINGS)*

# CONTENTS

# CONTENTS

# PREFACE

Christians have divided themselves into many denominations and sub-denominational groups. The strife created by doctrinal differences ranges from subtle rejection to all out war.

Opposing doctrinal positions can be reconciled only by higher truth. Lifting the spiritual eye from doctrinal debates to a higher level of practical, personal revelation of truth can help dissolve conflicts.

The practical **"gospel of the kingdom"** that Jesus preached is that higher truth. Focusing on the revelation of the **"kingdom of God"** can reconcile doctrinal differences. **And more importantly, the revelation of the "gospel of the kingdom" can enable Christians to overcome in this life.**

Christians are often subconsciously, denominationally trained to recognize and reject opposing views of doctrine. Hearing a certain "buzz word" or phrase may instantly trigger automatic rejection. The word or phrase may be a perfectly good Bible word, perhaps even spoken by Jesus Himself. Yet the hearer may identify it with an opposing denominational view and automatically reject the truth being stated.

The focus of this work is neither denominational, nor theological. No particular denominational view is proffered, nor assaulted. **The intent of this work is to focus on the higher truth of the "gospel of the kingdom", both individually and corporately.**

This work is the product of over sixty years experience. Over forty of those years have focused on seeking to serve the Lord. By intensely studying His Word, and personally applying the revelation and wisdom, I have sought to successfully overcome great and severe obstacles of life, and to assist many others in overcoming victoriously in their lives.

This book is not meant to be read, but rather to be studied. The reader is encouraged to fully digest each portion before moving on to the next. The reader is also warned not to spot read or scan this material.

**It is extremely important that the reader carefully complete the first portion on "Hear With The Ear In The Heart", and enter into the "Prayer Agreement" before investigating the text further. Until the reader can sincerely complete the prayer agreement, it is strongly recommended that he or she read no further into the material.** It will probably be a waste of time and can lead to confusion.

Many Christians who think they know, from a casual observation, what this book is about will be surprised at what they find if they systematically study the material in the order in which it is presented.

Your patience is solicited. Should you encounter different thoughts or ideas difficult to accept, please do not quickly discard them. But rather place them on the shelf in your heart and allow the Holy Spirit time to confirm or deny them.

*"HE WHO HAS AN EAR TO HEAR LET HIM HEAR!"*

# HEAR WITH THE EAR IN THE HEART
## (THE SECRET WEAPON FOR OVERCOMING)

There is only one source of direction for our lives that will always lead us into the overcoming life of righteousness, peace, and joy. Our quality of life is directly affected by the decisions we make, the roads we take, and the works we do. Our lives are a composite of all the decisions we have ever made. Our entering into and walking in the kingdom-of-God lifestyle depends upon our ability to hear God clearly. God's infinite wisdom and understanding of all things is available to direct our lives. Finite man and his very limited intellect at best do not begin to compare with God's total understanding.

*Isaiah 55:2-3,8-9: "Listen diligently to Me, and eat what is good, And let your soul delight itself in abundance. Incline your ear, and come to Me. **Hear**, and your soul shall live ... For My thoughts are not your thoughts, nor are your ways My ways," says the Lord. "For as the heavens are higher than the earth, So are My ways higher than your ways, And My thoughts than your thoughts."*

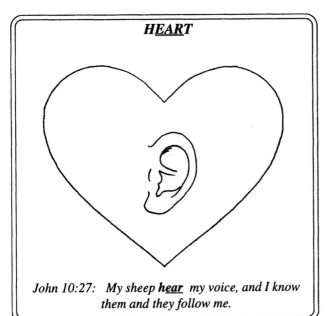

### HEART

*John 10:27: My sheep **hear** my voice, and I know them and they follow me.*

What exactly does it mean to hear God? How do we hear Him?

Don't we often lock up people who say, "God talks to me"? Aren't these the people who say, "God told me to kill all those people"? Am I saying you and I must become like these deranged, pitiable people? Certainly not! A counterfeit will always confuse or obscure the genuine.

Have you ever noticed that the devil almost always makes a bad copy of anything good that God does? Is his purpose perhaps to discredit the truth of God and to steer God's people away from it? Please lay aside the TV and Hollywood images that may cloud your mind and hide the truth. Let's look at this truth with an open mind.

The world does not understand Godly men. Abraham, Moses, Peter, Paul, and even Jesus along with most of the other great men of God in the Bible would probably be heavily medicated and locked up, with the key thrown away, if they were here today. Yet, today it is acceptable and common practice for individuals, law enforcement agencies, famous people, business leaders, and even government officials to call upon psychics, mediums, gurus, and other demonic soothsayers for guidance and assistance. Their objective is to hear from the spiritual realm what they cannot hear or see in the natural realm. This practice of looking to the devil and his copy for guidance and assistance is strictly forbidden in the Word of God. It may provide insight, but it is never without hidden costs! And it will never help to provide the good success of God in our lives.

We as Godly people hear God primarily through the revelation of His Word, the Holy Bible. God also speaks to us through other Godly people. He may even use natural creation, events, circumstances, dreams, visions, impressions in our spirit and any other method He chooses to communicate with His people. This is not to say that all events, circumstances, dreams, visions, and inner impressions are words from God. As an example, a dream might mean no more than having had too much pizza before bed. And a vision might just be your run-away imagination stimulated by the cold/flu medicine you took. It may even be an occult input from the enemy.

We can and must discern whether a word or thought is from God or from some other source. In order to do so, we must know God and his Word. We must learn to depend on God, the indwelling Holy Spirit, and the Word of God to discern light from darkness. God will never give us a word, thought, or direction that does not line up with His written Word and is not consistent with His character and nature. Therefore, if a word is not from God, we must exercise our ability to identify it and prevent it from entering our hearts or spirits.

Whether the input comes to us from the Bible or a spoken word from a teacher or some other source, we must **hear it with the ear in our hearts**. Hearing it with our natural ears is only a first step. It must be heard in our spirits to be effective and bring forth the work God desires.

Adam gave up the position of communicating intimately, one-on-one, with God when he decided to disobey God and partake of the tree of knowledge of good and evil. Adam chose to depend on using his own intellect to guide and direct his life, rather than hearing God. Jesus bought back for us the opportunity to turn to the tree of life and again communicate intimately one-on-one with Almighty God. **Prayer is both speaking to and hearing from God.**

There are different levels of hearing God. The first truth we are able to hear is that we are condemned by our sin and that Christ died for us to save us. If we have not received that revelation and acted upon it, we could read the Bible through once a week and still not hear any other word from God. After receiving that first word, we must continue on our journey with God, mature in Him, and begin to hear more.

Some Christians do not hear God at all. Many do not hear clearly and are never quite sure what they heard or where it was from. Others are not even sure that we are supposed to hear God. According to the Bible, it is natural for Christians to hear God. Some who love God above all else can accurately hear deep mysteries that move them from the ordinary to the extraordinary. To know God's plan and power, we must stop partaking of the tree of knowledge—trying to reason things out for ourselves—and start truly putting God first, above all else in our lives, to accurately hear Him.

*John 10:27: "My sheep **hear** my voice, and I know them and they follow me."*

*Psalm 85:8: I will **hear what God the Lord will speak**, for He will speak peace to His people and to His saints; but, let them not turn back to foolishness.*

*Acts 4: 19-20: But Peter and John answered and said to them, "Whether it is right in the sight of God to **listen** to you more than to God, you judge. For we cannot but speak the things which we have **seen and heard**."*

*John 16: 12-14: "I (Jesus) still have many things to say to you, but you cannot bear them now. However, when He, the Spirit of truth, has come, He will guide you into all truth; for He will not **speak** on His own authority, but whatever He hears He will speak; and He will **tell** you things to come. He will glorify Me for He will take of what is Mine and declare it to you."*

*John 16: 25: "These things I (Jesus) have spoken to you in figurative language; but the time is coming when I will no longer speak to you in figurative language, but **I will tell you** plainly about the Father."*

*1 Corinthians 1:20, 2:1, 2:12-16: Where is the wise? Where is the scribe? Where is the disputer of this age? Has not God made foolish the wisdom of this world? And I brethren, when I came to you, did not come with excellence of speech or of wisdom declaring to you the testimony of God.*

*Now we have received, not the spirit of the world, but **the Spirit who is from God, that we might know** the things that have been freely given to us by God. These things we also speak not in words which man's wisdom teaches but which the Holy Spirit teaches, comparing spiritual things with spiritual. But **the natural man does not receive the things of the Spirit of God, for they are spiritually discerned.***

*But he who is spiritual judges all things, yet he himself is rightly judged by no one. "For who has known the mind of the Lord that he may instruct Him?" But we have the mind of Christ.*

In 1 Corinthians, chapters one and two, the message is clear that God has not chosen the excellent speech of the wisdom of man to proclaim the deeper truths of the hidden mysteries of His kingdom. These mysteries are never received by the intellect of man, but must be revealed by the Spirit of God into the spiritual ear in the heart of man. Only by the Holy Spirit, may mortal man hear the things that immortal God has prepared for those who **love Him**.

*1 Corinthians 2:6-10: However, we speak wisdom among those who are __mature__, yet not the wisdom of this age, nor of the rulers of this age, who are coming to nothing. But we speak the **wisdom of God** in a **mystery**, the **hidden wisdom** which God ordained before the ages for our glory, which none of the rulers of this age knew; for had they known, they would not have crucified the Lord of glory. But as it is written: 'Eye has not seen, nor ear heard, nor have entered into the heart of man the things which God has prepared for those who love Him.' But God has revealed them to us through His Spirit. For the Spirit searches all things, yes, the deep things of God.*

There is hidden wisdom of God, deep mysteries that are going to be heard only by those who **really love Him**. Hearing the deep hidden wisdom of God will enable us to walk in His glory and freedom. If we are truly able to hear the deep, hidden mysteries of the wisdom of God, nothing will be impossible to us. True prosperity in every area of our lives will no longer elude us. It will no longer be just over the next horizon. We will not continue to search for the elusive will of God, but we can know His desire and direction for our lives. The power of God will no longer be only something that is about to happen in our lives, but will be manifested to accomplish His purpose in and through us.

The deep secrets of God are not revealed to those who love anything as much as, or more than, they love God. If the mysteries were revealed to them, they would use them to build their own empire or to please the god or gods that they love. **Only the spiritually-mature servant who loves God more than anything or anyone else can hear the deep, hidden mysteries** of God's wisdom which unlock His direction and power in life. Jesus taught the wisdom of God in a symbolic, figurative language that can be revealed only by the Holy Spirit. Those who are not spiritually-mature and do not love God above all else cannot hear and understand the deeper mysteries of God. Only a pure heart can hear the deep mysteries of God.

*Matthew 13:10-17: And the disciples came to Him and said to Him, "Why do You speak to them in parables?" He answered and said to them, "Because it has been given to you to know the **mysteries of the kingdom of heaven**, but to them it has not been given. For whoever has, to him more will be given, and he will have abundance; but whoever does not have, even what he has will be taken away from him. Therefore I speak to them in parables, because seeing they do not see, and hearing they do not hear, nor do they understand. And in them the prophecy of Isaiah is fulfilled, which says: 'Hearing you will hear and shall not understand, and seeing, you will see and not perceive; for the heart of this people has grown dull. Their ears are hard of hearing, and their eyes they have closed, lest they should see with their eyes and hear with their ears, lest they should understand with their heart and turn so that I should heal them.' But **blessed** are your eyes for they see, and your ears for they hear; for assuredly, I say to you that many prophets and righteous men desired to **see** what you see, and did not see it, and to **hear** what you hear, and did not hear it."*

**Mark 12:29: "You shall love the Lord your God with all your heart, with all your soul, with all your mind, and with all your strength."**

**Only the pure heart can truly hear the hidden mysteries** of the Word of God. The **desire** to have a pure heart does not make it so. The intent of the heart is not enough. It is from the abundance of the heart that the mouth speaks and our conversation of life emanates. In Matthew, chapter thirteen, the Lord compared a pure heart to good soil—soil cleared of weeds and rocks, and softened in preparation for receiving the word of the kingdom and maturing it to fruition. The wayside soil or hardened soil of the heart might be compared to the woundings of our life experiences which can harden our hearts as heavy footsteps of men and the wheels of their ox carts and chariots press down our "heart-soil". This hardened soil must be healed (softened) before the seed of the kingdom (God's kingdom patterns and principles for life) can enter the soil. Then the good soil can receive the deep, hidden, mysteries of God's kingdom wisdom.

The rocks in this passage may be likened to very firm convictions or hard, preconceived ideas. In other words, we already have fixed our minds about most matters in life. We already "know" what the Bible says: what men are like, what marriage is like, what to expect from life, what will happen if we trust someone, etc. We are not really willing to receive the new pattern or principle deep into our hearts and get rid of our old rocks. So, when we hear a word of the kingdom, it has no real root within us, and at the first sign of difficulty or opposition, it dies.

And of course, the thorns may be likened to the cares of this world. Self gratification through worldly things, such as: possessions, power, fame, position, control, and lust for sex or romance, will choke the kingdom-of-God life. In other words, we really like the principles and patterns that we are using now, even though they may not really be working for us in the long run. They are just too much fun to do away with. The kingdom-of-God lifestyle will be choked by these cares and there will be no fruition.

**Do we really love Him?**——Is there anything in our lives that we love as much as, or more than, we love God? What really abides in our heart? What fills our thought life? What desires truly are deep in our heart? What really is important to us? Where do we really get our delight? Do we really delight and abide in the Lord? Or do we just **say** we do? Do we **hope** we love God more than anything, and **hope** we delight in Him, and **hope** we abide in Him? Mature love knows that nothing else even comes very close to God. There is no very close second to the love for God in the spiritually mature.

The price we must pay to hear the deep, hidden mysteries of God's kingdom wisdom is a **willingness to lay aside everything** in our lives that is important to us, to figuratively sell all that we have to buy that "perfect pearl", that "field of hidden treasure". We must be willing to lose our lives to find the true life in God.

*Matthew 13:44-46: Again the kingdom of heaven is like treasure hidden in a field, which a man found and hid; and for joy over it he goes and **sells all that he has and buys that field.***

*Again the kingdom of heaven is like a merchant seeking beautiful pearls who when he had found one pearl of great price, went and **sold all that he had and bought it.***

*Luke 14:33: (And Jesus said), "So likewise, whoever of you does not forsake all that he has cannot be My disciple."*

*Matthew 16:24-25: Then Jesus said to His disciples, "If anyone desires to come after Me, let him deny himself, and take up his cross, and follow Me. For whoever desires to save his life will lose it, and whoever loses his life for My sake will find it."*

*Mark 10:29-30: "Assuredly, I say to you, there is no one who has left house or brothers or sisters or father or mother or wife or children or lands, for My sake and the gospel's, who shall not receive a hundredfold **now in this time**—houses and brothers and sisters and mothers and children and lands and, with persecutions—and in the age to come, eternal life."*

Let us purpose in our hearts this moment to release to God everything that is precious to us. Let Him have our wives, our husbands, our children, our ministry, our business, our hobbies, our health, our reputation, our need for acceptance of men, our religious convictions, our pet doctrines, all traditions, our secret desires, our very lives, anything in which we delight. Can we trust Him with these things? If we truly believe that He loves us and what He will do is best for us, we can release all to Him without reservation, to do with as He pleases.

If you are **willing,** or if you are **willing to be made willing** to release all that is in your hand, head, and heart, so that you may hear mysteries of the kingdom, pray the prayer on the following page from your heart. Fill in the blank with those special things you need to release. It is important for you to sign and date the prayer agreement. Entering into and signing the prayer agreement serves as a spiritual stake of commitment set in time. The signer is not seeking to hear a word from the author or even just to receive revelation from this work, but is specifically seeking to hear deep mysteries from God that will greatly impact and empower his or her life.

Mankind has searched in many areas for ultimate wisdom, peace, and fulfillment. We have built empires, compiled great knowledge, and pressed ourselves beyond reasonable limits in our search. Yet there remains a high level of frustration among the rich and the poor, the educated and the unlearned, the religious and the heathen, each and all alike.

Only hearing the deep hidden mysteries of God can end mankind's frustrations. Only as God's ultimate wisdom permeates our hearts can mankind know real peace and fulfillment. And only as we give our all to God, all we have, all we are, and all we care about, will we be given an **ear to hear** the deep hidden mysteries.

## Matthew 13:9: He who has ears to hear let him hear!

---

# PRAYER AGREEMENT

Heavenly Father, in the name of Jesus, by the power of the Holy Spirit, I repent and turn from all that is in my heart before you.

Now by an act of my will, I release to you all that is precious in my life. I specifically release to you my business, my family, my ambitions, my possessions, my _daughter_ _husband, finances, singing + writing dreams,_ and my _physical beauty_ .

God, I am one who truly loves you. Jesus, You are my Lord. I esteem You above all else. Nothing or no one else is my Lord.

In the name of Jesus, by the power of the Holy Spirit, I bind from me all the works of darkness, blindness, deception, delusion, man's traditions, and religion. I loose the Spirit of revelation in my heart.

Father, in the name of Jesus, I choose to open my spirit to receive that which was previously hidden, to receive Your wisdom. Grant to me the mind of Christ. Holy Spirit come in power, speak into my heart hidden mysteries of the wisdom of God. Fill my heart with the light and life of God. Give me an ear to hear in my heart. In Jesus name, Amen.

Prayed on this date _July 10_, _2014_, Signed _Lindsey R. Racy_

ADDITIONAL SIGNERS

Prayed on this date _____, _____, Signed _____

Prayed on this date _____, _____, Signed _____

Prayed on this date _____, _____, Signed _____

Prayed on this date _____, _____, Signed _____

# CHAPTER 2

## REVELATION LIGHT
### (GOD'S RAINBOW)

*1 John 1:5-6: God is **light** and in Him is **no darkness** at all.*

*Mark 4:22: "For there is nothing hidden which will not be **revealed**, nor anything been kept secret but that it should come to **light**."*

In these verses God speaks of Himself as light, pure light without any darkness. And He speaks of hidden secret truth being revealed as light. Obviously what God is saying here goes beyond His being the rays of the sun or the brightness of the electric light bulb in your lamp. If He were saying only this, we would have to do no more than flip the light switch on our wall, and God would appear.

God often uses language of natural things to communicate spiritual matters. Parables and symbolic or figurative language are common throughout the Bible. Jesus often taught unseen spiritual things by parable using visible natural things such as: grain fields, vines, branches, mustard seeds, pearls, soil, and many other natural things. He told stories of natural people doing natural things, all with deeper hidden spiritual meaning. These hidden truths must be revealed and become spiritual light to the hearer.

God has recorded spiritual truths in His natural creation. Creation may be thought of as an unwritten word of God, a natural expression of spiritual God.

*Romans 1:19-20: Because that which may be known of God is manifest in them; for God hath showed unto them. For the **invisible things of Him from the creation of the world are clearly seen, being understood by the things that are made** ... KJV*

*Hebrews 11:3: By faith we understand that the worlds were framed by the word of God, so that the **things which are seen were not made of things which are visible.***

In a discussion with a dear friend of mine, two positions of spiritual truth became evident. My friend

**RAINBOW OF REVELATION**
*1 John 1: 5-6: God is **light** and in Him is no darkness at all.*

*Mark 4:22: For there is nothing hidden which will not be **revealed**, nor anything been kept secret but that it should come to **light**.*

strongly held to a certain position. I was trying to explain my position—that there was perhaps greater truth and room for some balanced understanding. The discussion had become a bit intense and it seemed a good time for me to excuse myself for a bathroom break. As I left the room, my friend almost shouted to me, "Well it's either black or it's white".

I remember being alone in the other room and thinking that if it weren't black or white, then it must be gray, and that didn't sound too good to me. I began to pray and ask God, "Is it really black or white?." Instantly the reply to my question burst into my heart, my heart was flooded with light as God simply and profoundly spoke as only He can do and said "NO, IT'S A RAINBOW". The scripture "God is light and in Him is no darkness (black) at all", came to my mind. With God it is not black or white; it is all perfectly clear. Like the light of the sun, the whole clear light of God can be divided into all the colors of the rainbow. Yet when the whole light is together, it is perfectly clear light.

I'm afraid my friend was a bit shocked as I literally burst back into the room radiating my awe-struck excitement and bubbling out babblings about the rainbow of God.

"Black" and "white" are terms that relate to religious doctrines created by someone intellectually approaching and legalistically interpreting the Word of God. "Crystal clear" and "beautiful colors" are terms that relate to the revelation of the Word of God and the portions we personally receive by His Spirit.

Spiritual truth is revealed to us as we compare natural sunlight to the spiritual light of God. Sunlight as we see it is neither red, blue or yellow; it is perfectly clear. Yet it contains all of the colors of the rainbow. If that same clear whole light is broken down and separated through a prism it becomes red, blue, yellow, and every shade in between.

Did you ever wonder how so many men of God with apparent light from God could have so many different and seemingly opposing views of theology? Let's begin to answer that question with another question. **Does anyone have all the light?** Does God reveal all the light to any one person on earth today? I believe you will agree that He does not. Only Jesus has all the light. Our revelation is partial and therefore becomes as a color in the rainbow of God's whole clear light. We personally may be able to see one color: red, blue, or yellow; but we have not received by revelation the clear whole light of God.

We've probably all seen a color wheel with the pie-shaped sections of the primary colors of red, yellow, and blue, with all the blended shades between the primary colors. We can imagine that spiritual light from God, when broken down to its different parts, is like these pie-shaped sections of natural color. If we individually do not have all the light, but we do have some light, then we must have only a part. The portion that has been revealed to us may be a pie-shaped piece of red. But if God has not revealed the blue or yellow part to us, then we have a big empty space in our color wheel of spiritual understanding.

Many severe problems develop as we begin to fill in the empty spaces in our spiritual understanding apart from the revelation of God. He has not revealed it to us and yet we need answers. The question arises: "How can I fill in the rest of my circle of understanding?" We rationalize something like this: "I know what I will do. The Bible is written in my language. I will read and study it and figure out how to fill in the missing parts." We intellectually begin to discern the Word of God. But the Word of God cannot be understood and received by natural processes of the mind. Therefore, while we search for light, we find darkness. We begin to build religious doctrines of black or white by the tree of the knowledge of good and evil. We have now become a mixture of truth from God (our revealed pie-shaped, red part) and darkness (the other parts filled in with intellectual discernment).

Differences turn into denominations as we each from our own perspective of revealed color (red, for example) look at our brother's different color (blue or yellow) and decide he must be in darkness. We must recognize that we do not have all the light and must receive our brother's part to more completely fill out our circle of color.

We cannot go to the Bible and intellectually discern the Word of God and receive revelation. Intellectual discernment of the Bible is darkness and will never match up with revelation of the Word from God. We must receive our brother who has the true revealed color to fill in our circle. We must develop spiritual discernment. If we can, by the Spirit, discern truth, we need not fear darkness. We can receive our brother and his area of light without fearing that his darkness will contaminate our doctrine.

Many men of God have received an area of revelation from God, but then have filled in the rest of their color circle with intellectual discernment (darkness) rather than with the light (color) from their brothers. Only by receiving one another and **spiritually discerning** the color of revelation from our brother— while at the same time filling in his darkness with our color—will we ever come to the whole clear light of God.

Perhaps we can get new light from these verses as we see that not only does rejecting our brother indicate darkness within us, but it also assures our remaining in darkness because we cannot receive his color, his part of the light, unless we receive him. We do not need to receive **his** darkness, and **he** does not need to receive **our** darkness. By spiritual discernment we can know the difference. We cannot know the difference by holding on to teachings obtained from intellectual discernment. If we hold on to these religious teachings, we will reject every word that does not match up with them, including the revealed truth of God that our brother brings to us.

*1 John 2:8-11: "Again, a new commandment I write to you, which thing is true in Him and in you, because the darkness is passing away, and the true light is already shining. He who says he is in the light, and hates his brother, is in darkness until now. He who loves his brother abides in the light, and there is no cause for stumbling in him. But he who hates his brother is in darkness and walks in darkness, and does not know where he is going, because the darkness has blinded his eyes."*

## DIFFERENT MESSAGE FOR DIFFERENT SITUATION

One of the reasons for our different colors is that we have different jobs to do. We may not all come to the same balance of light. However, by working together in unity, with each of us being and doing our part, we will bring the whole clear light forth from the blending of the many colors. One important thing for each of us to realize is that our message is not the whole. We are only a part. Therefore, it's important that our message be delivered to the right part at the right time, and that it not be delivered where and when it should not be.

An example of the different messengers is what I call the "trumpeters of judgment" and "the singers of restoration". In the following verses, the message of judgment and the message of restoration is brought forth at the same time.

*DARKNESS & LIGHT*

*Isaiah 60: 1-3: Arise, shine; for your **light** has come! And the glory of the Lord is risen upon you. For behold, the **darkness** shall cover the earth, and deep darkness the people. But the Lord will arise over you, and His glory will be seen upon you. The Gentiles shall come to your light, and kings to the brightness of your rising.*

14

*Isaiah 60:1-3:* *"Arise, shine; for your **light** has come! And the glory of the Lord is risen upon you. For behold, the **darkness** shall cover the earth, and deep darkness the people; but the Lord will arise over you, and His glory will be seen upon you. The Gentiles shall come to your light, and kings to the brightness of your rising."*

*Matthew 13:41-43:* *"The Son of Man will send out His angels, and they will gather out of His kingdom all things that offend, and those who practice lawlessness, and will cast them into the furnace of **fire**. There will be wailing and gnashing of teeth. Then the righteous will shine forth as the sun in the kingdom of their Father. He who has ears to hear, let him hear!"*

These two distinct prophetic voices are sounding in the earth today. Clearly and loudly the trumpet of judgment is heralding across the earth, while at the same time the musical voice of praise is singing forth the message of restoration and revival throughout the land.

Hearing two different messages at the same time and observing the apparent conflict between the prophets can become confusing. Which is right: are we headed into "doom and gloom", or are we on the verge of glory and the greatest move of God ever on the earth?

Both messages are correct if they are delivered to the right people. The fiery message of judgment and doom is for Babylon (the Godless world system and the Harlot Church) and those who are walking in her. The message of glory and restoration is for New Jerusalem, the Bride Church—those who are being purified, having their hearts healed and coming to true holiness, those who overcome by the blood of the Lamb and the word of their testimony, and do not love their lives to the death. *(Rev. 12:11)*

The trumpeters of judgment and singers of restoration are currently not together as one because they have not yet fully accepted and received each other. Therefore, they are not able to receive one another's color of revelation. They assume that their own message is for a greater portion of the earth than God intended. So, erroneously, the trumpet of judgment is hurled at the Bride Church and the song of restoration is sounded to the Harlot Church. The resulting conflict and confusion further prevents the prophets from receiving revelation from each other. This results in

the judgment trumpeter having no view of the kingdom of God coming forth on earth now, and the restoration singer having no view of the vast destruction coming forth from the hand of God today.

As God further purifies His prophets and His Church by bringing forth healing to our hearts by the ministry of Jesus "to heal the brokenhearted" (Luke 4:18), we will see these voices of revelation come together. The glory of God will fill His kingdom Church even greater than He filled Solomon's temple.

*2 Chronicles 5:11-13:* *"And it came to pass when the priests came out of the Most Holy Place ( **for all the priests who were present had sanctified themselves, without keeping to their divisions** ), and the Levites who were the singers, all those of Asaph and Heman and Jeduthun, with their sons and their brethren, stood at the east end of the altar, clothed in white linen, having cymbals, stringed instruments and harps, and with them one hundred and twenty priests sounding with **trumpets**—indeed it came to pass, **when the trumpeters and singers were as one to make one sound** to be heard in praising and thanking the Lord, and when they lifted up their voice with the trumpets and cymbals and instruments of music, and praised the Lord, saying: 'For He is good, for His mercy endures forever,' that the house, the house of the Lord, was filled with a cloud, so that the priests could not stand to minister because of the cloud; for the glory of the Lord filled the house of God."*

The Church is to become the purified, cleansed and healed Bride of Christ, the New Jerusalem of God on earth. In her womb the kingdom seed (word) is planted and New Jerusalem, God's ruling city, comes forth on earth.

As the Bride Church is healed and purified, she is able to come together, bringing all colors of the rainbow of revelation back together, and her light becomes crystal clear. The glory of God is manifested in her and God's kingdom life rules on earth. *(Rev. 21: 2,9-11)*

We each have a part it the kingdom of God. As our hearts are purified we can reflect the bright color of revelation God gives to us. We are then well equipped to bring forth our part and to be blended with the others, forming the whole clear light of the Bride of Christ.

# CHAPTER 3

## MY PART IN THE KINGDOM

In the kingdom of God, if we are a part, we have a part. Scripture makes it clear that there are many parts. And though different parts have various functions, they all fit together to form the whole. Even those who are not joined to the body and are not a part of God's Israel, may have a function in the overall scheme of things (the universal kingdom, all creation). As an example, the ungodly may gather wealth for the righteous who will possess it later. Another obvious function is that of testing the saints of God and providing a source of strengthening and growth through experience. A weight lifter develops muscle as he overcomes the resistance of weights.

However, our focus at this time is understanding our individual parts in the kingdom, our parts in the body of Christ. We may try to function in the wrong area with little reward to ourselves or others if we don't know our parts. It's important that we be joined in the proper place in order to supply and receive from the joint next to us. In the natural, our whole body would suffer if any part of our body were dislocated.

*Ephesians 4:15b-16:  ...Him who is the head, Christ, from whom the whole body, **joined and knit together** by what every joint supplies, according to the effective working by which every part does its share, causes growth of the body for the edifying of itself in love.*

*1 Corinthians 12:4-7,18-21: Now there are **diversities of gifts**, but the same Spirit. There are **differences of ministries**, but the same Lord. And there are **diversities of activities**, but it is the same God who works all in all. But the manifestation of the Spirit is given to each one for the profit of all. But now God has set the members, each one of them, in the body just as He pleased. And if they were all one member, where would the body be? But now indeed there are many members, yet one body. And the eye cannot say to the hand, "I have no need of you"; nor again the head to the feet, "I have no need of you."*

One of the blunders of religion is that of trying to make each part exactly like all the other parts. As wonderful as an eye is, it would make a horrible toe. We must begin to realize that the nature of the body requires various functions be performed for various reasons. And different functions demand different tools, gifts, beliefs, abilities, emphases, and understandings. We, as individual parts of the kingdom, simply cannot all think exactly alike. We cannot all believe or understand the same things in the same way. We are neither equipped to, nor are we expected to be the same. Being different is not equated with being wrong. Religion has said "if you aren't like me, you're wrong and you're not a part".

Often we tend to pick a spiritual hero and begin to seek to be just like him or her. That might work pretty well, if we are supposed to be the same part as our hero. If, however, we are not that same part, we probably will not help ourselves or the body by seeking to act the part of our hero.

God made many kinds of trees for many different functions. Some bear delicious fruit, some nuts, some olives; some make great lumber; some make beautiful furniture; some are beautiful to look at; some make great shade; and others have other useful functions. All trees have some functions in common, but some functions are different and unique to each particular variety of tree.  All of these are trees—all members of the same family. All were created by the same God. All praise and worship God as they serve Him by serving His people and the world around them.

Each one serves in its own individual way. Even within the same type of trees, different characteristics exist: some peach trees are large; some are dwarf; some produce red peaches, some yellow; some have white flesh; some have deep yellow.  Some yield freestone peaches; some yield clingstone peaches.  But all the various peaches are still peaches. All have "their part". All peach trees have similarities, but none are exactly the same.  Even each leaf on the tree, if examined closely, will prove to be slightly different from every other leaf—on the same tree. No two are exactly alike.

Can you imagine the frustration of a peach tree if, it looked up and saw a walnut, pecan, or a tall pine tree, and thought it had to be and act like one or all of them? Haven't you sometimes felt frustrated as "mighty-oak" teachers and preachers declare "you must be like me"? Then next week a tall pine comes by and says, "be like me". Next, a prophetic olive tree comes by, and you think you've got to be like him also. Even if the trees are not saying, "Be like me and bear fruit like me," don't you sometimes assume you are supposed to be exactly like them?

Friend, the Word just does not teach it that way. Oh! For the FREEDOM to be who we are and to fit where we belong. We will be greatly blessed when we can allow our brothers and sisters to be different and stop trying to cut down every tree that is not just like us. God said **He** would cut down every tree that He has not planted. He does not need **us** to cut down what we deem to be "not of God" just because it's not exactly like us and does not teach exactly the same doctrine as we do. The word "doctrine" simply means teachings. It is a fruit from a tree. It is <u>made</u> by God. But it is <u>not</u> God!

We will each by revelation receive in our hearts the particular part of a teaching that will strengthen us in what we are supposed to be and do. We are not required to receive that part which is meant for another part of the body. If we did, we would become that part instead of the part that we are. We can all partake of the same Spirit and grow and bear unique fruit according to our tree. Every tree may receive the same rain, nutrition, and sunshine, but each tree will extract its part and may make different fruit from it. What is important is for each of us to determine what kind of a tree we are and what kind of fruit we are to bear.

It's obvious that more than anything else, the peach tree wants to bear peaches. Its whole reason for existing seems to be to bear all the peaches it can. All winter it's preparing to send forth blossoms early in the spring. And after the fruit season is over, it begins all over again to store the nutrients to make next year's fruit. Everything seems to indicate that the greatest desire of this tree's heart is to bear peaches. And year after year the desire of its heart is fulfilled.

What is **your** part in the kingdom? How can you know for sure? Simple. **What is the desire of your purified heart?** Psalm 37 says, *"Delight yourself in the Lord and **He will give you the desires** of your heart."* John 15 says, *"Abide in Him and you shall ask **what you will** and He will give it to you."* The key is in abiding and delighting in Him.

If we need or desire to get our delights from any source other than God, our hearts' desires will be adulterated. We will have difficulty in knowing our part. Some search all their lives trying to find themselves. Who am I? What is my purpose?

Only those individuals with healed hearts can be free from all need to delight themselves in something other than God. If we have unhealed pain stored in our hearts, we will always need something to make us feel better. As long as we have that need, our desires will be to fulfill it. We will get our delight in filling the needs of our hearts with money, power, position, fame, romance, sex, or whatever makes us feel better. Seeking these things will not produce the good fruit God intended. After being healed, we can choose to delight ourselves in the Lord, and our desire will be to bear the fruit God intended. We need only to follow these God-given desires, and we will walk in the middle of His plan. We each will know what kind of a tree we are and what our purpose is. We will simply carry out our heart's desire.

We are then free to do the will of God. We are no longer constrained to fulfill the needs of our hearts. **Freedom is the ability to live righteously in Christ Jesus by following the desire He has put into our hearts.** The bondage of trying to follow a religious order or set of rules is gone. Trying to be like someone else and do what they do, like they do it, is in the forgotten past.

## THE SERVANT GIFTS TO THE CHURCH

God has provided five special servant gifts to edify His people. The Bible refers to these offices as apostles, prophets, evangelists, pastors, and teachers. They are like five different types of trees. They are all servants. They each provide for God's people, but each in a distinctly different way. Each must think differently than the others. Each must have different tools, different revealed understandings of the Word. The pastor will always understand the Word as it relates to his office. The evangelist and the pastor may sit in the same conference, hearing the same Word from the same apostle, yet each will receive the part that feeds his calling.

*Ephesians 4:11-13: And He Himself gave some to be **apostles**, some **prophets**, some **evangelists**, and some **pastors**, and **teachers**, for the equipping of the saints for the work of ministry for the edifying of the body of Christ.*

The **apostle** tends to see the overall larger picture. Often he sees it, first in the spiritual, and then seeks to bring it forth into the natural realm. The **prophet** quickly sees anything that is being done wrong and what the future results will be. He may demand change to line up with what is right. The **evangelist** goes out to get the people to come to work on the vision. The **pastor** sees that all the people are well provided for, safe and as comfortable as possible. The **teacher** breaks the vision down into parts and begins to teach the specific details of each part.

These **gifts** function in the church, in business, and in all walks of life. The apostle in business may be thought of as one who starts businesses from nothing and serves as C.E.O. In business a prophet might be a trouble shooter. A pastor might be a personnel manager. An evangelist might be a traveling salesman. A teacher might be a technical instructor.

There are many other gifts, each having its unique function in God's overall scheme. All gifts and parts are needed. And they all need to be in their proper places doing their particular jobs. One of the greatest hindrances to each one of the parts doing its job is the lack of understanding and acceptance of the role God has given to each one of them. Often our temptation is to try to mold everyone into whatever we are. Pastors tend to seek to get everyone to function in pastoring. Evangelists want everyone to go out and gather. Apostles want everyone to come to the same level of spiritual understanding and commitment that they themselves must have to regularly work miracles to accomplish their purpose.

We don't need for everyone to be what **we** are. We need to help others to become what God has designed for **them** to be. We must resist trying to form people in our image and stop rejecting people because they are different. We must stop thinking that we are more important than others. We must learn to submit to the servant that God has sent in the area of spiritual grace God has gifted that servant in. Our ideas that we are superior because we have some status in the church or in a business can be a serious hindrance to our sub-

mitting to the one God has sent for a specific job. Pride in who we are and in what a great position we occupy is deadly. **There are no big-shots in the kingdom of God.** But when God sends someone with godly authority in a specific area, we must submit to them in that area and not think of ourselves more highly than we ought to think.

The need to be a big-shot comes from "unhealedness" in our hearts. If we are healed by the ministry of Jesus, we feel abundance in our lives and don't need to be bigger than our brother. We are free to allow the love of Jesus to flow to everyone. Love is the key that allows us to receive one another, to hear and see Jesus in our brother and to submit to the Jesus in them. Neither do we fear boldly stepping into the position of responsibility that He has called us to fulfill. In love, we serve one another.

Love is the greatest principle or law of the kingdom of God. God is love. Love causes the body of Christ to fit together and to "flow life" from joint to joint. Love produces true unity, and unity leads to production and prosperity of life. Love is the power of the kingdom. It is the single greatest motivational force in the world.

"Unlove" separates and starves the members of the body. It creates disunity which leads to a lack of production and poverty. Unlove flows death from joint to joint. Unlove is simply the lack of love. All sin flows from unlove. Love fulfills the law; unlove breaks the law. Every human conflict has its roots in unlove. Without unlove, there would be no church splits, no divorces, no wars, no crime, no bitterness, no angry hostility, no depression, no fear, no false pride, no rebellion, no evil lust, and no need for hell.

Our first and most important "part" in the kingdom is that of loving. Regardless of what our individual functions or offices are, we must be connected by love. Spiritual gifts, ministry, and good deeds are useless without the God-kind of unconditional love.

*1 Corinthians 13:1-3: Though I speak with the tongues of men and of angels, but have not love, I have become as sounding brass or a clanging cymbal. And though I have the gift of prophecy, and understand all mysteries and all knowledge, and though I have all faith, so that I could remove mountains, but have not love, I am nothing. And though I bestow all my goods to feed the poor, and though I give my body to be burned, but have not love, it profits me nothing.*

If we refuse closeness to another person because he has a different balance of doctrine, or attends another kind of church, are we showing love or unlove? What if we withdraw from someone because of rumors we heard about him? What if we see a brother or sister in sin and don't try to restore them? What if we think we sense something wrong about a brother or sister and talk to others about it, or maybe even preach about it, instead of honestly and humbly talking to the brother about it? Is that love or unlove? What if we refuse a spiritual gift from a brother because we don't think he's exactly right? Is that love or unlove? What does the scripture "bear one another's burdens" mean? — Someone once said, "He aint heavy; he's my brother."

As God gives revelation of His kingdom to a person the individual's focus moves from denominational doctrines and theological traditions that cause separation, and division. A revelation of the kingdom of God (kingdom of heaven) that Jesus taught in the Gospels will change one's life forever. Focusing on the revelation of the kingdom brings great harmony to understanding the Scriptures and helps unify the many parts.

# CHAPTER 4

## REVELATION OF KINGDOM

For many years I read and studied the Bible. It was the focal point of my life, my guide and source of direction. The living Word continued to amaze me day by day as old familiar passages continued to yield new light and meaning. To some degree I was accustomed to this wonderful phenomenon.

From time to time, as fresh revelation shed new light on the Word, it seemed that my whole Bible became new. When I was born again, the Bible suddenly spoke clearly of salvation by grace through faith in the cross of Jesus Christ. Later when a deeper experience occurred in my life, suddenly passages became alive to me that I'd some way not even noticed before. Many scriptures about healing, miracles, powers of darkness, casting out demons, healing the heart, and the baptism of the Spirit, "appeared" in my Bible.

These and other experiences, as great as they were, had not fully prepared me for what happened to me in January of 1986. I had left the ministry where I'd been serving and had no other occupation at the time. My day's were spent in a nice quiet travel trailer beside the house praying and studying the Word. I'd begun again to read the book of Matthew. This time one word seemed to be on almost every page—and again and again came from the lips of Jesus as He seemed to preface many of His teaching with this word. I knew I'd read it hundreds of times, but it had never really "been there" before. It had always just seemed to flow "under" or "behind" what was being said without adding meaning to the passage.

Because this word had suddenly "appeared," and because I knew little or nothing about it, I became curious. So I prayed a simple prayer. The answer to that prayer changed my entire life forever. Suddenly in a moment of time, it seemed everything I had ever known was shaken and began to take on a whole new light, a new meaning. Mysteries began to clear up about things I'd wondered about for years. Pieces began to fit together that I could never get to fit before. A deep satisfaction began to come into my heart as things began to become real and make practical sense for the present instead of religious ideas and doctrinal systems from the past or for the future.

I had simply prayed, "God, what does this word "kingdom" mean? What is the kingdom of God—kingdom of Heaven—Why did Jesus talk about it so much? That simple phrase, "kingdom of God", that did not even appear to be there before, has become the focal point of my life as it was with Jesus. In the days that followed this prayer, the heavens were opened to me. God was closer to me than ever before. Every question that I asked was instantly answered with staggering impact and clarity. I was amazed again and again and often overwhelmed, my mind reeling as God poured simple profound revelation of His kingdom into my heart. I became very careful about the questions I asked.

One of my reactions to all of this was that of thinking that people would surely come against me because many of the things God was revealing to me were different from the way my church had taught them. I'd never before heard a word of the kingdom message like God was giving it to me. I was afraid I'd be the only person with this radical message. Then God told me He was giving this message to certain men around the world and that it would eventually just seem to come up from everywhere like the grass in a field. In the years that followed, He allowed me to receive tapes from men in various parts of the world who had received the same message. Now, there are many churches preaching the gospel of the kingdom that Jesus preached. Praise the Lord!

Apparently, this is the season for the restoration of the preaching of the gospel of the kingdom. According to the Bible, the history of man is completing its six millennium and beginning the seventh millennium. Please do not let your mind begin to recall your version of end-time theology at this point. I don't know what all this means relative to end-time understanding, and I'm not bringing forth any particular "pre or post" view of anything. There does appear to be some relationship between the time in history and the preaching of the gospel of the kingdom.

*Matthew 24:14: "And this **gospel of the kingdom** will be preached in all the world to all nations, and then the end will come."*

When Jesus preached the gospel of the kingdom, many religious people had a hard time receiving it. The message he preached didn't fit their system of theology. Jesus warned them not to try to fit the new revelation into their old system.

*Luke 5:36-39: Then He spoke a parable to them: "No one puts a piece from a new garment on an old one; otherwise the new makes a tear, and also the piece that was taken out of the new does not match the old. And no one puts new wine into old wineskins; or else the new wine will burst the wineskins and be spilled, and the wineskins will be ruined. But new wine must be put into new wineskins, and both are preserved. And no one having drunk old wine immediately desires new; for he says, 'The old is better.'"*

Our wineskin is like a filing system. We each have within us a theological filing system, a system of mental file folders with headings and sub-headings. As an example, some of our headings might be something like: salvation, the cross, resurrection, Pentecost, Holy Spirit, baptism, healing, deliverance, second coming, and many more. Each piece of new theological data, when received, is analyzed, compared to the data in the system, and then filed under the proper heading.

The new wine of the gospel of the kingdom will not fit the old file system. We don't have a folder for it. And the revelation of the kingdom will not fit under any of our headings. We cannot simply make a new folder and stick it in somewhere. It will not fit under any other heading. The gospel of the kingdom becomes the system into which all other revelation and truth of God will fit. The kingdom that Jesus preached is the major heading under which all other God-given doctrine can be filed. We must have a new wineskin. If we try to patch in the gospel of the kingdom, we may become frustrated and burst our old wineskin, spilling out the contents with a big splatter.

All of the men that I know of personally who first began to receive the gospel of the kingdom were over fifty years old and some over seventy. They were all men who had experienced the moves of God over the past forty to fifty years. All were apostolic in the nature of their ministry. Some had planted hundreds of churches. Others had started Bible colleges. Some were prominent Christian educators in the secular educational systems of their nations. Some were Christian businessmen who had started many businesses. All were still actively involved in serving the Lord. They all seemed to be men with pure hearts toward God and no motives left except to serve Him. All of these men speak of a deep inner satisfaction as they received the kingdom of God revelation. Their souls were satisfied as different words and moves of God began to fit together in their minds. They seemed to have a more well-defined understanding of the purpose of man and our planet.

## KINGDOM OF GOD

Some people today have difficulty with the word "kingdom". There are many connotations attached to the word, "kingdom". Many religious views and some perversions may come to mind when we hear the word. Yet it is a very prominent Bible word. Jesus used the Greek word "basileia" which is translated "kingdom" in English, over one hundred times in the Gospels. The enemy would like for doubts and fears to enter our minds when we hear the word, "kingdom", because he greatly fears the kingdom of God coming forth in God's people.

One of the wonderful men of God who first began to hear the gospel of the kingdom said he had trouble with the word, "kingdom". He asked God for another word to replace kingdom. He heard the word, "government". A kingdom is a government ruled by a sovereign. Perhaps it will help us to think of the kingdom of God as the "government of God".

Most of the teachings of Jesus were aimed at defining the kingdom (government) of God, how it works, and how to enter it. For us to fully grasp the kingdom of God, we would need to digest all the teachings of Jesus and much of the rest of the Bible. But, the Holy Spirit, speaking through Paul in Romans 14:17, gives us perhaps the most clear, concise definition of the kingdom of God.

*Romans 14-17: ... for the **kingdom of God** is not food and drink, but **righteousness** and **peace** and **joy in the Holy Spirit**.*

The word translated "kingdom" in the New Testament is the Greek word "basileia" and comes from the root word "basis". "Basileia" means "foundation of power, realm, rule, or royalty. "Basis" means to walk, to pace, or foot".

## KING / DOM

"King" means "ruler or sovereign". "Dom" is the root from which we get words like "dominion, dominant, domain and dome". Thus the kingdom of God means the "sovereign ruler/dominion walk of God, the ruler/dom of God".

**The kingdom of God is a realm or walk, a lifestyle, sovereignly ruled by the foundational power of God, through which God's ruler/dominion is established on earth.** The kingdom walk or lifestyle is produced by the appearing or manifesting of Jesus through the Holy Spirit within God's people.

When the character and nature of Christ is developed in the hearts of God's people, they bring forth the purified bride of Christ. God's love flowing in and through His bride produces obedience, and righteousness prevails. Righteousness always leads to peace and joy. The bride or wife of Christ carries out her part as pictured in Proverbs 31:10-31, and the ruler/dominion of God is functioning in the world.

The secrets of how to rule our planet God's way are locked up in the revelation and understanding of the kingdom of God. They are extremely potent and can indeed produce the overcoming of any negative force in the world. There is nothing impossible to those who possess the understanding of the practical working of God's government on Planet Earth. This powerful understanding could be very dangerous in the hands of impure men who would seek to use it to establish their own kingdom, plan, or government. That is why God's kingdom ways will be revealed only to the purified bride. The kingdom of God begins with the purification of the motives of our heart.

Only a pure heart can hear the secrets of God's kingdom. This means a heart free from all other allegiances, a heart healed from all the enemy's wounds— a heart that not only intends to serve God only but also has the freedom to actually do it. It is a heart that has no needs or desires apart from God. That's why Jesus saves the lost, heals the brokenhearted, and proclaims liberty to the captives, and the opening of the prison to those who are bound. God will give us ears to hear His kingdom truth to the level that we are purified.

For about two years before I began to hear the word of the "kingdom", the Lord dealt with me extensively in what I call the personal ministry of Jesus. He led me to people who had gifts and anointings to assist in appropriating the ministry of Jesus to heal my brokenheartedness and bring about my deliverance.

For many years I had sought to serve the Lord with great zealousness and commitment. Yet, areas of serious lack and defeat were in my own life. The best I could do with all the help I could get was not enough. The zealous application of all the Biblical doctrines I knew could not keep me on track and bring me through. The firm directives to adhere more firmly to doctrine by my well-meaning brothers in Christ only worsened my condition.

It took a bold, fresh revelation from God to loose my bonds and set me on a road to restoration and greater heights than I'd ever before known. I will ever be indebted to those who have given of themselves to bring the personal ministry of Jesus to me—the ministry of healing the brokenhearted and setting the captives free. It's been my great pleasure and my means of repayment to those who ministered to me, to give of myself to carry the ministry of Jesus to others.

When the Lord revealed "kingdom" to me and commissioned me to plant the seeds of the kingdom in His people, it seemed He was directing me in two directions at once. One was the kingdom-now lifestyle, and the other was personal ministry. He's since shown me they are not at all different directions. **The personal ministry of Jesus is the cleansing process that we must go through before we can walk into the purified Bride of Christ, kingdom-of-God-now lifestyle.** Personal ministry and kingdom-now revelation are not separate directions, but are aligned in one direction toward the kingdom-of-God lifestyle.

**The goal of personal ministry is to eliminate, remove, or heal all hindrances to the manifesting or appearing of the life of Jesus in the person.** There are many needs, and stresses in the wounded hearts of people that drive them and hinder or prevent the appearing of Christ to produce the kingdom of God lifestyle in them.

*Colossians 3:3-4: For you died, and your life is hidden with Christ in God. When Christ who is our life **appears,** then you also will appear with Him in glory.*

*Galatians 2:20: I have been crucified with Christ; it is no longer I who live, but **Christ lives in me.***

As Jesus (appears) manifests His life in us, we walk in obedience to, and in harmony with the universal laws of God. Aligning with God's ways produces the favor of God in our lives, and overcoming in all areas of living becomes the norm in our lives.—Oh, God! I pray, Help me to hear and see clearly the revelation of Jesus in me, establishing your kingdom now on earth.

# CHAPTER 5

## THE ESTABLISHMENT OF KINGDOM

The kingdom of God was established on earth in Adam. From the ruling city of the Garden of Eden, Adam had dominion over the earth and lived in the presence and peace of God. Adam lost the dominion rights to Satan; the kingdom of God was taken captive, and the kingdom of darkness was loosed on earth. Though Satan functioned as a kingdom during this time, truly it was not a kingdom but a principality. He was **prince** of the power of the air **not king.** *(Ephesians 2:2)* The kingdom of God remained in captivity until Jesus came to redeem it. Christ Jesus came to earth to recapture the kingdom, to destroy the kingdom of Satan, and to re-establish the **kingdom of God from heaven, on earth.** *(Matthew 6:10)*

*John 18:36-37: Jesus answered, "My kingdom is not of this world. If My kingdom were of this world, My servants would fight, so that I should not be delivered to the Jews; but now **My kingdom is not from here."** Pilate therefore said to Him, "Are you a king then?" Jesus answered, "You say rightly that **I am a king.** For this cause I was born, and for this cause I have come into the world."*

God is and always has been in complete authority of all things. He chose to delegate the rule of earth to man. God limited Himself to work with what man would do on earth. He truly gave dominion and rule to man. Man is free to make right or wrong decisions and will live or die by them. Satan and his powers of darkness were present in the garden of Eden, but were totally powerless until man chose to disobey God and thereby release the power of Satan.

Positionally, the devil was completely defeated, and the kingdom, including mankind, was completely redeemed at the cross. In actual experience, Christ Jesus is now establishing in the natural what is already established in the spiritual. Man has not been removed as ruler of the planet. Jesus became man to redeem the kingdom. And then He *"became a life-giving Spirit"* to now indwell believers, empowering men to live in obedience and thereby establish His kingdom in the natural realm on earth.
*(1 Corinthians 15:45) (2Corinthians 3:17)*

Now on planet earth, including up to the second heaven around earth, the two kingdoms are operating in conflict. *(2 Corinthians 12:2, 1 Thessalonians 2:18, Daniel 10:13)* They are vying for control, each attempting to rule the earth. The kingdom of light and truth, (the kingdom of God), and the kingdom of darkness and lies, (the kingdom of Satan), are both seeking to sway the minds of men. Only mankind has the ability to decide which kingdom will be released and which will be bound.

**One of the greatest lies that the kingdom of darkness has perpetrated is that the kingdom of God is not available on earth today.** Satan's first attempt is to try to make us believe that there is no God, or that He isn't involved with us today. If that doesn't work, then he will try to convince us that God's kingdom is for another time, not today, or for another place, not earth. Satan would have us believe that the teachings and promises of God throughout the Bible, describing His glorious kingdom life is for heaven in the future, or maybe for earth someday, but surely not for you and me, here and now. A university professor in Texas was quoted as saying, "Everything in the Bible is in the nebulous past or possible nebulous future."

*Matthew 6:10:* ***"Your kingdom come, your will be done on earth as it is in heaven. Give us this day our daily bread."***

Just as Jesus taught us to pray daily for our daily bread, He taught us to pray daily for the kingdom of God to come on earth. Our daily bread is not just for the future sometime, but a very present-day issue. Neither is the kingdom (ruler/dominion) of God just for the future, but is indeed a very present-day issue.

The kingdom of God that Jesus taught about is the rulership of God on earth now. It is available to us now, with its righteousness, peace, joy, abundance and presence of God. The kingdom-of-God lifestyle is for us today, and many are missing it. That's why Jesus preached, "Repent for the kingdom of heaven (the ruler/dominion of God, from heaven) is at hand." Why

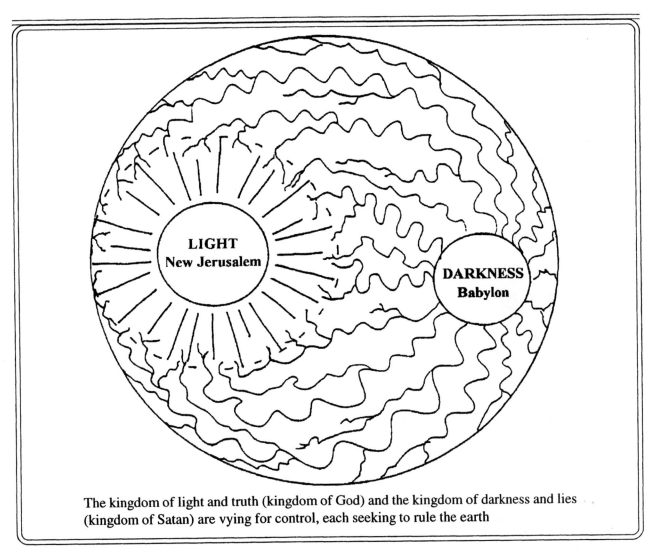

The kingdom of light and truth (kingdom of God) and the kingdom of darkness and lies (kingdom of Satan) are vying for control, each seeking to rule the earth

repent? **Repent because the kingdom lifestyle is here now** for us, and we've missing it. We've preached "repent" for many reasons: so you won't go to hell, so you can go to heaven, and others. All of these reasons are good reasons, but again they may seem a bit distant to the person who is suffering in this life now. The "at hand" kingdom promises life now as well as later.

*Matthew 4:17: From that time Jesus began to preach and to say, **"Repent, for the kingdom of heaven is at hand."***

*Mark 1:14-15: Jesus came to Galilee, preaching the **gospel of the kingdom of God,** and saying, **"The time is fulfilled, and the kingdom of God is at hand. Repent,** and believe in the gospel."*

*Matthew 4:23-24: Now Jesus went about all Galilee, **teaching** in their synagogues, **preaching the gospel of the kingdom**, and healing all kinds of disease among the people. ...they brought to Him all sick people who were afflicted with various diseases and torments and those who were demon-possessed, epileptics, and paralytics; and He healed them.*

Jesus taught and preached the gospel (good news) of the kingdom of God and demonstrated the authority of God's kingdom over the enemy kingdom of Satan by casting out the demon spirits, destroying their work, and healing the people.

*Matthew 12:28: "But if I cast out demons by the Spirit of God, surely the kingdom of God has come upon you."*

*Matthew 9:35: And Jesus went about **all the cities and villages, teaching** in their synagogues, **preaching the gospel of the kingdom,** and healing every sickness and every disease among the people.*

Multitudes began to come as they saw the authority of the kingdom of light overcome the kingdom of darkness. Jesus instructed and sent out the twelve disciples to *"preach the gospel of the kingdom is at hand, heal the sick, cleanse the lepers, raise the dead, and cast out demons..."* (Matt.10:7-8).

When Jesus sent out the seventy other disciples they were instructed to *"heal the sick who are there, and say to them, 'The kingdom of God has come near to you.'"* But for those who were aligned with the opposing kingdom and would not receive them, they were to wipe off the dust of their feet against that city and say, *"Nevertheless know this, that the kingdom of God has come near to you..."* (Luke 10:9-11).

Immediately prior to Jesus' ascending to the right hand of God, He spoke these words of instructions to His disciples, *"Go ye into all the world and **preach the gospel** to every creature..."* (Mark 16:15).

He went on to include casting out demons and healing the sick. What gospel was he talking about? Yes, He meant for them to **preach the gospel of the kingdom.**

Hearing the gospel (good news) of the kingdom-of-God life **now** with all its qualities and benefits, and realizing we are missing it, is the only sufficient reason for true repentance. This real repentance turns us toward salvation. Those who hear the gospel of the kingdom and believe will repent and be saved, *"but he who does not believe will be condemned"* (Mark 16:16). **When we see the goal, the abundant, overcoming kingdom-potential life of peace and joy, we will turn toward the light and persevere until we overcome.** We overcome the enemy kingdom in our personal lives and eventually overcome the enemy's hold on the world. In a practical real sense, we destroy the works of darkness and establish the works of the kingdom of light.

The devil and all the powers of darkness fear the gospel of the kingdom more than any other doctrine or teaching of the Word of God. The "dreaded" gospel of the kingdom will end the reign of darkness on the earth. As people realize the wonderful potential of Jesus Christ living in them now to destroy evil and bring forth true righteousness with all its joy and peace, they will persevere and overcome. The powers of darkness will do all they possibly can to prevent, delay, or pervert the teaching of the gospel of the kingdom.

Some of the enemy's tactics will include sending out a smoke screen of false teachings that look and sound something like the true message. These deceptive teachings will always have enough error in them to discredit the teaching when they are discovered. This sets the stage for the disciple to also reject the truth when it comes to him, because it looks much like the false doctrine. The disciple must, from his pure heart, spiritually discern the truth to determine the difference.

Another tactic is to discredit the teacher and his motives. The enemy will preach and teach a perversion of the kingdom message. The perversion will make it seem that the message is a means for men to take dominion to get what they want; to control as they desire from their own fleshly hearts.

The enemy will set up extensive snares to find grounds for discrediting accusations against the kingdom teacher. Insignificant incidents that would normally be dealt with and quickly forgotten will be blown out of proportion and used to slander godly men. When the enemy can find nothing, he will invent something from nothing. He will build an illusion from the impurities of a person's own heart and cause him or her to project that illusion on the man of God. Others will accept the illusion and corroborate the accusation.

Perhaps the most effective scheme of the devil is to assist men to develop alternate doctrines to replace the truth. For many years I personally accepted some of these alternate theological teachings. I was taught that the "at-hand kingdom" meant Jesus came and made an offer of the kingdom to Israel, which they refused. The kingdom was in Jesus and "at hand" at that time. But, since they refused the kingdom, Jesus returned to heaven, taking all potential for the kingdom with Him and would return at a later time and establish the kingdom of God. The best we could hope for at this time was to get people saved and try to hang on till He would come to take us out of this wicked world, or until we could die and go to heaven. It always bothered me that Jesus spent most of his brief ministry and most of the recorded Gospels teaching kingdom principles that we could not use until a future thousand-year reign.

Unfortunately many of us are testimonies of the enemy's effectiveness in hiding the gospel of the kingdom. We yet need to know; what is the gospel of the kingdom?

# CHAPTER 6

## THE GOSPEL OF THE KINGDOM

Jesus preached the gospel of the kingdom. He sent the twelve and the seventy disciples out to preach the gospel of the kingdom and told all disciples to preach this same gospel. Is the gospel of the kingdom any different from the gospel of salvation or being born again? We have preached the cross and personal salvation in Jesus for many years. Is that the gospel Jesus preached? Is it the gospel that the twelve and the seventy preached? Shouldn't we be preaching the gospel Jesus preached? God has been restoring revelation to His church in waves or layers. After one wave comes and men receive it and that layer is in place, then another wave of restoration brings another layer. The new layer does not replace the last one; it builds upon it.

In recent years, the gospel of the kingdom has been widely restored. The gospel we previously preached focused on missing hell and getting into heaven when we died. For the most part, there was little or no real help for living life today. We tended to write off this life and looked forward to dying to have victory, or to Jesus' coming back and rescuing us from this mess. Certainly the Lord's bodily return, and heaven with all its wonder, are primary to our Christian faith and foundation blocks of our understanding.

The gospel of the kingdom that Jesus preached focused on heaven's ways coming to earth more than our going to heaven. (*"Thy kingdom come, thy will be done, on earth as it is in heaven."*) He taught how to live in the highest order of life that would bring peace on earth and goodwill toward men. There is, however, another being on earth that desires his will on earth and not God's. I wonder who would like to cloud our minds and prevent us from seeing the potential of the will of God on earth?

Gospel means "good news"; kingdom refers to "ruler/dominion". The gospel of the kingdom of heaven or kingdom of God, means "the good news of the ruler dominion of heaven, or God". Or another way to say it is: "the good news of the government of God from heaven at hand on earth". The good news is that the blessings of God's rule are potentially available to His children.

Jesus announced the blessings of His kingdom in that portion of Scripture we call the Beatitudes. He had been preaching the gospel of the kingdom, healing the sick, and casting out demons all about Galilee. And **seeing the multitude,** He began to speak to His disciples, telling them that the needy people were blessed **now**. The kingdom is finally come, and those who are entering are blessed. Before the kingdom, those who mourned, just mourned. Now they will be comforted.

*Matthew 5:3-6:* *"Blessed are the poor in spirit, for theirs is the kingdom of heaven. Blessed are those who mourn, for they shall be comforted. Blessed are the meek, for they shall inherit the earth. Blessed are those who hunger and thirst for righteousness, for they shall be filled."*

Let me illustrate the difference between the gospel of being born again just to go to heaven and the gospel of the kingdom with this story:

A man had set out to cross a large swamp in a small boat. He had paddled well into the swamp and was attacked by several large alligators. The attack was so vicious that the small boat was damaged and it sank. The man was left standing in about waist-deep, murky water with only his paddle to fight off the alligators. The fight was so fierce that his paddle was broken. He was now left with only a stub of a paddle with which to jab and beat the alligators.

A voice heralded from a distant shore, "Hey out there! I've got good news for you. A big government man was here a while back and looked at this swamp. He promised to come back someday with a big crew and drain it."

Jesus' coming back and the "heaven someday" message is good news. But the gospel of the kingdom that Jesus preached can also help us with our alligators now. As we continue our story:

A man in a boat appeared and glided quickly to the man in the water and asked, "Do you need some help?"

"Yes! Please help me!," the man anxiously replied.

The man in the boat commanded the alligators to stop their attack. Immediately, the alligators swam away. The man in the boat helped the tired, wet and bloody man into his boat. He gave him dry clothes and medicine which quickly healed the wounds. As they were gliding toward their destination, the man in the boat told the rescued man. "Oh, by the way, have you heard, we are going to drain this swamp someday."

As mankind sees the reality of the kingdom message and its overcoming power the devil will be made powerless. This is why the kingdom of darkness so violently opposes the kingdom-of-God-now message. There is a violent pressing involved in entering the kingdom-of-God walk. It is not a pressing or violence toward or from God, but from the opposition, the kingdom of darkness.

*Luke 16:16: "The law and the prophets were until John. Since that time the kingdom of God has been preached, and everyone is **pressing** into it."*

*Matthew 11:12: "And from the days of John the Baptist till now the kingdom of heaven suffers violence, and the violent take it by **force.**"*

There is often more opposition toward the kingdom message than any other. The devil is much less threatened by a message of "heaven some day in the future". Our seeing the rule of God only in the future allows the devil to continue his dirty work now. The simple message of Jesus, "Repent, for the kingdom of God is at hand", the kingdom-is-now gospel, draws violent reactions from anyone who is, in some way, infected with or influenced by the opposing kingdom. The Lord spoke of kingdom rising against kingdom and nation (or tribe) against nation *(Matthew 24:7)*.

*Matthew 24:10-11: "... many will be offended, will betray one another and will hate one another. Then many false prophets will rise up and deceive many, and because lawlessness will abound, the love of many will grow cold. But he who endures to the end shall be saved. And this **gospel of the kingdom** will be preached in all the world to all nations, and then the end will come."*

*Matthew 10:21: "Now brother will deliver up brother to death, and a father his child; and children will rise up against parents and cause them to be put to death."*

*Matthew 10:34,36: "Do not think that I came to bring peace on earth. I did not come to bring peace, but a sword. And a man's foes will be those of his own household."*

Remember, the conflict is between the kingdom of God and the kingdom of darkness. *"We wrestle not against flesh and blood, but against principalities, against powers, against the rulers of darkness."* *(Ephesians 6:12)*

The spiritual battle is for the prize of entering and walking in the kingdom of God lifestyle; not just being born again, nor just going to heaven when we die.

# CHAPTER 7

## UNDERSTANDING KINGDOM

The rich understandings of the kingdom of God are hidden in the Word of God, veiled in **figurative symbolic language** that can be revealed to the mind only by the Spirit of God. For centuries we have read and studied the Bible, yet the understanding of "kingdom" will be revealed to us only at the level we are ready to receive it, and in the season that God desires.

**The Bible uses a <u>natural word</u> about a <u>natural thing</u> to represent a spiritual thing.** Once we have the spiritual meaning of the natural word, we can use that word to communicate the spiritual thought. For example, we have referred to the "Bride of Christ" several times. We all know that we are not referring to a literal bride. A natural bride is one female person who is being married to a husband. The "Bride of Christ" is a figurative term representing all "purified believers in whom Christ dwells". The believers may be male or female, old or young, of any heritage, and of any number. Yet they can all be described collectively in the term "Bride of Christ". We all know when the Bible speaks of the "milk of the Word", that it is not talking about a white liquid in a bottle, or when it speaks of the "meat of the Word", it is not talking about a beef steak.

*John 16:25: "These things I (Jesus) have spoken to you in figurative language; but the time is coming when I will no longer speak to you in figurative language, but I will tell you plainly about the Father."*

*John 16: 12-13a: "I (Jesus) still have many things to say to you, but you cannot bear them now. However when He, the Spirit of truth, has come, He will guide you into all truth ..."*

*Matthew 16:17b.19: "... for flesh and blood has not revealed this to you, but My Father who is in heaven. And I will give you the keys of the kingdom of heaven, and whatever you bind on earth will be bound in heaven, and whatever you loose on earth will be loosed in heaven."*

*Mark 4:22-23: "For there is nothing hidden which will not be revealed, nor has anything been kept secret but that it should come to light. If anyone has ears to hear, let him hear."*

There are certain key words that unlock the figurative symbolic language of the Word and open vast areas of kingdom revelation. Many of these symbols and types have been revealed for many years. But some are only recently revealed, and most of those that we have known for some time have a deeper freshly revealed kingdom meaning.

In the figurative Biblical language, much is revealed from simple symbols, from the "sea" (unstable masses of unsaved without structure), to the "fruitful plains" (the saved stable Christians), to "trees" (men's

*SOME SYMBOLIC LANGUAGE KEYS*

life-structures), to "hills" (authority structures), to the "high mountains" (great structures of authority), and on to the "highest mountain" (the ultimate authority of God).

To understand the Word of the kingdom from the Bible the disciple must be able to hear the spiritual meaning of the figurative or symbolic language from the Holy Spirit. When I study a passage of Scripture, I pray and ask the Holy Spirit to give me revelation of the hidden symbolic spiritual meaning of the words. Then I meditate the passage allowing quite time in my spirit and mind while waiting to hear from God. When enlightment or understanding comes then I begin to check out the concordance, Greek and Hebrew dictionaries, and other Scriptures for conformation or clarification.

The following are a few examples of Symbolic language. Try using these as you study and meditate the Word:

**Mountains**-Great structures of authority, may be godly or ungodly. The great churches of today are mountains.

**Hills**-Structures of authority as mountains, except lesser.

**Fields**-Lower structures of authority, but still firmament. Usually indicate those saved, as opposed to the sea of lost. As such, they are the fruitful production areas where grain and fruit trees, etc. are grown.

**Valleys**-Lower structure than fields, often fertile and well-watered by neighboring mountains.—Also may indicate a very low period, a time of difficulty and hard decisions.

**Sea**-No structure at all, fluid, blown about, sometimes roaring, unsaved masses of people.

**Trees**-Natural structures of life; individual men and their life-structure, ranging from great men or rulers as great cedars, strong stable men as mighty oaks, olive and fig trees as prophets or ministers, fruit trees and vines as fruitful Christians, to insignificant bramble bushes and ungodly thorns and briars.

**City**-A corporate structure of life. A spiritual community for the protection and well-being of its citizens, governed by spiritual laws, ruled by a spiritual hierarchy, which determines the personality of the city and the quality of life within the city. A city is structured by **patterns** of life. A **great city** is a capital or ruling city, whose patterns reach out beyond its city walls or limits to govern a greater area.

**Israel**-The overall church, including its ruling city, its many different cities, and wilderness areas.

**New Jerusalem**-The purified, holy, renewed ruling city of God, the remnant Bride Church, the Bride of Christ without spot or wrinkle.

**Babylon**-The ruling city of the kingdom of darkness. The great soulish system of man characterized by covetousness, immorality, and sorcery. The mother system of harlots and adulterers.

**Bride & Wife**-The obedient, perfected, faithful, and true, ruling city portion of the church, where reproduction takes place and mature sons are brought to glory. She is God-seeking and God-serving.

**Harlot**-The unfaithful rebellious mistress (person or church) who sells her purity to fulfill her own desires and meet her needs. She does not seek the true God, but is self-seeking and self-serving.

**Adulteress**-The unfaithful part of the church who has a husband and pretends obedience to him, but has other lovers. She seeks to fulfill her desires and meet her needs from sources other than her husband. She has a divided heart, and her desire is both self-seeking and God-seeking, self-serving and God-serving.

**Assyrians, Philistines, Canaanites,** etc.-Evil enemy spiritual forces, demons.

**Dragon, Serpent, Roaring Lion, Wild Beast, Fowls of the Air, Adverse Wind, Storms,** etc.- Satan and/or demon spirits.

**Seed**-A living pattern, word, thought, idea, vision, also the offspring made from the pattern. A word, vision, etc. from God is a **good seed**, A **bad seed** would be the same, except from the enemy.

**Soil, Land**-The heart of man. The spiritual/natural interface through which seeds from the spiritual realm are planted in the fertile creativity of the heart, to be brought forth into the natural realm.

**Holy Spirit may be represented in His different aspects or facets as: Oil, Water, Wine, Strong Drink, Light, Rain etc.**

**Oil**-Comfort, healing, joy, of the Holy Spirit.

**Water**-Cleansing, washing, or life-giving, Word or Holy Spirit.

**Wine**-Revelation from God, a rhema word from God, unveiled truths of God's Word, by the Holy Spirit.

**Old Wine**-Revelation from the past, usually a taste has been acquired for it. It is smooth and comfortable to the taste, and can put one to sleep.

**New Wine**-New revelation from God. It is fresh and exciting, but may be very different to the taste and cause discomfort for those who have not yet acquired a taste for the new. It can be intoxicating if we take too much of it by itself. One must continue to feed on the bread and meat along with the new wine.

**Strong Drink**-A hard word such as correction, rebuke, or warning etc. by the Holy Spirit.

**Light**-Understanding, discernment, life-giving, growth-stimulating Word or revelation by the Holy Spirit.

**Rain**-Outpouring of grace gifts of the Holy Spirit.

**Rivers**-Continuous flow of life, flow of Holy Spirit.

**Wineskins**-The container, or framework, the organized filing system for the revelation of God. Theological systems.

**Cloth**-A woven network of understanding of life. It may contain intricate patterns of design, each thread fitting together to make the whole.

**Flood**-A great outpouring of damaging words.

**Jewels**-Perfected sons or daughters.

**Fire**-Intense adversity for purification or judgment, judgmental or critical words.

**Stars**-Spiritual persons, men of God, **Bright Stars** are men of God with greater visibility than lesser stars.

**Heat**-Correction or judgment; the heat of the sun, particularly, is intense light that brings correction from God the Father.

**Angels**-Sometimes symbolizes men of God sent to the church, ministers, messengers, preachers of the message from God.

**Trumpets**-Sometimes are the voices of the prophets speaking forth the message of God, or calling an assembly, or focusing attention, and especially blasting forth the judgments of God.

**Grain and Grain Fields**-Production, particularly annual or periodical production.

**Green Grass**-Production of the fields, including grain.

**Birds**-Spirits, either godly or evil.

**Crowns**-Authority to rule.

**Temple**-A permanent dwelling place of God. The eternal heart of man where God dwells.

**Tabernacle**-A temporary dwelling place of God.

Consider the meaning of the figurative words used in *Luke 5: 36-39.* The Lord speaks of patching new **cloth** into old—and of putting **new wine** in **old wine-**

**skins.** He also mentions that a man having drunk **old wine** does not immediately desire the new. Using the key words, it is easy to discern what He is saying spiritually.

What is being said in Isaiah 55, when the **mountains** and **hills** are said to break forth into **singing**, and the **trees** of the **field** clap their hands?

One of the most devastating mistakes man makes when seeking to know God through His Word, is to take every passage which can be **literally** interpreted, and apply **only literal** interpretation to it. The spiritual man learns to **literally interpret** the true spiritual meaning of the passage through the **figurative** language of the Holy Spirit. Often there is both a literal meaning and a spiritual meaning. Much prophecy has had a literal historical fulfillment and a greater spiritual implication. One might think of this as a railroad with two tracks running side-by-side. One track is the literal meaning of the passage, and the other track is the spiritual. Many Old Testament terms and passages have a very literal, natural meaning, and, at the same time, have vital spiritual meaning to New Testament believers about the "kingdom of God". Many Old Testament events were recorded as examples to us.

*1 Corinthians 10:11: Now all these things happened to them as examples, and they were written for our admonition, on whom the ends of the ages have come.*

The nation Israel is extremely significant as God's chosen people. It was through this nation and the Jewish people that the Son of God came and the Bible was written. The many prophetic writings and historical events of Israel all have spiritual meaning to the church. God has chosen Israel and its ruling city, Jerusalem, as a living message to the world. God's dealings with **natural Israel and natural Jerusalem** become **spiritual messages to spiritual Israel and spiritual Jerusalem.** The spiritual kingdom, the Israel of God, is a new people, a spiritual people to whom origin of nationality, race, color, social cast, or political standing is of little or no significance. It is a kingdom in which all are adopted by the heavenly Father and become true brothers and sisters.

*Galatians 3:7,14b,29: Therefore know that those who are of faith are sons of Abraham ... that the blessing of Abraham might come upon the Gentiles in Christ Jesus, that we might receive the promise of the Spirit through faith. And if you are Christ's, then you are Abraham's seed and heirs according to the promise.*

*Galatians 6:15-16: For in Christ Jesus neither circumcision nor uncircumcision avails anything, but a new creation. And as many as walk according to this rule, peace and mercy upon them, upon the Israel of God.*

Spiritual Jerusalem, or New Jerusalem, is the ruling city of spiritual Israel, just as natural Jerusalem or old Jerusalem was the ruling city of natural Israel. As old Jerusalem was the natural figurative mother which birthed the kingdom into the earth, so now the New Jerusalem is the spiritual mother, the wife of God, the Bride of Christ that is birthing the wonderful spiritual kingdom of God into our world. The New Jerusalem is the Bride of Christ, the holy, purified, overcoming portion of the church.

*Revelation 21:9-11: Then one of the seven angels who had the seven bowls filled with the seven last plagues came to me and talked with me, saying, "Come, I will show you the bride, the Lamb's wife." And he carried me away in the Spirit to a great and high mountain, and showed me the great city, the holy Jerusalem, descending out of heaven from God, having the glory of God. And her light was like a most precious stone, like a jasper stone, clear as crystal.*

*Revelation 21:2: Then I, John, saw the holy city, New Jerusalem, coming down out of heaven from God, prepared as a bride for her husband.*

*Galatians 4:25b,26: Jerusalem which now is, and is in bondage with her children. But the Jerusalem above is free, which is the mother of us all.*

*Revelation 19:7-8: "Let us be glad and rejoice and give Him glory, for the marriage of the Lamb has come, and his wife has made herself ready. And to her it was granted to be arrayed in fine linen, clean and bright, for the fine linen is the righteous acts of the saints."*

New Jerusalem is coming down from the spirit realm now and is being formed on the earth. It is the Bride Church, the holy, purified, remnant people of God. Just as it is possible for a person to be in the nation of Israel, but not in the city of Jerusalem, it is also possible to be in the church, but not yet in New Jerusa-lem. Not everyone in the country of Israel is in the city of Jerusalem. Neither has everyone in the church become the purified holy Bride of Christ, the New Jerusalem.

In the beautiful, illustrative figurative language of God, (characteristically used by the Holy Spirit to communicate spiritual truths to mankind), God describes the kingdom-of-God lifestyle in the picture of New Jerusalem in *Revelation 21 & 22:1-5.*

In the New Jerusalem lifestyle, we live in the presence of God continuously as the tabernacle of God is with men. The glory and light of God fill our lives. Pain and sorrow are gone as God wipes away our tears. No more death as eternal abundant life prevails; we pass from life to life. Righteousness and holiness prevail in our lives as pure gold and clear crystal. There is no night; there are no dark, threatening seasons. There is no more curse. We are under the dome of His protection, and there is perfect peace. We serve Him and rule over the circumstances of life.

*Isaiah 62:5b,12: "...and as the bridegroom rejoices over the bride, so shall your God rejoice over you. And they shall call them The Holy People, The Redeemed of the Lord; And you shall be called Sought Out, A City Not Forsaken."*

In Isaiah chapter 60, Isaiah begins to picture and describe the glory and prosperity of **"The City of the Lord,** the Zion of the Holy One of Israel". (v. 14)

## THE KING-DOME

Let me share with you an illustration that helps me understand the concept of the spiritual city of New Jerusalem. Imagine a giant, glass dome filled with the glorious presence and light of God. Inside this huge spiritual dome, everything is like it should be. Everything is in perfect obedience to God's laws, and nothing that defiles can enter in. The environment is perfectly controlled, like a greenhouse. Those who overcome, enter and abide inside the dome where they enjoy all the victorious aspects and attributes of New Jerusalem. The enemy has no part and can do no harm inside the dome.

The bright light from inside the dome flows out to the countryside in a large circle of light around the

## THE KING-DOME

*Romans 14:17: ...for the **kingdom of God** is not food and drink, but **righteousness** and **peace** and **joy** <u>in the Holy Spirit.</u>*

lifestyle. Many people in the church are now beginning to see the kingdom lifestyle, and are now moving toward the Holy City.

Just as it is possible to be in the nation, but not in the ruling city, it is possible to be in the outer court of the tabernacle, but not in the holy place. Many have entered the tabernacle into the outer court, but now must be purified to enter the holy place. The presence of God is in the holy place; all the promises of New Jerusalem are in the holy place. We must come in the gate and partake of the brazen altar, the blood sacrifice for our sins, the atoning blood of Jesus. Next we must be washed by the water at

dome. Everywhere the light reaches, the darkness must flee and cannot return unless the light is lessened or drawn back. People who sit in darkness may see the light from a distance and begin to move toward it. At the point that they actually leave the darkness and enter the light, they have entered the Israel of God, but have not yet reached and entered Jerusalem, the city of God. They have come out of darkness into the light and must continue on the journey to the dome. Their goal is to enter the king-dome, the New Jerusalem-purified-holy-Bride-of-Christ lifestyle.

*Matthew 4:16: The people who sat in darkness saw a great light, and upon those who sat in the region and shadow of death light has dawned.*

*Hebrews 12:22: But we have come to Mount Zion and to the **city** of the living God, the **heavenly Jerusalem,** to an innumerable company of angels, to the general assembly and **church** of the first-born..."*

We must, through a purifying growth process, come to maturity and walk into the New Jerusalem

the brazen lavar in preparation for entering the holy place. We must journey on to the candle sticks of the Holy Spirit ministry and on to the show bread being broken—before arriving at the altar of incense and the Holy of Holies, the intimate communion with God (the king-dome).

*Psalm 15: Lord, who will abide in Your tabernacle? Who may dwell in Your holy hill? He who **walks uprightly,** and **works righteousness,** and **speaks the truth in his heart;** he who does not backbite with his tongue, nor does evil to his neighbor, nor does he take up a reproach against his friend; in whose eyes a vile person is despised, but he honors those who fear the Lord; he who swears to his own hurt and does not change; he who does not put out his money to usury, nor takes a bribe against the innocent. He who does these things will never be moved.*

*Hebrews 12:28: Therefore, since we are **receiving a kingdom** which cannot be shaken, let us have grace, by which we **serve God acceptably** with reverence and godly fear.*

# CHAPTER 8

## ENTERING THE KINGDOM

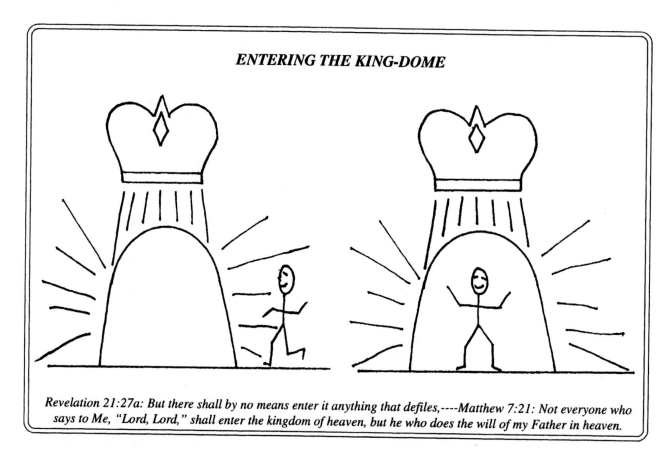

*ENTERING THE KING-DOME*

*Revelation 21:27a: But there shall by no means enter it anything that defiles,----Matthew 7:21: Not everyone who says to Me, "Lord, Lord," shall enter the kingdom of heaven, but he who does the will of my Father in heaven.*

Jesus taught much about entering the kingdom and walking or abiding in it. Jesus preached and taught more about what the kingdom of God is like, how it works, and how to enter it, than any other subject. The parables that Jesus taught in the four Gospels are the richest teaching on the kingdom of God in the Bible. However, what the kingdom of God (the ruler/dominion of God) is like and how it works spans the entire Bible, and is the predominant theme of the Word of God.

Jesus was not greatly concerned with teaching us how to live in heaven someday. His great concern was revealing to us how to live on the earth in this life now. God's plan is the establishment of His kingdom on earth in and through redeemed man.

Many people have great difficulty in truly understanding the good-news message of the kingdom of God because they must first lay aside the strong convictions (rocks in the heart) that "kingdom" means heaven only someday, or in a future millennial reign. This mentality leads to a focus on what we refer to as the "salvation" or "born-again" experience, after which, we do the best we can to "hang on" until we die and go to heaven or until Jesus comes to rescue us. In Matthew 13, Jesus referred to these types of strong convictions as "rocks" in the heart-soil that prevent the fruit of the kingdom from coming to completion.

The Gospel of the kingdom does not do away with the gospel of being born again. It includes the gospel we have preached for years, as well as all true Bible doctrines. Jesus focused on preaching the Gospel of the kingdom because it encompassed all the parts of revealed doctrines and is the umbrella that covers them. Some doctrinal groups have referred to themselves as "full gospel", because they received and incorporated into their structure the latest revelation. God is still restoring His message on earth. As each new area is restored, we are tempted to think that we now have it all. But about the time we get comfortable with what we have, He gives us more. When He gives more light, some of the error that we previously believed was accurate and complete then begins to melt away.

We must come to grips with the reality that heaven is not just for dead people, and that the kingdom of God \ kingdom of heaven is not just for them, but is also for the people living on earth now —that entering the kingdom does not mean just going to heaven when we die. We are not waiting for Jesus to come back to earth to establish His kingdom. Jesus has already returned to earth in the Holy Spirit to indwell and empower the people of God to rule and reign, to overcome, to retake and possess the land. Yes, He is coming back as Lord of lords and King of kings to receive His prepared Bride. Yes, His bodily return to rule and reign with His purified bride is the fulfillment of the kingdom. But the establishment time is now! Jesus has already done all that is necessary to defeat the devil and his rule. He now lives in us by the Holy Spirit to empower His purified Bride to overcome. According to *Romans 14:17*, the kingdom of God is righteousness, peace, and joy **in the Holy Spirit.**

Is there any wonder why there is so much conflict, confusion and controversy about the baptism of the Holy Spirit? It's easy to see why the enemy comes against it so, when we recognize the role of the Holy Spirit in walking in the kingdom-of-God potential now. **The kingdom of God** is righteousness, peace and joy **in the Holy Spirit.** The potential for experiencing the Bride-of-Christ life **now** is in the Holy Spirit.

The kingdom-of-God potential first returned to earth in Jesus at the time of His baptism. The Holy Spirit descended on Jesus and remained on Him, in an experience of Spiritual life in a different dimension from what had been known before. The heavens opened to Him. Jesus saw into the spirit realm, the heavenly realm; and the voice of God spoke clearly to Him, affirming Him as His Son, and expressing His pleasure in Him. The kingdom-of-God age came into the earth. The potential to communicate with God intimately returned to the earth into Jesus, in that moment.

The Baptized was to become the Baptizer and baptize many with the Holy Spirit, opening for them the potential to walk in a new level of obedience and power, enabling them to walk in the glorious Bride-lifestyle. John was the last great prophet of the captive kingdom, but did not experience the greater kingdom life available to us.

*Matthew 11:11:* *"Assuredly. I say to you, among those born of women there has not risen one greater than John the Baptist; but he who is least in the kingdom of heaven is greater than he."*

*Mark 1:7-8:* *And he (John the Baptist), preached saying, "There comes One after me who is mightier than I, whose sandal strap I am not worthy to stoop down and loose. I indeed baptized you with water, but **He will baptize you with the Holy Spirit."***

*Matthew 3:16-17:* *Then Jesus, when He had been baptized, came up immediately from the water; and behold, **the heavens were opened to Him,** and He saw the Spirit of God descending like a dove and alighting upon Him, and suddenly a voice from heaven, saying, "This is My beloved Son, in whom I am well pleased."*

*John 1:32-34:* *And John bore witness, saying, "I saw the Spirit descending from heaven like a dove, and He remained upon Him. I did not know Him, but He who sent me to baptize with water said to me, 'Upon whom you see the Spirit descending, and remaining on Him, **this is He who baptizes with the Holy Spirit.'** And I have seen and testified that this is the Son of God."*

From this point forward, the kingdom was now on the earth in Jesus. Jesus was empowered to demonstrate the kingdom authority, and His earthly ministry began. When He later left the earth, the kingdom potential went with Him. The King promised before He left that He would soon return with His kingdom to His disciples.

*Matthew 16:28:* *"Assuredly, I (Jesus) say to you, there are some standing here who shall not taste death till they see the Son of Man coming in His kingdom."*

*Luke 9:27:* *(And Jesus said), "But I tell you truly, there are some standing here who shall not taste death till they see the kingdom of God."*

These verses plainly and emphatically state that some of the people there were going to be alive and see Jesus coming in His kingdom, the kingdom of God. Jesus made it clear that He was going away and coming back quickly, bringing the kingdom with Him. This is a strong statement by the Lord that He was returning to earth, bringing His kingdom with Him, during their lifetime. When did this happen? Or did it not happen as the Lord said it would?

In the past, the only way I could get around this statement was to assume that He was speaking of the mount of transfiguration when the disciples caught a glimpse of His glory. It was always a bit of a stretch for me to believe that the brief glimpse of Jesus in His glorified state was what He had in mind when He said they would  "see the Son of Man coming in His kingdom". The revelation of "kingdom" brings much seemingly difficult scripture into such sweet harmony.

Jesus returned to earth as a "life-giving Spirit" at Pentecost. How many Gods do we have? We have only one God! He manifests Himself in three persons: Father, Son, and Holy Spirit. Jesus made it clear that "if you have me, you have the Father, and if the Holy Spirit dwells in you, so does the Son and the Father." Many Christians who will quickly tell you that Jesus lives in their heart don't realize that **He could not be in their heart if He had not returned to earth.**

When Jesus walked on earth as a man, He could be in only one place at one time. He bodily returned to the right hand of the Father and then returned as Spirit and can now be everywhere at once. He can indwell all believers at one time, empowering us to walk obediently in His kingdom lifestyle.  Thus the will of God can be done on earth as it is in heaven. Many are yet looking for Jesus to return to do what He has already done or is now here to do.

In *John 14:15-28*, and *John 16:12-25*,  Jesus is speaking of the Holy Spirit that is to come after He (Jesus) goes back to heaven. He makes it clear that He will return to His disciples. When He says, "I'm going away and coming back to you",  He does not mean to their descendants thousands of years later.

*John 14:18:  "I will not leave you orphans; I will come to you."*

*John 14:20:  "At that day you will know that I am in the Father, and you in Me, and I in you."*

*John 14:21:  "I will love him (those who love the Father) and manifest Myself to him." (Or "manifest myself in him")*

*John 16:14:  "We (Jesus and the Father) will come to him and make Our home with him."*

*John 14:28:  "I'm going away and coming back to you."*

*John 16:14:  "He (the Holy Spirit) Will take of what is Mine (or Me) and declare to you."*

Jesus finishes up the discussion in *John 16:23-24* by saying, *"In that day you will ask me nothing ... whatever you ask the Father in my name, He will give you."*  Obviously, the day he is talking about is today, and not some future day when He bodily returns.

Jesus came to earth, reclaimed the kingdom, was crucified and resurrected, ascended to the right hand of the Father, **returned to earth** in the Holy Spirit and now lives in believers to establish His kingdom on earth. Yet, He is still at the right hand of the Father making intercession for us. Though Jesus possessed the fullness of the kingdom potential after His baptism with the Holy Spirit, He was not omnipresent in His natural body on earth. Now that He has returned to earth in the Holy Spirit, He is omnipresent.

Christ Jesus in us, by the Holy Spirit, will produce righteous obedience to God. Real holiness, true righteousness, perfect obedience is the only way to enter the fullness of the kingdom of God and become the Bride of Christ. Positional righteousness does not in itself cause us to enter or become the purified Bride. Only practical righteousness, practical obedience will enable us to live on earth in the kingdom of God. We enter and walk in the kingdom by obedience to the will of the Father.

*Matthew 5:20:    "For I say to you, that unless your righteousness exceeds that of the Scribes and Pharisees, you will by no means enter the kingdom of heaven."*

*Matthew 7:21-23:  **"Not everyone who says to Me, 'Lord, Lord,' shall enter the kingdom of heaven, but*** *he who does the will of My Father in heaven. Many will say to Me in that day, 'Lord, Lord, have we not prophesied in Your name, and done many wonders in Your name?' And then I will declare to them, 'I never knew you; depart from Me, you who practice lawlessness.'"*

*Matthew 19:17b: "...But if you want to enter into life, **keep the commandments."***

Remember, we are not talking about being born again; nor are we talking about going to heaven when we die. Those are "parts", but what Jesus is talking about in these verses is entering and living in the kingdom of God **now**. We enter and walk by obedience to the Father. Only Jesus, by the Holy Spirit living in us, will always obey the will of the Father. Even though Jesus was seated in heaven, He was, and still is, available to carry out miraculous works of God through His disciples.

*Mark 16:19-70: ...He was received up into heaven, and sat down at the right hand of God. And they went out and preached everywhere, **the Lord working with them** and confirming the word through the accompanying signs. Amen.*

*Luke 17:20-21: "The kingdom of God does not come with observation; nor will they say, 'See here!' or 'See there!' For indeed the kingdom of God is within you (or in your midst)."*

As Christ Jesus manifests Himself in our being, we truly become the body of Christ, a body for Jesus to live in on earth. Jesus the Christ has returned to earth and lives in us. We can now rule and reign over the kingdoms of the earth, as His glorious life, His love, His power, His wisdom, His peace, and His faith, rule and reign through our being. We take dominion over all the earth, and over all the powers of darkness. We reclaim every area of the kingdom, and nothing is impossible to Jesus in us.

When God's messengers receive the kingdom-of-God-now truth in their hearts and proclaim it with their mouths to all the world, then the kingdom of God is established. But as long as it is preached as a "someday kingdom", it will not be fully established on earth. The other kingdom, **the kingdom of darkness, can continue to run the governments, businesses, finance, religion, arts, music, media, sports, educa-** tional systems, entertainment industry, etc. of our world. **Evil can continue to poison the minds of our people, inflicting pain, perverting, killing, and destroying men, women, and children of our land.**

**Wake up, Christians! Wake up, preachers!** The saints who have gone on to heaven are not going to take back the earth, reclaim it and establish the kingdom of God on the earth. Yes, they are cheering us on. Yes, their work is made perfect in us. We are establishing what the great men of faith have begun—building upon the foundational heritage of generations of men of faith. But, only those alive on earth have the opportunity to cleanse their hands and purify their hearts. It is then that the Spirit of Christ Jesus can come forth in their lives in power and glory sufficient to overpower the kingdom of darkness and establish the kingdom of light. This new generation has the potential now to see the kingdom of God established in hearts today, individually, and then in the earth.

All who have gone before and paid a great price are looking to the people of God on earth today to **make perfect** their works and sacrifices by bringing forth the kingdom of God on earth.

*Hebrews 11:37-40: They were stoned, they were sawn in two, were tempted, were slain with the sword. They wandered about in sheepskins and goatskins, being destitute, afflicted, tormented - of whom the world was not worthy. They wandered in deserts and mountains, in dens and caves of the earth. And all these, having obtained a good testimony through faith, did not receive the promise, God having provided something better for us, that **they should not be made perfect apart from us.***

*1 Corinthians 10:11: Now all these things happened to them as examples, and they were written for our admonition, **on whom the ends (purpose) of the ages have come.***

We are each in one kingdom or the other. We are being ruled by either the kingdom of darkness or the kingdom of light. We are bringing forth, from our hearts, either one kingdom or the other into the earth.

There is great conflict between the two kingdoms and keen competition for the hearts of men. The propagation of either kingdom depends on the hearts of men. Men must cast the deciding vote as to which kingdom will rule the earth. Only in the heart-soil of man is the potential for ruling the earth. **Whichever kingdom rules the hearts of men, rules the earth.**

Boiling it all down, man has one great continuous **"yes and no"** decision to make He must decide "yes" to the kingdom of light and **"no"** to the kingdom of darkness. Many generations ago, mankind decided "yes" to the kingdom of darkness and "no" to the kingdom of light. Men need make no further decision to remain in the kingdom of darkness. A decision not to come to the light is a decision to remain in darkness.

God will furnish all the power, all the direction, and do all the work to establish His kingdom; but man must decide by his own will. God has given us the rule of the earth and has chosen not to overrule our will. What we bind is bound, and what we loose is loosed.

*Matthew 16:19, "And I give you the keys of the kingdom of heaven, and whatever you bind on earth will be bound in heaven, and whatever you loose on earth will be loosed in heaven."*

The Bride of Christ is prepared by practical obedience and holiness. Now is the time for the church to make herself ready and become the perfected Bride, the New Jerusalem. Each of us must go through a process of becoming obedient and holy, or "growing up" in the kingdom walk. We must receive true understanding of the kingdom of God by spiritual revelation of the Word of God.

For anyone who might have a tendency toward thinking "this is something I can humanly do," please be aware, it is all by the grace of God. Grace can be defined as unmerited favor. **The grace of God is the empowerment of Christ within the individual to live righteously.** The grace of God is not a whitewash covering for our continued disobedience.

Grace is freely given but never forced upon an unwilling individual. Our part is to become willing to lay down our own way, our selfish desires, our religious order, our inner needs, to empty ourselves of ourselves that the grace of God may fill us with Christ. We must be born into the kingdom as a child and grow into the maturity of the kingdom lifestyle.

# CHAPTER 9

## SEVEN STAGES OF KINGDOM

1. In the Womb Stage

2. With The Mother Stage

3. The Independent Stage

4. The Suffering Stage

5. The Obedient Stage

6. The Servant Stage

7. The Seated Stage

Spiritual birth, growth, and the maturing process into the kingdom-of-God lifestyle is taught in the Bible in parables of the natural. Remember, we can receive insight and understanding of spiritual things by looking at natural things. Again the figurative language of Scripture speaks of natural things to communicate spiritual kingdom-truth to those who have an ear to hear. We can identify seven stages of development into the maturity of kingdom living by looking into the Word and comparing natural development.

Each of us must go through a process of becoming obedient and holy, or "growing up" in the kingdom walk. It is not enough to be born spiritually, anymore than it is enough to be born in the natural. Before ruling as a man, one must go through a growth process, be nourished and be trained in order to grow from a baby to a man. Likewise, in the spiritual, we cannot rule or even walk in the kingdom of God as a baby.

Jesus said we must enter the kingdom as a child. He said that we must be born into the spiritual kingdom as we were born into the natural world.

*Matthew 18:3: "Assuredly, I say to you, unless you are converted and become as little children, you will by no means enter the kingdom of heaven."*

*John 3;3, 5-6: Jesus answered and said to him, "Most assuredly, I say to you, unless one is born again (or from above), he cannot see the kingdom of God. Most assuredly, I say to you, unless one is born of water and the Spirit, he cannot enter the kingdom of God. That which is born of the flesh is flesh, and that which is born of the Spirit is spirit."*

## IN THE WOMB STAGE

In the natural, there must be conception before there can be birth. Life does not begin at birth but at conception in the womb of the mother. There must be a mother and a father coming together in intimacy. A seed from the father comes together with an egg in the mother and conception occurs; life begins. Is the new life in the world at this point? Yes, it is in the world. It is in the womb of the mother who is in the world. But it is not yet birthed or released into the world by itself.

In the spiritual kingdom, the father is God and the mother is the church, the Bride and wife of God. The seed is the Word, the living pattern of God. The egg is the heart soil of a person. The Holy Spirit is the womb of the church; that tender, caring, sensitive, praying, loving, presence of the Spirit in the purified Bride.

When the church is properly related to God, that intimate communion produces children. As the Word (the seed) enters the heart-soil (the egg) prepared by the Holy Spirit in the church (the mother), conception takes place—at the time the word is received (believed) in the heart.

*Hebrews 4:2: For indeed the gospel was preached to us as well as to them; but the word which they heard did not profit them, not being mixed with faith in those who heard it.*

Life has begun when the **Word and faith** come together, but the new life must be protected and nurtured in the womb. This new life is unable to sustain itself. It is dependent on the purified bride, the mother

church to breathe for it, to receive and digest food, to provide protection from the elements, and to flow love, comfort, and acceptance. The embryo cannot walk in the kingdom on its own. It can only go where the mother carries it in her womb.

*Galatians 4:26: ...but the Jerusalem above is free, which is the mother of us all.*

*Isaiah 44:2: "Yet hear now, O Jacob My servant, and Israel whom I have chosen. Thus says the Lord who made you and formed you from the womb, who will help you."*

When the word comes and is received in faith (believed), we repent of the old and are conceived—a new creation. We must then go through a season of being formed and developed in the womb of the church before being birthed into the kingdom. Remember we are talking about walking in the kingdom lifestyle that Jesus taught, not just getting into heaven when we die. In relation to kingdom living, what we may have viewed in the past as being born again is really only conception.

## WITH THE MOTHER STAGE

Birth is that time at which we begin to breathe on our own. Spiritual breathing is spiritual communion, praying to and hearing from God on our own. In natural birth, we are suddenly pressed forth from our warm protected environment in the womb into the real world. No longer are we protected from all cold or heat. Shocks and bumps are no longer cushioned by our mother's body. No longer does all the nutrition and oxygen we need flow effortlessly into us from the mother. We must, for the first time, begin to breathe on our own. For the first time, we will feel the exhilarating rush of life sustaining air into our own lungs. We will, for the first time, begin to taste food given to us in our own mouth.

Many people who received Christ as an adult can remember a short season after they first received the Lord in which everything seemed to be perfect. Love was all around. All prayers were quickly answered. Church was a great joy and peace was everywhere. Life seemed effortless. If you can remember, the season probably lasted about nine months. We were being formed in the womb of the Holy Spirit.

As it is in the natural, so it is in the spiritual. We are birthed into the kingdom life when we begin to breathe on our own spiritually, when we can first begin to **speak to God and hear Him** ourselves. We are separated from the womb, but must now be carried in the mother's arms, nurtured at her side, and nourished with milk from her breast. We are not ready for meat, but can partake of the milk of the word. We know to draw the word from the breast of the church into our own mouths. And soon we can receive more solid food from the spoon in the mother's hand.

*Isaiah 46:3: "...all the remnant of the house of Israel, who have been upheld by Me from birth, **who have been carried from the womb.**"*

*Genesis 49:25b: "Blessings of the **breasts** and of the **womb.**"*

*Isaiah 66:8b-11: **"For as soon as Zion travailed, She gave birth to her children.** Shall I bring to the time of birth and not cause delivery?" says the Lord. "Shall I who cause delivery shut up the womb?" says your God. "Rejoice with Jerusalem and be glad with her, all you who love her; rejoice for joy with her, all you who mourn for her; **that you may feed and be satisfied with the consolation of her breasts,** that you may drink deeply and be delighted with the abundance of her glory."*

This is a stage of nurturing by the mother, a time of feeding, bathing, and changing diapers—a time of affection and tender loving care from the purified mother church.

In the natural realm, if you have been around small children, you are well aware that they will make some stinky messes from time to time. Thank God for the grace given to loving parents who patiently, again and again, clean up the messes, doctor what is hurt, and fix or replace what is broken, all the while lovingly reassuring the child. It is no different in the spiritual realm. The church must have grace from God to care for the spiritual children.

This is a time of rapid growth and a time to begin to receiving instruction. We begin to learn to eat on our own and bathe ourselves. Then we begin to practice doing things, watching others and trying out our own wings a little.

Remember, we are on a journey to the holy place, the City of God. We are moving through the process of maturity and holiness that will lead to true success and prosperity, to the establishment of the kingdom (ruler/ dominion) of God in our lives and then in the world.

## THE INDEPENDENT STAGE

**Well, we've finally made it!** We're ready to move out and begin to minister on our own. We can leave the close confines of the mother. Our intense training period is over. We're ready to go out to save all the lost, and conquer the world or make our fortune. Our life is filled with the excitement of doing and building. Our goals are clear and our ambitions and confidence are high. We know beyond any doubt that we can do all things through Christ who strengthens us.

We are really doing great. We have the respect of everyone: those we minister to, our peers, and our authority. Everyone seems to want us on their team. We're really cruising. Almost all our ideas work; we think to ourselves, "This kingdom life is great; I've got to remember to try to be humble, and to be kind to all the little people."

We flex our spiritual muscles and with firmness let the world know that we have arrived. Our convictions are even more firm than our muscles. If there is anything that we don't know, it probably isn't worth knowing anyway. Our doctrinal position is so rigid and complete that nothing can be changed or added. It's inconceivable that anyone would be dumb enough to have a different position. Surely part of our calling must be to correct all those older fuzzy-minded men who seem to border on being liberal fools. We know we have it right. After all, haven't we accomplished more in the one year we've been working than they have in their thirty plus years of service.

We are blind to the fact that our harshness and lack of real love may be tearing down as much of the kingdom as our wonderful preaching or intense labor is building. While we are out pounding people with our Bible, the wife and kids are trying to live over the wounds of neglect and rigid authority we've harshly administered to them. What does it profit a man to save the whole world or make a great fortune and lose his own family? Our empire will surely crumble. Thank God He does use us even in spite of ourselves.

Praise God for His mercy. No one could tell us the truth; that we've not even entered the kingdom-of-God walk yet; that our real training is about to begin. Oh yes, we've heard those sermons on suffering and the testimonies of enduring hardship, but we surmise that some way those guys must not have things quite right. We quickly learn to deal with backbiters and to kick the devil off our heels. **So we think that we are overcoming warriors, mighty men of valor!**

## THE SUFFERING STAGE

*Acts 14:22:* **We <u>must</u> through <u>many</u> tribulations enter the kingdom of God.**

"It seems so strange! It doesn't make sense! I was doing everything right! My desire was to serve God! I thought they would like me!"

Suddenly we are cut to pieces and run through the stomach with a sword— not through the back, but right to our face—from those close to us—those we've helped and even loved. Then the big rocks begin to smash us even from above. The authority that was so pleased with us suddenly does not seem to understand us any more. We are accused and abused from every direction. We are chewed to pieces with razor-sharp teeth of steel. And the more we do, the more we say to try to let them know that they are making a mistake, that we really didn't do anything wrong—the worse it gets.

Now! We are really about to enter the kingdom walk. Remember, we enter and walk in the kingdom by obedience. And though we are sons, we must learn obedience by the things we suffer. We will never really know the love of Christ until we've learned to love those who persecute us. This is our great opportunity to really die to self and to see the love of Jesus mani-

fest within us. The love, the great blessing, the presence of God in our lives that will come through this experience is the manifestation of the **glory of God.**

*Luke 24:26:* *"Ought not the Christ to have **suffered** these things and to **enter into His glory ?"***

*Hebrews 5:7-9:* *...who, in the days of His flesh, when He had offered up prayers and **supplications, with vehement cries and tears** to Him who was able to save Him from death, and was heard because of His godly fear, **though He was a Son, yet He learned obedience by the things which He suffered.** And having been perfected, He became the author of eternal salvation to all **who obey Him.***

*1 Peter 4:12-14:* *Beloved do not think it strange concerning the fiery trial which is to try you, as though some strange thing happened to you: but rejoice to the extent that **you partake of Christ's sufferings,** that when His glory is revealed, you may also be glad with exceeding joy. If you are reproached for the name of Christ, blessed are you, for the **Spirit of glory and of God rests upon you.***

*Matthew 5:10-12:* *"Blessed are those who are persecuted for righteousness' sake, for theirs is the **kingdom** of heaven. Blessed are you when they revile and persecute you, and say all kinds of evil against you falsely for My sake. Rejoice and be exceedingly glad, for great is your reward in heaven, for so they persecuted the prophets who were before you."*

*2 Corinthians 12:9-10:* *"My grace is sufficient for you, for **My strength is made perfect in weakness."** Therefore most gladly I will rather boast in my infirmities, that the power of Christ may rest upon me. Therefore I take pleasure in infirmities, in reproaches, in needs, in persecutions, in distresses, for Christ's sake. For when I am weak, then I am strong.*

*1 Thessalonians 1:4b-5:* *...for your patience and faith in all your persecutions and tribulation that you **endure,** which is manifest evidence of the righteous judgment of God, that you may be counted **worthy of the kingdom of God** for which you also suffer.*

*1 Peter 2:19-23:* *For this is commendable, if because of conscience toward God one endures grief, suffering wrongfully. For what credit is it if, when you are beaten for your faults, you take it patiently? **But when you do*** *good and suffer for it, if you take it patiently, this is commendable before God. For to this you were called,* because Christ also suffered for us, leaving us an example, that you should follow His steps; who committed no sin, nor was guile found in His mouth, who when He was reviled did not revile in return; when He suffered, He did not threaten, but committed Himself to Him who judges righteously.

*Romans 8:18:   For I consider that the **sufferings of this present time** are not worthy to be compared with the **glory which shall be revealed in us.***

In the suffering stage, our motives are further purified. If we are serving God for comfort or fleshly benefit, or out of a guilt motivation, we will not endure this stage except our motives be changed. If there remains a need for healing from the past in our hearts, we will experience bitterness being formed from the pain we are suffering. If we are not dead to self in any area, we will react or revile back when the pain becomes severe.

We may not be able to stay on top of things and remain up in our spirit or emotions during severe suffering. We may wish to die and despair of our lives. But let patience have her perfect work. **Endure** suffering as a good soldier. When the man Jesus suffered to the limit, he cried out, *"My God, My God, why have You forsaken Me?"  Matthew 27:46.*

Paul said in *2 Corinthians 1:8: "For we do not want you to be ignorant, brethren, of our trouble which came to us in Asia; that we were burdened beyond measure, above strength, so that **we despaired even of life.**"*

Elijah, in *1 Kings 19:4: "prayed that he might die,"* and said, *"'It is enough!  Now, Lord, take my life.'"*

After we are broken, through the endurance of suffering, and have no further kingdoms of our own to build; we are ready to be used by Him to build His kingdom. All of our independent desires and inner needs must die. His desires must replace those that drove us during the independent stage. When it does not matter to us whether men respect us or not, when we really are completely fulfilled in knowing that the Lord is pleased with us, then we are free to follow the Lord and are not moved by men. Man, the world, or the devil

have no place in us to hang their hook of control. We are very dangerous to the kingdom of darkness when there is no fear in us except the fear of disappointing our loving heavenly Father. If we fear men, we do not yet fear God. If we truly fear God, we have no fear of anything else.

## THE OBEDIENT STAGE

When our motives are right and our hearts are being healed, **the pain we feel is converted into love** and not bitterness. There is no other way <u>to have</u> and <u>know that we have</u> the perfected love of Jesus manifested in our everyday life. Being persecuted, suffering wrongfully, being wronged, and patiently enduring and forgiving, is the method by which we have love. **Pain, plus forgiveness, equals love. Pain plus resentment equals bitterness.** When we really love our enemies, God's love is perfected in us. This perfected love causes us to obey the commandments of Jesus and to do the will of the Father, thus entering by obedience into the kingdom-of-God walk.

*John 15:12: "This is My commandment, that you love one another as I have loved you."*

*1 John 2:5: "But whoever keeps His word, truly the love of God is perfected in him. By this we know that we are in Him."*

*1 John 5:3-4a: "For **this is the love of God that we keep His commandments.** And His commandments are not burdensome. For whatever is born of God overcomes the world."*

*Galatians 5:14: For **all the law is fulfilled in one word,** even in this: "You shall **love your neighbor** as yourself."*

Our obedience and pure motives make us worthy or trustworthy to receive the kingdom of God. We can be trusted with the riches and power of God. He can safely release to us secrets of how to rule in the earth. We will use all that He gives us to serve Him according to His directions. The enemy will not be able to tempt us to use the power of God to provide for our own needs or wants. Our love for Him and our desire to please Him will so outweigh any other wants or needs in our lives that we would sacrifice everything we have and even our own lives to obey Him.

Love is the greatest law of the kingdom. Every other law or principle is held together by love and works by love. It is the strongest force in creation. By love, one can be motivated to pay the supreme sacrifice and do what he would not do for all the riches in the world. The kingdom of God is characterized and held together by God's love. We can truly thank God and call it all joy when persecutions and suffering come to break us down to love.

## THE SERVANT STAGE

Now we are ready to really accomplish something in the kingdom, not from our own zealousness, as in the independent stage, but from a **love motive to serve.** We serve Jesus by serving His people. We really become humble servants, serving from the heart, producing heartily and reaping great blessings as a result. We are no longer trying to build our dream or "do our thing". As He pours out His grace to empower us and His wisdom to guide us, we are more humbled.

*Matthew 25:34-40:* *"Then the king will say to those on His right hand, 'Come you blessed of My Father, **inherit the kingdom** prepared for you from the foundation of the world. For I was hungry and you gave Me food; I was thirsty and you gave Me drink; I was a stranger and you took Me in; I was naked and you clothed Me; I was sick and you visited Me; I was in prison and you came to me.' Then the righteous will answer Him saying, 'Lord, when did we see you hungry and fed you, or thirsty and gave you drink?... And the King will answer and say to them, 'Assuredly, I say to you, **inasmuch as you did it to one of the least of these My brethren, you did it to Me'"***

The business in the kingdom of God is serving. It is serving God by serving His people. The more profitably we serve, the more we rule. Through the love of Jesus made perfect in us by suffering, we become obedient, which causes us to become profitable servants to God as we do only His will. The Father can specifically direct our lives through the Holy Spirit when our self-desires are dead. Then, we are able to hear His voice and receive direction that will cause us to align with His desires, and to prosper in the kingdom.

## THE SEATED STAGE

*Matthew 8:11:* *"And I say to you that many will come from the east and west, and **sit down** with Abraham, Isaac, and Jacob **in the kingdom of Heaven."***

We shall not be seated until we have entered the kingdome where we will be seated at the table of the Lord. We will sit in His presence and have supper time communication with the Lord. The goal of the entire journey has been to be spiritually seated at His table in His kingdom—to sit down and cease from our own labor. It is to be completely at rest in our soul while His life flows through us. Our goal is to be intimately present with the Lord and to faithfully carry out His will, to rule and reign with Him.

The seated-in-the-kingdom stage is the **mature-son** stage, the time of entering into the **rest** of God. It is the time for **ruling** in the kingdom on earth from that special spiritual place of closeness to the throne of God. It is leading the people of God and **interceding for them before God.**

*Galatians 4: 6-7: And because you are sons, God has sent forth the Spirit of His Son into your hearts ... Therefore you are **no longer a servant but a son,** and if a son, then an heir of God through Christ.*

*Romans 8:14: For as many as are led by the Spirit of God, these are (full grown) sons of God.*

*Romans 8: 18-19: For I consider that the sufferings of this present time are not worthy to be compared with the glory which shall be **revealed in us.** For the earnest expectation of the creation eagerly waits for the **revealing of the (mature) sons of God.***

The world is groaning and waiting for us to become the holy, purified, obedient, mature sons who will release the power of God to restore the kingdom of God on earth. It is waiting for us to heal and deliver our planet from the rule of darkness and oppression—to break, forever, the cruel bondage of Satan from the earth—and to establish the reign of righteousness, peace and joy—the kingdom of God. Thus we, as the mature sons, are to extend the king-dome and its light to the whole world. *Romans 8:21-22.*

The seated stage is a time of resting in closeness with God. We are no longer in the outer court, nor cast into outer darkness, but we serve as a pillar in the temple of God. We have a quiet, confident assurance as the power and love of God effortlessly flows through us, to heal the brokenhearted, set the captives free, and rebuild the ruined cities.

*Hebrews 3:18: And to whom did He swear that they would not enter His rest, but to those who did not obey?*

*Hebrews 4: 6b, 9-11: ...those to whom it was preached did not enter because of disobedience. There remains therefore **a rest for the people of God**. For he who has entered His rest has himself also ceased from **his** works. Let us therefore be diligent to enter that rest, lest anyone fall after the same example of disobedience.*

In the seated stage, faithful servants become rulers in God's kingdom. We serve by ruling after having faithfully served in obedience to God in smaller matters.

*Matthew 25:21: "His lord said to him, 'Well done, good and faithful servant; you were faithful over a few things. I will **make you ruler** over many things. Enter into the joy of your lord.'"*

*Luke 19:17: "And he said to him, 'Well done, good servant: because you were faithful in a very little, **have authority** over ten cities.'"*

*Luke 12:44: "Truly, I say to you that he will **make him ruler** over all that he has."*

*Luke 22: 26b-30: "...he who is greatest among you, let him be as the younger, and he who governs as he who serves. For who is greater, he who sits at the table, or he who serves? Is it not he who **sits at the table**? Yet I (Jesus) am among you as the one who serves. But you are those who have continued with Me in My trials. And I bestow upon you a kingdom, just as My Father*

*bestowed one upon Me, that **you may eat and drink at My table in My kingdom**, and sit on thrones, judging the twelve tribes of Israel."*

The highest order of ruling is intercession. Those who are seated at the table of the Lord have the opportunity and the responsibility to make intercession; to serve as an advocate for the Israel of God. It is bringing the people of God with their needs to Jesus, and bringing the Word from the Lord to His people—that they may also be brought to the table of the Lord. As seated, mature sons, we reign with Jesus Christ on earth.

*Romans 5:1 7b: ... those who receive abundance of grace and of the gift of righteousness will **reign in life** through the One Jesus Christ.*

*2 Timothy 2:12: If we endure, we shall also **reign with Him.***

*Revelation 5: 9b-l0: ... and have redeemed us to God by Your blood out of every tribe and tongue and people and nation, and have made us **kings and priests** to our God; and we shall **reign <u>on</u> the <u>earth</u>.***

Jesus has provided and is providing full redemption and restoration. It is more than spending eternity with Him in heaven and missing hell, though certainly this would be more than sufficient reason to endure. But the Word says that by His abundance of grace and gift of righteousness we will **reign in life with Him if we endure (overcome).** Jesus has provided and is providing all we need to reign as kings and priest on the earth, as He ever lives to make intercession for us. He is bringing many sons to glory. *Hebrews 7:25.*

*Hebrews 2:10: For it was fitting for Him, for whom are all things, and by whom are all things, in **bringing many sons to glory**, to make the author of their salvation perfect through sufferings.*

Seeing the goal of ruling and reigning with Him in this life now, encourages us to continue during the difficult life purification and reformation processes. Though we are sons on our way to the seated stage, we may encounter experiences of what the Bible refers to as "outer darkness."

# NOTES

# CHAPTER 10

## OUTER DARKNESS

*Matthew 25:30:* *"And cast the unprofitable **servant** into **outer darkness**. There will be weeping and gnashing of teeth."*

The illustration we used earlier of the king-dome helps me to understand this principle. You remember the gigantic glass dome filled with the presence and light of God. The light flowed out in all directions and dispelled the darkness. Everywhere the light is, the darkness must flee. But everywhere the light has not yet reached, the darkness remains. Envision the light reaching out in a large circle around the dome. As far as it reaches, there is light; at the point where the light stops, the darkness begins. These outer regions from the dome could be referred to as "outer darkness".

The powers of darkness lurk in that darkness around the light, waiting to do their dirty work. They concentrate in the area around the light to try to prevent people from entering the king-dome light. That is why Jesus said the kingdom of heaven suffers violence, and the violent take it by force. There is a "pressing" involved in entering the kingdom—not a violence from, or force toward, God, but a violence from the enemy, and a pressing or taking it by force by those who enter.

*CAST INTO OUTER DARKNESS*

*Revelation 21:27: But there shall by no means enter it anything that defiles, or causes abomination or a lie.*

*Matthew 8:12:* *"But the **sons of the kingdom** will be **cast out into outer darkness**. There will be weeping and gnashing of teeth."*

*Luke 16:16:* *"The law and the prophets were until John. Since that time the kingdom of God has been preached, and everyone is **pressing** into it."*

*Matthew 11:12:* *"And from the days of John the Baptist till now, the kingdom of Heaven suffers **violence,** and the violent take it by force."*

If disobedience is found in us, even though we are sons and are well into our journey in the light toward the Holy City, we are returned to outer darkness for more suffering. God loves us and is faithful to allow us to repeat this cycle as many times as is necessary to bring us to spiritual maturity. The devil is predictable and will always be waiting for us in the outer darkness to inflict fresh pain—until we are able to reckon ourselves dead to self—that Jesus may be manifested in us. Then, with repentance and fresh love, we return to our journey into the light, toward the Holy City of God.

This does not mean we are eternally destroyed. The powers of darkness mean their dirty work for our death. But God limits what the enemy can do to His children, and all things work together for good. *Romans 8:28*. It is not for our death; it is for our purification. As we walk closer and closer to the dome, the light becomes brighter and exposes impurities or imperfections that we could not even see in the lesser light. As these are exposed, we always have two choices. We must either repent and allow the light to purify us further, or deny the fault, and blame someone or something else. If we do anything other than quickly repent, we are again on our way to outer darkness for more pain and suffering. In the pain of outer darkness we may think something like this, "It sure didn't hurt this much back in the light. I believe I will become obedient." We repent, die to self some more, and are returned to the light on our journey to the king-dome.

I am very sorry to say that in my own experience, it has required many of these cycles to deal with my independence. The secret is to humbly repent very quickly; for while we debate it in our mind, we are already slipping back toward the darkness.

It is very easy once we are out of the suffering stage to again begin to feel our muscles and go back to the independent stage. We think something like, "Wow! I'm glad that's over. I've got it now. It's all working again now. I can really do it this time. Here comes the

man of faith and power for the hour." Guess what stage we are just about to enter again?

*Revelation 21:27: But there shall by no means enter it anything that defiles, or causes abomination or a lie.*

*Matthew 8:12:* *"But the **sons of the kingdom will be cast out into outer darkness.** There will be weeping and gnashing of teeth."*

*Matthew 22:11-13:* *"But when the king came in to see the guests, he saw a man there who did not have on a **wedding garment.** So he said to him, 'Friend, how did you come in here without a wedding garment?' Then the king said to the servants, '**Bind him hand and foot,** take him away, and **cast him into outer darkness;** there will be weeping and gnashing of teeth.'"*

*Revelation 7:13-17: Then one of the elders answered, saying to me, "Who are these arrayed in **white robes,** and where did they come from?" And I said to him, "Sir, you know." So he said to me, "These are the ones who came out of great **tribulation,** and washed their robes and made them white in the blood of the Lamb. Therefore they are before the throne of God, and serve Him day and night in His temple. And He who sits on the throne will dwell among them. They shall neither hunger anymore nor thirst anymore, the sun shall not strike them, nor any heat; for the Lamb who is in the midst of the throne will shepherd them and lead them to living fountains of waters, and God will wipe away every tear from their eyes."*

*Revelation 19:8: And to her (the Lamb's wife) it was granted to be arrayed in fine linen, clean and white, **for the fine linen is the righteous acts of the saints.***

The wedding garment we must have on is "the righteous acts of the saints". True righteousness is the white robe washed in the blood of the Lamb. The wedding garment was customarily furnished by the host, the lord of the feast. The man who is not wearing the garment is without excuse. It is only by his independent thinking that he elects to refuse the offer and provide his own garment. Self-righteousness in its purest form will not be good enough to enable us to walk into the Holy City. The Pharisees did not make it. The spirit of pharisee will not enter the kingdom walk today and, unfortunately, will hinder all that it can from entering. Religion and its pharisaical laws and traditions are part of the darkness that must be pressed through. The kingdom disciple can expect violent resistance from people affected by the spirit of pharisee.

*Matthew 23:13: "But woe to you scribes and Pharisees, hypocrites! For you shut up the kingdom of heaven against men; for, you neither go in yourselves, nor do you allow those who are entering to go in."*

As we enter and continue our progress, we must continue to become less and less—that Jesus the Christ may live in us more and more. Christ living in us provides all the love and power of heaven to work God's obedience in us. This is the only garment, the white robe of fine linen that we must wear on our journey to becoming "New Jerusalem", and living the overcoming life.

# CHAPTER 11

## GOD'S JEWELS

As the Israel of God (the church) attains practical obedience and holiness through inner empowerment of the grace of God, the Bride of Christ is prepared. Now is the time for the church to make herself ready and become the perfected Bride and City of God on earth. The church for the most part has thought that the kingdom isn't for today, and has focused on getting in the gate and hanging on till Jesus comes, or until we die and go to heaven. Therefore, we have multitudes of Christians hanging around the gate in the outer court. We've expected these neophytes to demonstrate the "Christian life". It's no wonder that most of the church has had to disregard kingdom teaching as not being for this time, since, seemingly, no one has the power to fully live it. Therefore, we have reasoned, the kingdom must be for heaven when we die or some other day.

Another beautiful figurative word God uses to describe His mature "sons of the kingdom" is **"His jewels"**. His children are being perfected into beautiful jewels. It is so amazing that a God, who has all the gold and precious stones in the world, considers His kingdom people as jewels, jewels now being perfected, cut and polished to reflect His Glory.

*Malachi 3:17a: "They shall be Mine," says the Lord of host, "on the day that I make them **My jewels.**"*

*Isaiah 61:10b: For as He has clothed me with garments of salvation, He has covered me with robes of righteousness, as a bridegroom decks himself with ornaments, and **as a bride adorns herself with jewels.***

The remnant church is being prepared as precious jewels to reflect the glory of God. The spotless, perfected Bride Church will reflect the glory of God in every facet of life. There must be no internal imperfections or flaws if we are to perfectly reflect His glory. Each facet must be cut to perfect shape and polished to perfection, if we are to become one of the jewels of New Jerusalem—one of the adorning stones set on the foundation of the twelve apostles of the Lamb.

In God's pictorial language, the twelve tribes of Israel are the "gates" of entry to the city of God. The purified church (the Israel of God) is the "gateway" as it brings forth the ministry of Jesus in the world. The twelve apostles of the Lamb are the "foundation" of the spiritual city of God.

*Revelation 21:12,14: Also she had a great and high wall with twelve gates, and twelve angels at the gates, and names written on them, which are the names of the twelve tribes of the children of Israel. Now the wall of the city had twelve foundations, and on them were the names of the twelve apostles of the Lamb.*

*Revelation 21:18-23: "And the construction of its wall was of jasper; and the city was pure gold, like clear glass. And the foundations of the wall of the city **were adorned with all kinds of precious stones:** the first foundation was jasper, the second sapphire, the third chalcedony, the forth emerald, the fifth sardonyx, the sixth sardius, the seventh chrysolite, the eighth beryl, the ninth topaz, the tenth chrysoprase, the eleventh jacinth, and the twelfth amethyst. And the twelve gates were twelve pearls: each individual gate was of one pearl. And the street of the city was pure gold, like transparent glass. But I saw no temple in it, for the Lord God Almighty and the Lamb are its temple. And the city had no need of the sun or of the moon to shine in it, for the **glory of God illuminated it, and the Lamb is its light** .*

*Isaiah 62:1,3,5b: "For Zion's sake I will not hold My peace, and for Jerusalem's sake I will not rest, until her righteousness goes forth as **brightness**, and her salvation as a lamp that burns. You shall also be a **crown of glory** in the hand of the Lord, and a **royal diadem** in the hand of your God. And as the bridegroom rejoices over the bride, so shall your God rejoice over you."*

As God is perfecting us, the finished jewel may be much smaller than the initial, damaged, rough stone. But when He is finished, there will be no impurities to impede the glorious light of God from flowing out every window or **"facet"** of our life. If there are imperfections yet within us, a need for further healing or dying to self, they will block or hinder the flow of God's glory and keep it from being reflected in one or more of our "facets". For example, we may be able to reflect His glory in the area of prosperity, but not in the area of enjoyment, etc.

Another word demonstrating the unimpeded ability to "flow" the glory of God from all the facets of our jewel is **freedom**. In the <u>natural</u> dimension, a cut diamond that has an impurity in it, such as a carbon deposit, is not free to "flow" the light out all of its facets. Also, if that diamond is not cut properly or has blemishes in its surface, the light flowing through it will be distorted. In the <u>spiritual</u>, if we, the children of God, have some spot of impurity remaining in our hearts, we will not be free to "flow" the glory of God in that area of our lives. Also, if we are not yet perfectly cut and polished, we are not free to "flow" His light without distortion. The process of being formed, cut, polished, and purified might be considered very difficult by the diamond that is experiencing the cutting and grinding.

The overcomer will want to locate these imperfections and allow God to deal with them. Jesus came to fix our imperfections and repair the work done to us by the devil and by our own foolishness. We can learn to recognize the problem area by the lack of the glory of God flowing through a particular area or facet of our life or daily walk. There are seven easily-defined general areas or facets of freedom in each of us.

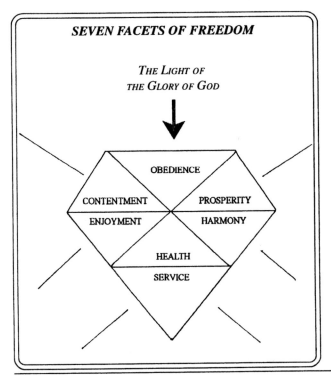

**SEVEN FACETS OF FREEDOM**

THE LIGHT OF
THE GLORY OF GOD

OBEDIENCE

CONTENTMENT     PROSPERITY

ENJOYMENT     HARMONY

HEALTH

SERVICE

*Zechariah 3:9, Amp.:* "*For behold, upon the stone which I have set before Joshua, upon that one stone are seven eyes or facets* " [the all-embracing providence of God and the sevenfold radiations of the Spirit of God]. "*Behold, I will carve upon it its inscription,*" says the Lord of host, "*and I will remove the iniquity and guilt of this land in a single day.*"

Freedom is having all hindrances to receiving and reflecting the light of His glory removed. If freedom in a certain facet does not exist, we will know to look in a corresponding area in the heart for impurities or imperfections to be healed or removed. We must know how to appropriate the ministry of Jesus to heal the brokenhearted and set the captives free, to allow Him to burn out impurities or cut away a portion of our stone to eliminate the impurity in our jewel. In love He may use the chisel and hammer of traumatic events and abrasive relationships to cut and polish our jewel.

The facets of a jewel are "windows". Light flows <u>in</u> some and <u>out</u> others. When the jewel is moved, the light shifts from window to window and sparkles brightly as it reflects the light from each facet. The jewel has no light of its own, but does a beautiful job of reflecting available light.

The major facet of our jewel is **obedience**. Usually the larger facet on top of a jewel receives the light <u>in</u> to be reflected <u>out</u> the other smaller facets. We will reflect whatever light we turn our obedience toward. If we turn our obedience toward evil, we will reflect the darkness of evil. If we turn our obedience toward God, we will reflect His glory. **Freedom is both freedom <u>from</u> reflecting evil and freedom <u>to</u> reflect good.**

## SEVEN FACETS OF FREEDOM

**Seven facets of freedom are obedience, contentment, prosperity, enjoyment, harmony, health and service.** Probably all needed areas of freedom are defined under these seven headings. If we have these freedoms, we can walk in the kingdom-of-God, New Jerusalem, purified, Bride-of-Christ, life-style.

## OBEDIENCE IS FREEDOM

FREEDOM FROM —Rebellion, Stubbornness, Self-will, Perversion, Arrogance, Compulsiveness, Impulsiveness, Pride, Impatience.

FREEDOM TO BE —Submissive, Yielding, Faithful, Loyal, Humble, Repentant.

## CONTENTMENT IS FREEDOM

FREEDOM FROM —Want, Lust, Needs that cause stress, Fear, Doubt, Worry, Anxiety, Insecurity, Suspicion, Distrust, Hopelessness, Nervousness, Tension, Confusion.

FREEDOM TO BE —Satisfied, Thankful, Fulfilled, Secure, Trusting, Believing, Hopeful, Peaceful, Stable.

## PROSPERITY IS FREEDOM

FREEDOM FROM—Lack, Poverty, Wastefulness, Fruitlessness, Loss, Not having enough to complete God's plan.

FREEDOM TO BE —Adequately supplied to complete God's plan, Fruitful, Flourishing, Receiving, Increasing, Conserving.

## ENJOYMENT IS FREEDOM

FREEDOM FROM —Ungodly Pain & Sorrow, Torment, Guilt, Boredom, Condemnation, Depression, Self-pity, Shame, Withdrawal, Loneliness, Frustration.

FREEDOM TO BE —Experiencing Pleasure in the blessings of God, Delighting in the Lord, Being Joyful, Happy.

## HARMONY IS FREEDOM

FREEDOM FROM —Strife, Contention, Jealousy, Envy, Hostility, Discord, Rejecting, Rejection, Resentment, Retaliation, Criticizing, Hate, Selfishness, Manipulation, Gossip.

FREEDOM TO BE —Unified, Compatible, In Accord, Friendly, Open, In Fellowship, Accepted, Accepting.

## HEALTH IS FREEDOM

FREEDOM FROM —(Physical, Emotional, or Spiritual) Sickness, Disease, Wounding, Disorder, Malfunction, Malformation, Perversion, Weakness.

FREEDOM TO BE—(Physically, Emotionally, or Spiritually) Whole, Well, Healed, Strong, In Order, Sound, Able-bodied, Hearty.

## SERVICE IS FREEDOM

FREEDOM FROM —Unproductivity, Slothfulness, Uselessness, Incapability, Lack of Purpose, Worthlessness, Futility, Vanity, Hindering.

FREEDOM TO BE —Productive, Purposeful, Providing, Useful, Capable, Valuable, Helpful.

Remember: We must turn our facet of obedience toward the light and away from darkness. We will reflect whatever light we turn our obedience toward. If we turn our obedience toward evil, we will reflect the darkness of evil. If we turn our obedience toward God, we will reflect His glory. **Freedom is both freedom <u>from</u> reflecting evil and freedom <u>to</u> reflect good.**

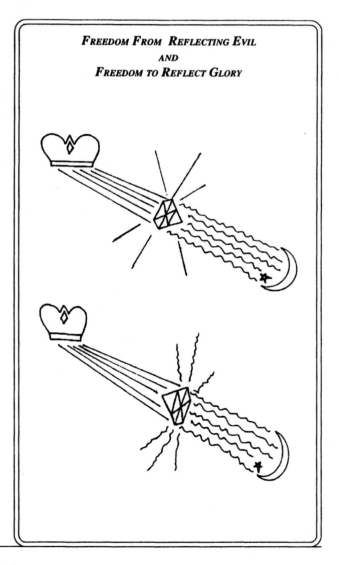

*FREEDOM FROM REFLECTING EVIL*
*AND*
*FREEDOM TO REFLECT GLORY*

If we have impurities in our jewel, we feel very uncomfortable when we turn fully toward the light. The bright light generates heat within as it contacts the impurities and is blocked from flowing out. For comfort's sake, some will turn their "obedience facet" away from the light, away from the closeness of God.

*Romans 6:16-18: Do you not know that **to whom you present yourselves slaves to obey, you are that one's slave whom you obey,** whether of sin to death, or of obedience to righteousness? But God be thanked that though you were slaves of sin, yet you **obeyed from the heart** that form of doctrine to which you were delivered. And having been **set free** from sin, you became slaves of righteousness.*

Some will lift up a **shield of unbelief or self deception** to keep the light from burning within them. The enemy will provide the shield for us if we will use it. He has a whole suit of armor for those who will obey him.

*Luke 11:20-22: "But if I cast out demons with the finger of God, surely the kingdom of God has come upon you. When a strong man, **fully armed,** guards his own palace, his goods are in peace. But when one stronger than he comes upon him and overcomes him, he takes from him **all his armor** in which he trusted, and divides his spoils."*

The armor of Satan is the opposite of God's armor. Those who obey the enemy have their waist girded with lies, a breastplate of unrighteousness; their feet are shod with the bad news of conflict; they carry the shield of unbelief and self deception ; they take the helmet of damnation; and they wield the sword of evil spirits, which is the words of accusation and condemnation.

**Self-deception begins with replacing what God has said with human rationalization and self-justification.** Rather than repent and change, some will attempt to alleviate their uncomfortable feelings of guilt through self-deception, by denying their own guilt and blaming others. They will accuse and condemn others for their own inner-impurities and imperfections. The enemy will assist with the development of belief systems and doctrines which seem to justify one's faults, rather than change them.

Only by turning directly toward the light of God and continuing to move toward the light, can one's inner-impurities and imperfections be exposed and dealt with. Only by repenting and allowing the power of God to change, will one become purified. **Belief and obedience causes man to be conformed to God. Unbelief and self-deception attempt to conform God to man.**

If we are to become the jewels of God, there are things in each individuals life that must be overcome. As we journey toward becoming His jewels the damage previously done to us by the enemy and the resulting negative life patterns must be overcome. We must become overcomers.

# CHAPTER 12

## THE OVERCOMING LIFE

The crowd at the finish line leans forward and peers intently down the track to see which one of the well-trained cyclists is leading as they all come into view over the last hill of the race. The young men who have trained diligently are now pushing their bodies to the very limit. Their lungs work to the fullest capacity to gather oxygen for pounding hearts to rush it to their powerful, muscular, sinewy legs—legs pumping like engine pistons in an effort to push their bicycles ahead of the others.

The burst of applause and cheers from the crowd are delayed for an instant. The crowd is shocked into silence for a split second while their minds try to accept what their wide-opened eyes are seeing. Gaping mouths begin to burst forth cheers and shouts of jubilation as the momentary disbelief of their own eyes is dispelled. Many eyes fill with tears as the crowd wildly applauds the young man with only one leg and one arm as he crosses the finish line first.

At another time and place in a high school auditorium, hundreds of children gasp and draw back a little as they get their first look at a man walking out on stage. After only a few minutes, the man behind the disfigured face seems like one of their best friends. And they are hardly aware of the massive scars or the knurled, maimed hands. The children are mostly aware of the gentle love and real, caring attitude they feel coming from their new friend. Soon they are laughing hilariously with him as he humorously relates true stories of being burned almost to death in a military ordeal. All are moved and must consider the God that he tells them about. His joyous love proclaims overcoming victory over the years of intense pain and great loss, and testifies of the powerful grace of the love of Jesus.

Many such true stories of people overcoming tremendous obstacles could be told. Our hearts would probably be touched by each of them. Something inside us seems to be excited. In some way we begin to feel encouragement in our own soul? Is it possible that our own problems may seem to be a little less of a mountain when we consider their victories? Is there perhaps a new ray of hope released in us? Perhaps something like this thought crosses our minds, "If God helped them to overcome, maybe He can also help me." Perhaps our doubt that God will do anything about our world is challenged a little. If He will work in these individuals' lives to overcome, isn't it possible that He might work in many lives across the world? What might be the result of multitudes, one at a time, overcoming? Is there perhaps hope birthed in our hearts for our own lives and for the world by these examples of overcoming?

How did they do it? How can I do it? Many books are written to attempt to answer these questions. We surely don't have all the answers, but one common denominator is always present. In a word, it is **faith**. What the individual believes, how he views God, Himself, and the problem is the key. Most overcomers will say something like, "I never thought of myself as handicapped—only challenged." Or, "It never entered my mind that it could not be done". A challenge seems to be there for the purpose of our overcoming it. Therefore, it is temporary, and if temporary, then temporal, not eternal. The temporal must yield to the eternal. The power for overcoming is the eternal God. "Handicap" implies a forever negative condition that we cannot overcome, but must succumb to. In faith, overcomers see God as greater than the problem and believe He is working with them. When God is working on the problem, it does not matter that it is too big for us. We know we could never do it alone. **How we see God, ourselves, and our problems makes the difference!**

Many lives have been damaged or crippled by bad things that have happened. Sin is always at the root of every bad thing. We each have been harmed to some degree by the results of someone's sin. If we view our problem as a challenge that Jesus came to help us with, we can overcome. Our world view can change if we see that the world's crippling sin problem is no greater than the individual's sin problem. There is just more of it. A brick layer can lay one brick in a few seconds. It takes longer to lay an entire brick wall, but it is still the same problem and can be done only one brick at a time. If many brick layers are working on the wall simultaneously, the wall is built much faster. If it is possible for one person to overcome, then it is possible for the world to overcome through faith in God.

**"Overcoming"** is one of the major teachings of the New Testament. Yet it has not been well-understood or applied in past generations. Overcoming has been seen, for the most part, as pertaining only to the area of personal sin. Once we receive revelation of the "at-hand" kingdom, our overcoming begins to take on a much broader scope. Jesus has not only provided the potential for His children to overcome personal sin; but, He has also provided a way for our overcoming to have an effect on the Church, the community, the nation, and eventually the planet. Some think there are also implications in the Word that the results of overcoming reach into eternal and celestial realms of the future.

Surely, the lack of overcoming in God's people is heavy on God's heart as it is on every loving pastor and true believer. **Those who do not overcome are overcome**—overcome by negative emotions of depression, hopelessness, pride, anger, rage, violence, fear, worry, insecurity, jealousy, etc. These negative emotions lead to being overcome in lust of all kinds, and bondages of immorality, drugs, alcohol, sexual perversions, selfishness, greed, etc.

This is not the lifestyle for which Jesus gave His life. He did not die to purchase failure for His people. If we are to ever see the overcoming of poverty, racial hatred, injustice, political aggression, child abuse, family violence, abortion, gang violence, and every other social sickness and evil, we must begin to understand the overcoming power of Christ. We must grasp in reality the ability to appropriate the great mystery of the overcoming work of Jesus.

The enemy wants you to believe that the earth is his and the fullness thereof. He wants you to hide out and just try to hang on till you die and go to heaven. The enemy sure doesn't want you to know that in appropriating the work (the ministry) of Christ Jesus, you have the power to overcome him and all of his dirty work. The truth is that the earth is the Lord's, and all that is in it.

*Psalm 24:1: The earth is the LORD'S, and the fullness thereof; the world, and they that dwell therein.*

The only right that the devil has to this world and all its people is the right that we give him. His only power is the power of deception. If he can make people believe his lies, then he can carry out the lies. The Word is clear. Jesus has overcome the enemy and all of his work. We do not belong to the devil. We do not need to believe or obey him in any area. Neither the earth nor anything in it belongs to the enemy, and we do not have to give up anything to him. He has no right to cause the earth to be burned in judgment. He has no right to the governments of the world. The world system does not belong to him. It is God's. God gave His only Son to repurchase it. He is waiting for His people to overcome and possess His world. Is there any mission on earth more important than overcoming?

Perhaps there is no more vital word in the Bible relative to overcoming than the following verse. If we can receive revelation light of the meaning of this verse, we will be on the way toward overcoming.

*KEY VERSE: Revelation 12:11:* **"And they overcame him by the blood of the Lamb and by the word of their testimony, and they did not love their lives to the death."**

The Greek work translated "overcame" is "nikao" (nik-ah'-o) meaning "to subdue", or "to get the victory". It comes from the word "nike" (nee'-kay), a prime root meaning "conquest", or "means of success".

The Greek word translated "testimony" is "marturia" (mar-too-ree'-ah), meaning evidence". It comes from "martus" (mar'-toos) meaning "witness" and implies "a martyr".

Our overcoming begins with the blood of the Lamb. It is only by the cross that the enemy's power was and is broken. When the perfect sinless Son of God gave up his pure life on the cross to die for all sin, the penalty for all sin was and is forever paid. From that point forward, the enemy has no further hold, no further right to impose evil on any person on earth except as we allow it. In our ignorance of the work that Jesus has done, and because of our doubt and unbelief, mankind continues to suffer needlessly. As the blood flowed from Jesus' body on the cross and was absorbed by the soil of the earth, the earth was forever changed. God's economy relative to man, the earth, and the devil was, for all time and eternity, changed.

God's full acceptance and acknowledgment of the completed work of the cross as payment for the penalty of all sin is proved in the resurrection of His Son.

Had the work of redemption not been perfect, had the law not been totally satisfied, there would have been no resurrection. It is forever settled. The enemy has no further right to impose evil without our (mankind's) approval. That's why the Scripture says, *"the devil goes about as a roaring lion seeking whom he **may** devour."*

Jesus then ascended to heaven and sat down at the right hand of the Father to make intercession for us. The finished work of the cross, the blood of Jesus the Lamb, is ever before God to plead our case. The enemy has no rights. The case is always decided by the blood of Jesus, **if we so plead.** The matter is in our hands. We can deny the blood. We can plead our own case. We can, if we choose, deny our sin. We can choose to do it our way. We can walk in unbelief toward the blood of Jesus. This is disobedience to God and is our invitation to the devil to impose evil upon us. We then become one he may devour.

Not only is Jesus interceding for us at the right hand of the Father, He has also returned to earth in the Holy Spirit to personally indwell each of His children. The word says he became a life-giving Spirit. *(1 Corinthians 15:46, 2 Corinthians 8:17.)* Living in us, He is our source of power and righteousness for daily living. He is always with us, always available to communicate with us regarding every situation we encounter. His love in us causes us to desire to walk in obedience to God. It also grants us the capacity of His life enabling us to walk in the practical reality of being and doing exactly as He is and does. And He always obeys the Father.

There are many things that can affect our ability to walk in the Spirit of Christ, but our walk must begin with our desire to lay aside any and every thing that hinders.

One of the hindrances might involve our need to do things our way. Our will must take second place to His will. Eventually **His will must become our will.** We can daily try to live righteously on our own. We can strive to keep rules and laws. We can seek religious orders, systems, and practices to cause us to live righteously. In doing so, we deny the Lord. We deny His Holy Spirit living in us.

The evidence **"or word of our testimony"** comes forth from Jesus living in us. As we **"do not love our own life to the death"**, we give up our own way and allow the Holy Spirit of Jesus the Christ to live in us instead of allowing our own life to live in us. As He lives in us and we listen to and obey Him, we overcome.

*Revelation 2:7b: "To him who overcomes I will give to **eat from the tree of life** which is in the midst of the Paradise of God."*

Eating from the tree of life means hearing, receiving living revelation of God, as opposed to reasoning things out from the tree of knowledge of good and evil. And it means experiencing eternal (abundant) life now.

*John 10:10: The thief does not come except to steal, and to kill, and to destroy. I have come that **they may have life, and that they may have it more abundantly.***

Eternal life is a **quality** of life, not just a quantity. The Greek word translated "abundantly" is (per-is-sos') and means "beyond", "super abundant (in quantity)", " superior (in quality)", or "preeminence".

*Revelation 22:14: Blessed are those who **do His commandments,** that they may have the right to the **tree of life** and may enter through the gates into the city.*

Western culture has taught us to depend on our intellect. Education is seen as the answer to mankind's social ills. The basic theory seems to be that if we have enough knowledge, we will become smart enough to rule our own lives successfully. Independence is very important to our way of thinking. We feel if we are intellectually sharp enough and have enough money, we can do what we want and have all we want. We think surely this will produce peace and happiness. This is partaking of the tree of knowledge of good and evil. Yes, education and mental skills are important aspects of life. But they alone cannot bring us the abundant, overcoming life we seek.

Several years ago a man in his fifties came to me for personal ministry. We will call him Dr. Smart. I chose this name because he was one of the most intelligent men I've met. He held several doctors degrees, including a theological degree. Dr. Smart had come looking for help with great emotional problems. I don't believe I ever saw a more miserable person. He was dealing with great inner pain and strife. Personal and professional relationships would not function properly in his life. He was intensely frustrated, lonely, and angry.

As we talked, I mentioned a scripture. He quickly told me where it was found, who wrote it to whom, the intent of the writer, and the cultural conditions at the time and place it was written. Yet, this poor man had no spiritual revelation of the Word. He did not have the first revelation of Jesus as savior, and would hear nothing of spiritual revelation at all. He would debate and even become angry with any suggestion of spiritual revelation. His whole understanding came from the tree of knowledge of good and evil and he had no part with the tree of life. Jesus is the only source of abundant life.

## JESUS THE OVERCOMER

The Bible teaches us that Christ Jesus has overcome the enemy and the world. The gospel of the kingdom which Jesus himself taught in the Bible deals primarily with the experience of overcoming in life now. Man seems to have been left with the awesome responsibility of finishing the job of making all God's enemies His footstool. Certainly Satan and his demonic hosts are totally defeated in the finished work of the cross and resurrection of Christ Jesus. Yet we live in a practical world in which it seems the enemy is still killing, stealing, and destroying. Many Christians are severely wounded and at least have their lives partially destroyed by the enemy.

*Psalm 110:1-3: Jehovah (self existing, eternal one) said to Adoni (sovereign, ruling, controlling one), "Sit at My right hand, till I make Your enemies Your footstool." Jehovah shall send the rod of Your strength out of Zion. Rule in the midst of Your enemies! Your people shall be willing (volunteers) in the day of Your power. In the beauties of holiness, from the womb of the morning...*

This and other scriptures make very clear that the final responsibility for overcoming power comes from Jehovah. The people of Christ are to be willing volunteers to "flow" the rod of Jesus' strength out of Zion (the purified, holy, bride-Church), in the beauties of holiness, from the womb of the morning.

There is no other method for overcoming apart from the blood of the Lamb and the expression of His strength through His people. There is no enemy, no power on earth, which cannot be overcome by the Spirit of the Lord working through His willing and obedient people.

You are greatly blessed to be a part of the awakening generation of believers who are throwing off the old garment of a defeated life, which only hopes to escape. We are putting on the new garment of praise and power of the overcoming life in the beauty of holiness. The morning is birthed. Let it be birthed in your heart. Pray for the Morning Star to arise in your heart. The freedom of the kingdom of God is available. Let's get in on it. Let's go on to all the fullness of the kingdom-of-God lifestyle, the overcoming life.

All of the relics of religious rules, traditions of man, and our striving to keep them will never overcome. The law has no power to fulfill itself. Christ Jesus is the one who fulfills the law. The power of the law is to make us aware of our sin. The law that is set into nature brings forth the natural penalty of our sin. The law kills; the Spirit brings life. *Romans 3:20, 2Corinthians 3:6, Galations3:13-14.* Trying hard with all our strength can make us very tired but will not enable us to keep the rules and overcome.

Only as we are willing to die to our self-life and our own strength, take up our cross, and to trust in His life, can the Morning Star (His own law-fulfilling life) be birthed in us. Then we can begin to live righteously by His strength. Overcoming is a natural result of the Spirit of Christ Jesus living in our mortal body.

Our method is not to try to know rules and keep them. It is not to try to know about God and about His word. Our method is to know God Himself in intense personal intimacy. We must know Jesus, the Word from God. We seek the God of the Word, not just the words about God. Intimacy with Jesus the Christ—a personal, intimate, real, penetrating covenant relationship as the bride of Christ—is the overcoming life.

## SAVED BY HIS LIFE

The penalty of our sin was paid by **His death** on the cross, reconciling us to Holy God. Our **life** is being saved, healed, made whole, and we are being delivered now by the indwelling **resurrection life** of Christ Jesus through the Spirit.

*Romans 5:10: For if when we were enemies **we were reconciled to God through the death of His Son,** much more having been reconciled, **we shall be saved by His life.***

The Greek word translated **"saved",** is "sozo" (sode'zo) which means "to save, deliver or protect"; it is also translated, "heal, preserve, do well, to be whole, or to make whole".

Two aspects of our redemption are referred to in this and other verses. One is **through the death of Jesus;** the other is **by the life of Jesus.** The cross of Jesus provides reconciliation. His resurrection life saves (heals, makes whole, delivers, protects, and preserves) us.

*Romans 7:23-25a: But I see another law in my members, warring against the law of my mind, and bringing me into captivity to the law of sin which is in my members. O wretched man that I am! **Who will deliver me** from this body of death? I thank God—through **Jesus Christ our Lord!***

*Romans 8:9-11, 14,16-17: But you are not in the flesh but in the Spirit, if indeed the Spirit of God dwells in you. Now if anyone does not have the **Spirit of Christ,** he is none of His. And if **Christ is in you,** the body is dead because of sin, but the Spirit is life because of righteousness. But if the Spirit of Him who raised Jesus from the dead dwells in you, He who raised Christ from the dead will also give life to your mortal bodies through His Spirit who dwells in you. For as many as are led by the Spirit of God, these are **sons of God.** The Spirit Himself bears witness with our spirit that we are children of God, and if children, then heirs —heirs of God and **joint heirs** with Christ, if indeed we suffer with Him, that we may also be **glorified together**.*

Speaking of those who are not entering into the overcoming kingdom-of-heaven lifestyle, the Lord said in *Matthew 7:23, "And then I will declare to them, **I never knew you;** depart from Me you who practice lawlessness!"*

We may know Him to some degree, but does He intimately **know us**? Unless we are related to Him as His bride and his life is actually within us, He does not know us in the sense of this verse.

Paul in *Philippians 3:7-16*, speaks of suffering the loss of all things, and that he counts them only as rubbish that *"I may **gain Christ** ",* and *"that I may know Him and the power of His resurrection, and the fellowship of His sufferings, being conformed to His death, if by any means, I may attain to the resurrection from the dead".*

As we are conformed to His death now in this life, we may attain His resurrection life now in this life. Verse 16 says, *"to the degree that we have already attained let us walk."* Suffering plays a part in being conformed to His death and attaining His resurrection life. The important thing for us is to ***"press toward the goal for the prize of the upward call of God in Christ Jesus".*** Intimately knowing Him and being known by Him **is** the power for the overcoming life.

## ENDURE TO THE END

Overcoming means we must finish the course. We have not totally overcome until we have overcome to the end. Overcoming is the victory of finishing.

Years ago I heard a story that supposedly took place some time in the early nineteen hundreds. Several schools had come together for a track meet and field day. The grand finale was a mile foot race, four times around a quarter-mile cinder track. The runners all got a good start and were still running as a pack together after the first lap. A careful look at the runners revealed that one boy was having a harder time keeping up with the pack. His face was showing signs of stress more than the others. In the second lap the boy began to fall behind the pack. The third lap saw the pack spread out as the strongest runners begin to pull away. But this one boy was now almost half a lap behind the last runner.

When the crowd cheered the winners across the finish line, this boy was far behind on the back side of the track. It was obvious to everyone that he was badly fatigued and could hardly keep going. Suddenly the crowd moaned a little as the young man stumbled and fell on the track. Every one watched as the boy struggled, got up and on wobbly legs, and with bleeding knees and hands, continued to try to make it around the track. All of the other runners were finished. Only the one wobbly runner remained on the track. He was finally rounding the last curve and headed toward the finish line when, apparently, he got a second wind and began to run a little better.

He crossed the finish line and immediately collapsed face down on the track. Those nearby ran to him and rolled him over. A doctor arrived and began to do what he could. The doctor called for a stretcher and moved the boy from the track to a shady spot on the grassy infield. As the young man began to recover, the doctor working over him asked the question that the crowd had been asking each other. The doctor asked, "Son why didn't you just step off the track? There was no chance for you to win the race. No one would have paid much attention if you had stepped off the track on the back side."

The boy replied, "You see, Sir, it was this way. A bad sickness hit my school, and all of our best runners that had trained for this race were too sick and weak to come. I was the best my school had to send. Sir, I couldn't let it be said that my school could not even finish the race."

You are the best God had to send to be you, to accomplish the purpose of your life. Only you can do and be what God has sent you to this race of life to do and be.

God is not so interested in our being first across the finish line. His primary concern is not that we run the race of life with perfect form. He does not count us out if we fall down on the track. The only way we can lose is to step off the track. No matter how far behind we are or how many times we fall, we can, we must, get up and keep moving toward the finish line. God has a significant purpose for our lives that may not be known to us fully now. Who knows what future multiplied results may come in the generations ahead from your overcoming and finishing the course God has set for you? Who knows what eternal matters may be affected?

We are not in competition with our brothers and sisters to be as good as, or better than, they. The race is not against others. God just wants us to be all **we** are meant to be. We are not here to please the crowd. We are here to finish the course and hear, "Well done, good and faithful servant."

In the following verses, the Greek word translated **"endure"** is "hupomeno" (hoop-om-en'-o), which means "to stay under or behind, remain, undergo, bear trials, have fortitude, persevere".

The Greek word translated **"end"** is "telos" (tel'-os), which means "to set out for a definite point or goal", "the point aimed at as a limit", by implication "conclusion or termination", literally or figuratively "result or purpose".

*Matthew 24:12-14: "And because lawlessness will abound, the love of many will grow cold. But he who endures to the end shall be saved. And this gospel of the kingdom will be preached to all the nations, and then the end will come."*

*Matthew 10:22: "And you will be hated by all for My name's sake. But he who endures to the end will be saved."*

*1 Corinthians 13:7-8a: (Love)—bears all things, believes all things, hopes all things, endures all things. Love never fails.*

In contrast, a different Greek word is used in the following verse which simply means "is or are".

*Mark 4:17: "And they have no root in themselves, and so endure only for a time. Afterward, when tribulation or persecution arises for the word's sake, immediately they stumble."*

Overcoming (subduing, having victory) means being delivered **from** some things and being delivered **through** some things. To strive to be delivered from all tribulation and persecution may be an unfruitful endeavor. Also, who can explain why some are delivered from having a divorce, and some are delivered from the devastation through and after a divorce? Both the one delivered from getting sick and the one delivered through a disease are overcomers if they endure. Perhaps it would be best to seek to know God's plan and purpose in each situation.

Overcoming may mean having victory in and during the fire. It means living in Him, in His peace and joy, for example, even in the midst of divorce, slanderous attacks, defaming accusations, and vile insinuations about our moral character and inner motives, even by those we may have loved the most.

Paul and many other men of God have been overcomers while in prison, being stoned, mocked, and falsely accused. Many have been free in prison, while many others have been in bondage walking the streets.

Overcoming has to do with peace that passes understanding and does not always mean a change in our external circumstances.

Overcoming and enduring to the end often eludes Christians. Though we strive hard to learn and obey the apostle's doctrine, we may experience a break down in our fortitude. *"Many are called but few are chosen"*. Only the finishers are chosen to receive the promises to the overcomers.

**We will overcome only by our covenant relationship with the Overcomer.** Only as we are braided into one with Jesus, will His strength become ours. We trade our strength (weakness) for His strength to overcome and endure. **We must intimately relate to Him continuously if we are to overcome consistently.**

The impact and results of overcoming in the individuals life can be tremendous. It is hard for many individuals to even imagine the beauty of walking in daily peace, joy, and prosperity, of spirit, soul, and body. The end of financial stress, marital stress, and other forms of stress seems an unattainable dream to many people who have come to accept stress as normal life.

The frustrations of life endured by mankind are generated by man's lack of walking in God's ways (kingdom living). The mountains of frustrating problems and insurmountable obstacles will melt away as the power of Christ by the grace of God flows in and through the individuals life. The corporate effect of many individuals overcoming and living God's way will greatly impact everyone and everything on the planet.

# CHAPTER 13

## CORPORATE KINGDOM

One of the results of personal individual kingdom righteousness is that the corporate patterns of life will begin to be ordered by the ways and will of God. Men begin to rule everything over which they have authority according to the ways of God instead of the fallen ways of man.

Only a very few people are just beginning to realize the degree of dominion and potency delegated to mankind for ruling the world systems and the planet. Man is not at the mercy of "mother nature" nor any other aspect of the world. On the contrary, the world systems and the planet are at the mercy of mankind. The combined effect of multitudes of people living their lives according to the ways of the Babylonian kingdom of darkness is great disorder and stress on all the systems of man and earth. Left unchanged it would eventually lead to destruction. In contrast, the combined effect of multitudes of people living their lives according to the ways of the New Jerusalem kingdom of God is great peace, order, and prosperity for mankind and the planet.

All systems of life on earth will be positively affected by the kingdom of God lifestyle in men. **Social, economical, political and ecological systems** will prosper and come into peaceful order. The negative trends of destruction and disorder, brought about by selfishness will reverse and the earth can become renewed. Even the weather will improve as delicate ecological balances damaged by man's selfishness and greed are repaired. Storms will decrease in number and intensity as global warming is reversed and stabilized, causing tropical temperatures to moderate slightly.

*Romans 8:19,21-22: For the earnest expectation of the creation eagerly waits for the revealing of the sons of God...because the creation itself also will be delivered from the bondage of corruption into the glorious liberty of the children of God. For we know that the whole creation groans and labors with birth pangs together until now.*

With the natural understanding we can not see or understand the link between man's beliefs and actions and the natural systems of the planet. Even with all the knowledge we have acquired man can not see very far into the spiritual realm. Therefore we have little understanding of the impact of what we believe, say, and do has upon the natural occurrences of the planet. We can however with the application of some wisdom begin to see the cost of the negative ways of man upon the social, economic, and political systems of our world.

It may be impossible for us to imagine all the ramifications of mankind living in obedience to God. There is more than plenty of everything on the planet that mankind would ever need. Consider what good could be done with vast amounts of money, resources, and manpower that mankind would no longer spend on wars. What about the many billions of dollars and man hours spent on sin-related diseases like Aids, or on injuries, and on property loss due to violence or negligence. Consider the tremendous cost of crime. Unbelievable effort and resources currently go toward providing law enforcement agencies, many costly prisons, and an expensive judicial system, not to mention the tremendous property loss. And what about the therapy and counseling needed to try to put back together the confused psyche of masses who are damaged by stress and fear. Who can even imagine the total cost of productive lives lost due to drugs and alcohol. The list of costs for disobedience goes on and on. If all this cost could be saved and reapplied to doing good and loving one another, there would be plenty of everything for everyone.

"Oh!" You say! "This is an impossible dream and can never really happen." **Tell that to Jesus! This is why He came to earth and taught the kingdom-of-God way of life. This is why He died on the cross, was resurrected, ascended into heaven, and returned to earth in the Holy Spirit to live in man and produce His kingdom lifestyle!** You tell Him it can't be done! Personally I know by the authority of His Word, **it is being done!**—One heart, one life at a time, He is establishing His rule, His kingdom. God is looking for and finding men who will give up their ways, their greed, their needs and wants, just to obey the Lord.

Yes, the wicked are becoming more vile. Yes, the numbers of greedy men who despise the way of God are increasing. Yes, the enemy is having a blast stealing, killing, and destroying men, women, and innocent children, while much of the church seems powerless to do anything about it, and sometimes, even becomes a part of the problem. Yes, we see governments faltering and unable to even slow down the degradation of society. Yes, we see mankind on the verge of destruction by his own ways. No doubt the fires of judgment are kindled on earth and the wrath of God is stored up against this evil. Yes it may get worse before it gets better. But as Christ Jesus lives in Godly men it will get better.

**What part of this worldly wickedness is greater than God?** Even during all this rampant evil, there are many extremely godly men and women that God is raising up in the world. These are men and women with a level of commitment toward God and a sense of destiny that compels them to live godly in Christ Jesus. These are not just churchly religious baby Christians. They are a mighty army of mighty men and women of God. These are people of valor that God is raising up— in business, in the military, in government, in the family etc., as educators, scientists, apostolic ministers, prophets, evangelists, pastors, and kingdom teachers. Their primary purpose in life is to intimately know the Lord and serve Him totally. People of God, it is not time to draw back or to be downcast. We are entering the most victorious season of earth—The season in which **the wrath of God's love** will cleanse the earth. And the season when **the mercy and grace of God's love** will cause the righteous, mature sons to shine forth as the sun. *(Matthew 13:40-43.)*

The focus of Christians has been so diverted by theological teachings toward future events that many have missed and are yet missing the ominous potential of God's provision for today. We are now living in the "end of the age". This is the time looked forward to by the writers of the New Testament. God is ready and everything is in place to restore His ways to our world. Many individuals are bringing forth the kingdom of God on earth in their own lives and families without even realizing what they are really doing. Enlightenment and understanding of the kingdom will move our focus from "future end time theology" to overcoming the kingdom of darkness and bringing forth the kingdom of God now on our planet.

## THE END TIMES

End-time theology is an area that I have not received great revelation on or that I greatly enjoy looking into. By no means do I think that I have all the answers. Bible school and years of being taught different teachers' views have given me traditional knowledge through other men. Please do not think that the things that will be presented here are because of ignorance to the traditional views as taught by the "pre's and post's" of eschatology. Though I know the views and at different times have held different ones I'm not sure that I can completely rest in any of the many camps of theological traditions.

Though end-time theology has not been an area of great personal interest to me, the revelation of the gospel of the kingdom that Jesus preached and taught began to have a disruptive effect on my end-time views. This fact and the pressure of Christians who have strong solid positions of one camp or another lodged in their hearts seem to demand that the Spirit of God reveal to us more specific truth regarding **the day of the Lord, the bodily return of the Lord, the judgment of the wicked,** and the **removal of the wicked or the saints.** We are not embarking on a study of these things in this work, but trust you will seek more truth from God in these areas.

We must begin with the firm realization that the kingdom of God is now, always was, and forever shall be. We must also fully recognize that Jesus has completely and forever defeated the devil and given authority to believers in His name over all the power of the enemy. There is no more for Jesus to do apart from mankind to establish His kingdom over the kingdom of darkness on earth. He does not need to bodily return to die on the cross again to defeat the devil. Does He need to return bodily to beat up the devil and set His people free from the devil's bondage? He certainly is not planning to bodily return to beat on Christians who are not yet perfected. Neither has He surrendered this planet or His people to the devil. Does He need to plan another rescue attempt for His children? Jesus has already gained the victory and now lives in believers as the Victor. He waits only for us to stop listening to the deception of the devil and begin to hear and believe the good news of the sovereign ruler/dominion of God in us.

Before getting deeply involved in what happens next, believers need to fully grasp what is happening now. The urgent matter is not when or exactly how the next theological event will occur. The most important thing by far is that we get a real revelation of who we are in Christ now according to the Word and the Spirit of God.

We would think it was very strange if some people were seated at a table filled with wonderful, tasty food, including all their personal favorite dishes prepared just the way they like them, and yet all they could think or talk about was what they were going to have for supper later. We would think it a real shame and loss for them to miss the wonderful meal prepared for them. The one who prepared the delicious meal would probably be very disappointed as the bountiful gift was ignored in favor of what might be happening later.

If I were an enemy and wanted to steal a bountiful meal from you, one of the things I might do is to try very hard to divert your attention elsewhere. Diversion is a trick used by every pickpocket or slight-of-hand artist. **God help me not to be tricked out of your wonderful provisions. Open my eyes to see who I really am and what I really have in Christ Jesus NOW.**

## THE NOW TIME

### I AM THE RIGHTEOUSNESS OF GOD IN CHRIST JESUS!
*2 Corinthians 5:21: For He made Him who knew no sin to be sin for us, **that we might become the righteousness of God in Him.***

### I'M BLESSED WITH ALL SPIRITUAL BLESSING IN HEAVENLY PLACES!
*Ephesians 1:3: Blessed be the God and Father of our Lord Jesus Christ, **who has blessed us with every spiritual blessing in the heavenly places in Christ.***

### AS JESUS CHRIST IS IN THE WORLD SO AM I!
*I John 4:17b: **as He is so are we in the world.***

### I'M BORN AGAIN BY THE WORD OF GOD!
*1 Peter 1:23: ...having been **born again,** not of corruptible seed but incorruptible, **through the word of God** which lives and abides forever.*

### I'M REDEEMED BY THE BLOOD!
*Ephesians 1:7: In Him we have **redemption through His blood,** the forgiveness of sins, according to the riches of His grace.*

### I AM COMPLETE IN JESUS!
*Colossians 2:9-10: For in Him dwells all the fullness of the Godhead bodily; and **you are complete in Him,** who is the head of all principality and power.*

### MY SINS ARE NAILED TO THE CROSS!
*Colossians 2:14b: And He has taken it out of the way, having **nailed it to the cross.***

### I'M SEALED WITH THE HOLY SPIRIT OF PROMISE!
*Ephesians 1:13b: in whom also, having believed, **you were sealed with the Holy Spirit of promise.***

### I RULE AND REIGN IN THE NAME OF JESUS!
*Romans 5:17b: those who receive abundance of grace and of the gift of righteousness **will reign in life through the One Jesus Christ.***

### I AM MORE THAN A CONQUEROR!
*Romans 8:37: Yet in all these things **we are more than conquerors** through Him who loves us.*

### I TAKE DOMINION!
*Genesis 1:28: Then God blessed them, and God said to them, "Be fruitful and multiply; fill the earth and **subdue it; have dominion"***

### I CAN DO ALL THINGS THROUGH CHRIST WHO STRENGTHENS ME!
*Philippians 4:13: **I can do all things through Christ who strengthens me.***

### I AM STRENGTHENED IN ALL MIGHT BY HIS GLORIOUS POWER!
*Colossians 1:9b-10a: being fruitful in every good work and increasing in the knowledge of God; **strengthened with all might according to His glorious power** ...*

### ALL THINGS ARE UNDER THE FEET OF THE LORD JESUS CHRIST! HE HAS BEEN GIVEN TO BE THE HEAD OF ALL THINGS TO THE CHURCH!
*Ephesians 1:22-23: And **He put all things under His***

*feet, and gave Him to be head over all things to the church, which is His body, the fullness of Him who fills all in all.*

MY WEAPONS ARE MIGHTY IN GOD, TO THE TEARING DOWN OF STRONGHOLDS, CASTING DOWN IMAGINATIONS, SPECULATIONS, EVERY HIGH THING THAT EXALTS ITSELF AGAINST THE WORD OF GOD! I BRING EVERY THOUGHT CAPTIVE TO THE OBEDIENCE OF CHRIST!
*2 Corinthians 10:4-5: For the weapons of our warfare are not carnal but mighty in God for pulling down strongholds, casting down arguments and every high thing that exalts itself against the knowledge of God, bringing every thought into captivity to the obedience of Christ.*

THE LORD JESUS CHRIST HAS ALREADY APPEARED FOR THIS REASON, TO DESTROY THE WORKS OF THE ENEMY!
*1John 3:8b: For this purpose the Son of God was manifested, that He might destroy the works of the devil.*

HE DISARMED HIM, MADE A PUBLIC DISPLAY OF HIM!
*Colossians 2:15: Having disarmed principalities and powers, He made a public spectacle of them triumphing over them in it.*

HE HAS GIVEN ME AUTHORITY, WITH THE WORD AND IN HIS NAME TO HAVE POWER OVER ALL THE POWER OF THE ENEMY!
*Ephesians 1:19,3:20b,6:10: and what is the exceeding greatness of His power toward us who believe, according to the working of His mighty power, — according to the power that works in us, Finally, my brethren, be strong in the Lord and in the power of His might.*
*Philippians 2:10: ... that at the name of Jesus every knee should bow...*
*Colossians 2:9-10: For in Him dwells all the fullness of the Godhead bodily; and you are complete in Him, who is the head of all principality and power."*
*Hebrews 4:12a: For the word of God is living and powerful...*
*Luke 10:19a: Behold, I give you authority to trample on serpents and scorpions, and over all the power of the enemy...*

I ALWAYS TRIUMPH IN JESUS' NAME!
*2 Corinthians 2:14a: Now thanks be to God who always leads us in triumph in Christ...*

HIS WORD NEVER RETURNS VOID!
*Isaiah 55:11: So shall My word be that goes forth from My mouth; it shall not return to Me void, but it shall accomplish what I please, and it shall prosper in the thing for which I sent it.*

I COME BOLDLY BEFORE THE THRONE OF GRACE! I RECEIVE MERCY AND GRACE!
*Hebrews 4:16: Let us therefore come boldly to the throne of grace, that we may obtain mercy and find grace to help in time of need.*

IN THE NAME OF JESUS I COMMAND THE POWERS OF DARKNESS!
*Mark 16:17a: And these signs will follow those who believe: In My name they will cast out demons ...*

What I bind on earth is bound from heaven, and what I loose on earth is loosed from heaven. *(Matthew 16:19,18:18.)* If any two agree on earth, they have what they ask. *(Matthew 18:19.)* If I believe in my heart when I pray and doubt not, I shall have what I say. *(Mark 11:24.)* All things are possible to him who believes. *(Mark 9:23.)* If I abide in Him, I ask what I will, and it shall be done. *(John 15:7.)* I receive the finished work of the cross, proclaim liberty and freedom, and speak peace. **God, help me to realize my potential and to be who I am in Christ NOW.**

These atributes are promised in the Word of God. If you are not experiencing them in your life pray in faith and ask God to make them real in your life. Believe you receive them when you pray and you will have them. *(Mark 11:24.)* If you have difficulty believing them in your heart begin speaking them out loud repeatedly. You will find that your heart will begin to believe the truth that you are speaking and eventually you will have what you say. *(Mark 11:23.)*

With the heart we believe unto righteousness and with the mouth confession is made unto salvation. *(Romans 10:10.)* It will greatly benefit our life to plant these truths of the Word in our heart. A good way to do that is to stand and speak them out loud with strength until they become planted in our spirit.

# NOW:

I AM THE RIGHTEOUSNESS OF GOD IN CHRIST JESUS!

I'M BLESSED WITH ALL SPIRITUAL BLESSINGS IN HEAVENLY PLACES!

AS JESUS CHRIST IS IN THE WORLD SO AM I!

I'M BORN AGAIN BY THE WORD OF GOD!

I'M, REDEEMED BY THE BLOOD!

I AM COMPLETE IN JESUS!

MY SINS ARE NAILED TO THE CROSS!

I'M SEALED WITH THE HOLY SPIRIT OF PROMISE!

I RULE AND REIGN IN THE NAME OF JESUS!

I AM MORE THAN A CONQUEROR! I TAKE DOMINION!

I CAN DO ALL THINGS THROUGH CHRIST WHO STRENGTHENS ME!

I AM STRENGTHENED IN ALL MIGHT BY HIS GLORIOUS POWER!

ALL THINGS ARE UNDER THE FEET OF THE LORD JESUS CHRIST! HE HAS BEEN GIVEN TO BE THE HEAD OF ALL THINGS TO THE CHURCH!

MY WEAPONS ARE MIGHTY IN GOD, TO THE TEARING DOWN OF STRONGHOLDS, CASTING DOWN IMAGINATIONS, SPECULATIONS, EVERY HIGH THING THAT EXALTS ITSELF AGAINST THE WORD OF GOD! I BRING EVERY THOUGHT CAPTIVE TO THE OBEDIENCE OF CHRIST!

THE LORD JESUS CHRIST HAS ALREADY APPEARED FOR THIS REASON, TO DESTROY THE WORKS OF THE ENEMY!

HE DISARMED HIM, MADE A PUBLIC DISPLAY OF HIM!

HE HAS GIVEN ME AUTHORITY, WITH THE WORD AND IN HIS NAME TO HAVE POWER OVER ALL THE POWER OF THE ENEMY!

I ALWAYS TRIUMPH IN JESUS' NAME! HIS WORD NEVER RETURNS VOID! I COME BOLDLY BEFORE THE THRONE OF GRACE! I RECEIVE MERCY AND GRACE!

IN THE NAME OF JESUS I COMMAND THE POWERS OF DARKNESS!

We must recognize our potential and become the purified powerful Bride. Now is the time for the church to lay aside her powerless religious traditions and be prepared as the Bride of Christ, the body in which Christ dwells. There is a need for healing in the church. The concepts of Babylon have become unhealthy traditions within the church. The faith and practices of individuals has been perverted by relentless attacks from the enemy. God has provided and is providing all that is needed to heal and prepare His Bride.

# NOTES

# CHAPTER 14

## PREPARING THE BRIDE

The mature church must become the body of Christ, a living organism, a network of spiritually-connected cells and parts—individuals emptied of self, filled with Christ. It must be without man's leadership or man's structure. There will be no human hierarchy. One individual will not rule over another, but all will serve one another. **Christ Jesus will spiritually rule within each individual and serve as overall head of the kingdom, thus establishing spiritual structure, not human.** Just as the head rules the healthy body, life from the head sends signals to each individual part, and every cell responds in obedience to the head.

Much of the church of today is sick, much like a person would be sick if any part failed to obey the head. The great apostasy of the past continues to affect the health of the body today. Men establish themselves as heads and develop hierarchical systems of church rule. This defection from the true head is fostered by the enemy and is carried out by the spirit of antichrist, opposing Christ as head. Spirits of spiritual blindness, darkness, deception, and delusion are sustained by religious spirits in the church.

The enemy has effective tools for stirring men and causing them to have strong desires to rule. The enemy must work on and through the individual parts of the "body" because he can have no effect on the true Head. Our purpose in this part of this work is to expose the enemy's schemes and his plan to rule and to recognize the true patterns of God's rule, which can produce the overcoming life, the kingdom-of-God lifestyle.

Let us now focus on the individual. The church is sick because individuals are sick. The enemy's plan is to cause strong needs or desires within the individual. To accomplish this, he must prevent the individual from being in contact with the knowledge of the love of God. He uses negative life-experiences and deceiving spirits to blind individuals to God's love and power. This causes the individual to become keenly aware of his own needs and to look only to himself to supply them. This self focus becomes self-centeredness. Selfish thoughts and actions lead to fear, pride, greed, lust, and disobedience to the true Head.

Once the disobedient lifestyle is established, the enemy can bring much inner turmoil and outer conflict, causing increasing emotional wounds and spiritual deception. Spiritual darkness, deception, and delusion opens the door for occult and demonic influence. The inner turmoil will eventually produce negative behavior such as aggressiveness, defensiveness, or withdrawal. This can produce conflict, marital strife, racial strife, religious strife, and power struggles in the church as well as in the world.

The strife, turmoil, and conflict causes stress and deteriorates the mental, emotional, and eventually the physical health of the individual. Often the individual will seek escape from the inner turmoil and stress. Many avenues are available that seem to offer some temporary escape, but often lead to more stress. Drugs, alcohol, immorality, some music, some sports, gaining wealth, entertainment, withdrawal, overworking, overeating, violence, and religion are some of the common escapes used today. The buildup of stress will often lead to greater conflict, strife, and more intense power struggles, which will become violent, leading to beatings, murders, and suicides. Sickness and premature deaths become normal in the resulting violent society.

Remember, the enemy's purpose in all this is to cut us off from the knowledge and reality of the love of God. It is easy to see how difficult it will be for a child growing up in this violent culture to even imagine the love of God. Power and strength are seen as synonymous with "mean and violent". God is often seen as only judgmental, and except the individual be healed, he cannot begin to know the love of God. He is, therefore, locked into the bondage of the enemy, doomed to live and die in the torment of inner turmoil and stress. There is no rest for the wicked. Unbelief cannot enter into His rest. *Hebrews 3:11-12.*

Most churchgoers today feel that if they can control their stress, and in some way contain it, they are doing as well as can be expected, under the circumstances. But as someone once said, "Why are you under the circumstances?", thus implying that there is a potential life in Jesus that is over the circumstances. It is really true. Jesus can totally remove our turmoil and stress—not just help us to live with it until we die and are relieved of it in heaven someday. We are not talking about perfect circumstances, even though they may improve in time. We are talking about living above them **now** in the real peace of God. As we live in real peace, we become a part of the solution, instead of part of the problem. As our lifestyle changes, we stop affecting those around us for bad and start affecting them for good.

Until we can see Jesus the King as He really is, we do not have the power or motivation to move toward ultimate closeness with Him. When we see the true abundant love and magnificent glory of the King, we will decide to move toward Him. Once we experience the reality of the glorious peace and eternal joy of being in the presence of the King, we will repent, as needed, to enter intimately into His glorious presence.

Preaching the Cross, personal salvation, and the baptism of the Holy Spirit, (the indwelling Spirit of Christ), are foundational building blocks of the overcoming life. Preaching the kingdom of God **now** establishes the goal or objective. Teaching God's kingdom patterns and exposing the enemy's schemes allows us to see where we are and what changes need to be made. Jesus the Anointed One is our source of power for change.

## THE RESTORATION MINISTRY OF JESUS

*Luke 4:18-19: "The Spirit of the Lord is upon Me, because He has anointed Me to preach the gospel to the poor. He has sent Me to heal the brokenhearted, to preach deliverance to the captives and recovery of sight to the blind, to set at liberty those who are oppressed, to proclaim the acceptable year of the Lord."*

The restoration ministry of Jesus serves as the cleansing process that we must go through before we can walk into the Holy City, the New Jerusalem, purified, Bride-of-Christ, kingdom-of-God lifestyle. It is the work of Jesus by His grace and power through the Holy Spirit. It is not of man "that any should boast". Our part in helping one another is to bring forth the Word and the anointings of Christ through the Spirit of Jesus, the Holy Spirit.

Christ Jesus destroys all the work of the enemy, the work the devil has done, and the work he is doing.

Jesus repairs, renews, and rebuilds all the damage done by the enemy. Jesus will establish righteousness, peace, and joy in those who seek Him with their whole heart. He will set those free who are in bondages created by the enemy. He will bring an end to mourning and a beginning to joy and praise.

*1 John 3: 8b: For this purpose the Son of God was manifested, that He might **destroy the works of the devil.***

*Isaiah 61: 1-4: "The Spirit of the Lord God is upon Me, because the Lord has anointed Me to **preach good tidings** to the poor; He has sent he to **heal the brokenhearted,** to **proclaim liberty** to the captives, and the **opening of the prison** to those who are bound; to **proclaim the acceptable (favorable) year** of the Lord, and the **day of vengeance** of our God; to **comfort** all who mourn, to console those who mourn in Zion, to **give them beauty** for ashes, the oil of joy for mourning, the garment of **praise** for the spirit of heaviness; that they may be called **trees of righteousness,** the planting of the Lord, that He may be glorified, and they shall **rebuild** the old ruins, they shall raise up the former desolations, and they shall **repair** the ruined cities, the desolations of many generations."*

The enemy has inflicted much damage on individuals and subsequently on the entire planet since Adam released him thousands of years ago in the garden. Primarily, he uses his powers of darkness to affect people and cause them to affect others negatively. If he can prevent someone from knowing and experiencing the love of God, he can devastate their life and cause them to wound many others.

The only real power that he has since Jesus defeated him is deception. He seeks to prevent us from knowing and believing the power we have over him in Christ. One of his favorite tricks on Christians is to make them believe that he and his demons are not really around any more. He likes to disguise himself as a religious angel of light and works under cover as a "religious spirit". This way he can influence Christians away from truth that will expose him—and, undetected, he can move them toward a false doctrine that will protect him. He can then fan the flames of natural differences to cause painful rejections. Through the pain he can excite the flesh to anger, bitterness, and many kinds of negative works.

*2 Corinthians 11: 14-15: And no wonder! **For Satan himself transforms himself into an angel of light.** Therefore it is no great thing if **his ministers also transform themselves into ministers of righteousness,** whose end will be according to their works.*

*1 Timothy 4:1b: ... some will depart from the faith, giving heed to **deceiving spirits and doctrines of demons.***

The enemy does not have a vast number of schemes. He really doesn't need very many. The ones he uses are highly-perfected by thousands of years of practice and work very effectively on unbelievers and uninformed Christians. His schemes are always designed to **pervert** the truth of God in order to **divert** man from the plan of God.

God's kingdom patterns for man's life always lead to an abundant life of love, righteousness, peace, and joy. The enemy's perversion of these patterns always produces unlove, evil, pain, affliction, and despair. Christians may be easily deceived and diverted to an alternate plan if they do not have a clear foundational understanding of God's kingdom patterns. The best way to recognize a counterfeit is to thoroughly know the real thing. If the enemy cannot totally pervert, he will attempt to divert by drawing our attention to some other less important matter.

The restoration ministry of Jesus must always involve two processes. One is the tearing down of the old life-structure, and the other is the building up of the new. To help us recognize and tear down the work of the enemy, and to help us avoid the schemes of the enemy, it is important to uncover and expose his work and methods.

In order to begin rebuilding, we must renew our minds to God's kingdom patterns of abundant life. The world system currently is highly affected by the enemy's deception. Therefore it is very easy to be trained in the devil's perversions and diversions. One need only grow up in a modern secular family, watch TV and movies, and attend public schools to be grounded in the perversions and diversions of the enemy.

We must be retrained to recognize what is kingdom of God living, and what is not kingdom of God living. Our understanding must be renewed to the Word of God. Kingdom life patterns must be revealed to us. We must learn to recognize the enemy's patterns for our lives, and the schemes he uses to press us into his perverted patterns.

Unfortunately, the local church doesn't often seem to have the power to effectively answer the situation and sometimes fosters the deception by joining the world system. Churchgoers often respond with hypocritical, legalistic attacks on people, while allowing the same or other perversions to operate in their own lives. Often a Christian who is under conviction for their own hidden problem will attack others in whom they see the same problem. This legalistic attack further wounds people and often drives them out for the enemy to further afflict.

Some of my readers at this point are agreeing. "Yea! I've sure seen that over there, or in that particular person." One scheme of the enemy is to divert attention from **our** need to the problem of **others**. As the Spirit of God reveals God's kingdom patterns, the enemy's work to pervert them will be uncovered. We must unmask ourselves as the Spirit of Jesus uncovers and exposes the enemy. We must agree with God about our own need and be willing to allow our old life-structure to be cut down and uprooted, that the new may grow and flourish in its place.

*Matthew 3:10: "And even now the ax is laid to the root of the trees. Therefore every **tree which does not bear good fruit is cut down** and thrown into the fire."*

*Matthew 15:13: "Every **plant which My heavenly Father has not planted will be uprooted."***

*Isaiah 61: 3b-4a: ...that they may be called **trees of righteousness, the planting of the Lord.** that He may be glorified, and they shall rebuild the old ruins.*

# CHAPTER 15

## THE HEART TREE
### *(THE LIFE STRUCTURE OF MAN)*

Trees are often used in Scripture to symbolize men or the life-structure of a man. In the figurative language of Scripture, the tree, the root, the soil it grows in, and the seed that the tree grew from are all important to understanding God's plan (kingdom pattern) for the individual, and exposing the enemy's scheme for causing affliction.

*Isaiah 55:12: For you shall go out with joy, and be led forth with peace; the mountains and the hills shall break forth into singing before you, and all the **trees** of the field shall clap their hands.*

*Isaiah 61:3: To console those who mourn in Zion, to give them beauty for ashes, the oil of joy for mourning, the garment of praise for the spirit of heaviness; that they may be called **trees of righteousness**, the planting of the Lord, that He may be glorified.*

In the parable of the sower and other Scriptures, the heart of man is referred to as soil. Our heart is our spirit and soul. Our spirit is who we are and relates to the spiritual realm. Our soul is our mind, will, and emotions, and relates to the natural realm through our bodies in which we live.

The heart of man, like soil, will grow whatever is planted in it. **The soil does not determine the type of tree that will grow. The seed does.** The same soil that will grow a pecan tree when a pecan is planted in it, will grow a peach tree if a peach seed is planted in it. A thorn tree will grow if the soil is planted with the seed of a thorn tree. Our heart-soil does not in itself determine our tree or life-structure—but rather the seed that is planted will determine the nature of our tree or life-structure. The fruit (our actions or deeds) is determined by the type of tree (life-structure).

*Matthew 7:16-20: "You will know them by their fruits. Do men gather grapes from thornbushes or figs from thistles? Even so, every good tree bears good fruit, but a bad tree bears bad fruit. **A good tree cannot bear bad fruit, nor can a bad tree bear good fruit.** Every*

**THE HEART TREE**

*Trees are often used in Scripture to symbolize men or the life-structure of a man.*

*tree that does not bear good fruit is cut down and thrown into the fire. Therefore by their fruits you will know them."*

*Matthew 12:33-35: "Either make the tree good and its fruit good, or else make the tree bad and its fruit bad; for a tree is known by its fruit. Brood of vipers! How can you, being evil, speak good things? **For out of the abundance of the heart, the mouth speaks.** A good man, out of the good treasure of his **heart**, brings forth good things, and an evil man, out of the evil treasure, brings forth evil things."*

In the above passages, the Lord speaks of the tree (life-structure) and its fruit (deeds) coming forth from the soil of the heart of man. The "Heart-Tree" of our life is either good or bad and will bear either good or bad fruit according to the tree. The type of tree has been determined by the seed planted. As we see in *Matthew 13:19*, **the seed is a word.** A word is more than just letters arranged on a page; it is a **pattern** that is alive, and can grow into a structure of life that bears fruit. It can be a vision, picture, image, an action, or a combination or series of these things. A communication in any form is a word or seed. Since there are two kinds of trees and two kinds of fruit, obviously there are two kinds of seeds, good and bad. **Good seeds are good words or patterns that are alive, and bad seeds are bad words or patterns that are alive.**

All words or seeds ultimately have their origin from either the tree of life, or the tree of knowledge of good and evil, which produces death. Every word, seed, action, or communication of any form has its source in either God or the devil. A child planted with inordinate premature sexual activity will grow a life-structure of sexual confusion and disorder. A child planted with legalistic rigid harshness will grow a life-structure of frustrated perfectionism. A child planted with violent acts will grow a life-structure of fear and aggression. A child planted with unconditional love and peaceful security will grow a healthy, happy life-structure.

The seed of the kingdom of God is a special good seed that will grow the rule of God.

## THE ENEMY'S SCHEME

### UNGODLY HERITAGE
*(OPEN TO BAD SEED)*

**Our ungodly <u>heritage</u> causes our heart-soil to be born with an openness to bad seed.**

The ungodly heritage of Adam has passed down through the generations. We were each conceived and born with a heritage that goes back to Adam. Sin and the curse of death entered through Adam and spread to all men. Through our forefathers, the sin of Adam reaches to each of us.

*Romans 5:19: Therefore just as through one man sin entered the world and death through sin, and thus death spread to all men, because all sinned.*

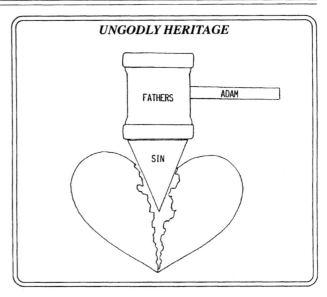

UNGODLY HERITAGE

*Psalm 51:5: Behold, I was brought forth in iniquity, and in sin my mother conceived me.*

Though we bear no personal accountability for the sin of our parents and forefathers; we each are born under the curse of sin and must at some time become personally accountable for our own sin. However, we <u>are</u> directly affected by the inheritance of the iniquity (tendency to sin) of our forefathers.

*Exodus 20: 5-6:   "....visiting the **iniquity of the fathers** on the children to the third and fourth generations of those who hate Me, but showing mercy to thousands to those who love Me and keep My commandments."*

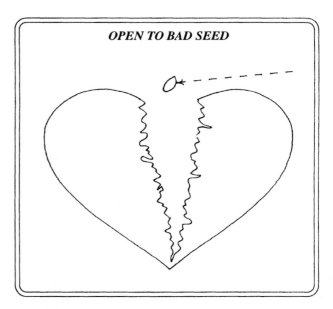

OPEN TO BAD SEED

*Leviticus 26: 39:* *"And those of you who are left shall waste away in their iniquity in your enemies' lands; also **in their fathers' iniquities;** which are with them, they shall waste away."*

*Exodus 34: 7b:* *"... visiting the **iniquity** of the fathers upon the children and the children's children to the third and the fourth generation."*

The sin of Adam, working through our heritage, (the iniquity or perversion of our forefathers), serves as a big hammer to drive the wedge of sin into our own heart-soil, causing an openness to receive bad seed. Then in our own experience, the seeds are planted, and our life-structure (Heart-Tree) grows—and eventually our lives bear the fruit of it.

## UNGODLY LIFE EXPERIENCE
### *(CLOSED TO GOOD SEED)*

**Our ungodly experience causes our heart-soil to be unable to grow the kingdom-of-God seed (the good seed).**

*Matthew 13:3-9:* *Then He spoke many things to them in parables, saying; "Behold, a sower went out to sow. And as he sowed, some seed fell by the **wayside;** and the birds came and devoured them. Some fell on **stony** places, where they did not have much earth; and they immediately sprang up because they had no depth of earth. But when the sun was up, they were scorched, and because they had no root, they withered away. And some fell among **thorns,** and the thorns sprang up and choked them. But others fell on **good ground** and yielded a crop: some a hundredfold, some sixty, some thirty. He who has ears to hear, let him hear!"*

### THE WAYSIDE SOIL

*Matthew 13:19:* *"When anyone hears the **word of the kingdom,** and does not understand it, then the wicked one comes and snatches away **what was sown in his heart.** This is he who received **seed** by the wayside."*

**The word of the kingdom cannot be received or understood in the hard-pressed soil of our heart.** The heavy-wounding footsteps of man and his ox carts have pressed down the soil of our heart and made it hard. These wounding experiences, and the hard-press of life have damaged our soil and our ability to receive

the good seed that could have produced a good life-structure. Because it cannot penetrate the hardened soil, the kingdom word is easily and quickly taken from us by the enemy. The wayside heart must be plowed to break up the hardened soil, and then healed by the gentle rain of the Holy Spirit before it can receive the good seed.

**UNGODLY LIFE EXPERIENCE**
**(THE BAD SOILS)**

### THE STONY SOIL

*Matthew 13:20-21:* *"But he who received the seed on stony places, this is he who hears the word and immediately receives it with joy; yet he has no root in himself, but endures only for a while. For when tribulation or persecution arises because of the word, immediately he stumbles."*

**The word of the kingdom of God cannot be brought to fruition in a stony heart.** The stones represent hardened, firm, previous convictions. If we are so certain that we already know how things are (what the Bible says, what life is like, what people are like, what we ourselves are like, etc.), then we will not grow the new life-structure to maturity. We will let it go when challenged, because negative, hardened, previous convictions will not let it take root deep in our heart. The stony heart must have the rocks of previous, hardened convictions either thrown out or smashed, before it can bring the kingdom life to fruition.

## THE THORNY SOIL

*Matthew 13:22:* *"Now he who received seed among the thorns is he who hears the word, and the cares of this world and the deceitfulness of riches choke the word, and he becomes unfruitful."*

**The Word of the kingdom cannot be brought to fruition in a heart growing thorn bushes of the cares of this life.** If we must have anything of this life in addition to, or apart from what God desires for us, we have thorn bushes. We must love God above all else and be totally sufficient and content with God, and his desired provision for us. The thorn bushes must be pulled up and thrown out before the kingdom-life can come to fruition.

## GOD'S KINGDOM PATTERN

### THE GOOD SOIL

*Matthew 13:23:* *"But he who received seed on the good ground is he who hears the word and understands it, who indeed bears fruit and produces; some a hundredfold, some sixty, some thirty."*

**The word of the kingdom of God will be received and grow to fruition in the good heart-soil.** The good soil is the heart that is healed of wounds, has had its stones of hardened previous convictions thrown out, and the thorn bushes of cares of this life pulled up and thrown out. This heart can produce the kingdom-of-God life style. It will be fruitful in production of the kingdom of God on earth. It will not receive the bad seed but is ready to grow the good seed.

We are told in Scripture to be careful what we hear, what we plant in our soil. It is God's plan for us to receive good seed. If we are filled with the peace of God, our hearts will receive only good seed, which will grow a good tree (life-structure). This will produce good fruit (deeds or actions). It is the peace of God that guards our hearts from bad seed.

*Philippians 4: 7b-9:* *...and the **peace of God,** which surpasses all understanding, will **guard your hearts and minds through Christ Jesus.** Finally, brethren,* *whatever things are **true,** whatever things are **noble,** whatever things are **just,** whatever things are **pure,** whatever things are **lovely,** whatever things are of **good report,** if there is any **virtue** and if there is anything praiseworthy, **meditate** on these things. The things which you learned and received and heard and saw in me, **these do,** and the **God of peace will be with you.***

*Proverbs 23: 7a: For as he **thinks in his heart,** so is he.*

We will be formed by the thoughts we think, by the words in any form we receive. Our heart-soil will grow whatever we allow to be planted in it, whether good or bad. Whether it is a spoken word, or some action carried out against us, if we allow it to be planted in our heart-soil it will determine our life-structure and, thereby, determine our feelings, our self-image, our attitude, and eventually our actions—whether good or bad. We will live in peace, or we will live in turmoil and stress, according to what we decide to allow to be planted in our heart-soil.

What are you allowing to be planted in your soil? What are you watching, listening to, and thinking about?

What did you plant in your heart-soil from the time you were born until you were about six years old? Obviously you had no choice at that young age. Someone else decided what would be planted in your heart-soil at that time. It is a known fact today that most of our life-structure was formed in us as small children. Before we developed the ability to choose, the seeds that would determine the majority of our life-structure were already planted. What kind of seeds were planted in our soil from the time we were in our mother's womb until five or six years old?

Unfortunately, we did not all grow up surrounded by the peace of God. Many of us did not have our heart-soil planted with seeds of unconditional love and acceptance. On the contrary, we may have received seeds of a conditional, performance-based kind of love and felt unaccepted. Or, we may have felt little or no love at all. Anything short of unconditional, affirming love and acceptance becomes a bad seed. If so, then a seed of unlove and rejection sown into our heart-soil began to grow into our life-structure.

God's kingdom pattern is that we be planted with good seed and grow a good life-structure. If, however, we were not, then Jesus came to uproot our bad life-structure (The Bad Heart-Tree), heal our heart soil, and replant it with His good seed to grow His good life-structure (The Good Heart-Tree).

God has given us the ability to take the cover off and see the method or scheme the enemy has and is using to afflict individuals and cause them to afflict others. We know his plan is to kill, steal, and destroy. Once we see his plot to kill us, steal all we have, including our faith and joy, and to destroy the plan and work of God, we can make the adjustments necessary to appropriate the ministry of Jesus to destroy all the schemes of the enemy and establish God's kingdom patterns.

Understanding God's kingdom patterns for the individual, family, business, and all aspects of life, and planting them in our heart will produce abundant life. Learning to personally appropriate the ministry of Christ will bring about the uprooting of the old and the planting of the new tree. Jesus has provided and is providing everything we need to completely destroy the old work of the enemy and establish the new work of God in our life.

We are absolutely without excuse. The enemy would like to make us believe that because it was planted in us, we can do nothing about it. To say, "I can't help it; someone did it to me", is to say, "Jesus is not sufficient to meet my need. His blood, resurrection life, and omnipotent power is not enough to fix me."

If we attempt to avert our responsibility by placing the blame on others ("the ones that did it to me"), then we are deceived. It really doesn't matter who did it; ultimately, it was the enemy who did it. And the Lord Jesus the Anointed One has been and is manifest to destroy the work of the enemy. He is no respecter of persons. His freedom-giving ministry is available to

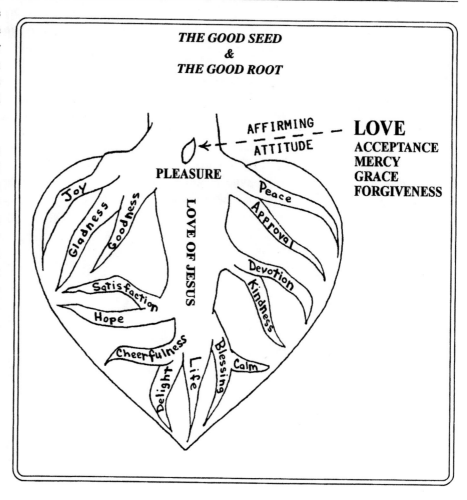

all. His ministry begins with our real repentance, not our phony excuses. Our escape and defense mechanisms are designed by the enemy and brought forth in our soul to prevent true repentance.

## THE GOOD SEED

The seed that will produce the **good heart-tree** when planted in good heart soil is LOVE. The unconditional God-kind of real love flowing through an **affirming attitude** is received in the heart as **pleasure** or comfort.

The heart perceives love primarily as **ACCEPTANCE,** along with **mercy, grace,** and **forgiveness** for our shortcomings. We find love, acceptance, mercy, grace, and forgiveness in God through Jesus Christ.

*John 3:16:  For God so **loved** the world that He gave His only begotten Son that whoever believes in Him should not perish but have everlasting life.*

*Ephesians 2:4-5: But God, who is rich in **mercy**, because of His great **love** with which He loved us, even when we were dead in trespasses, made us alive together with Christ (by **grace** you are saved).*

*Ephesians 1:6-7: ... to the praise of the glory of His **grace**; by which He has made us **accepted** in the Beloved. In Him we have redemption through His blood, the **forgiveness** of sins, according to the riches of His grace...*

The heart must experience the love of Jesus filling our spirit by the Holy Spirit. The heart also needs to experience the love of Jesus in our souls through the manifest love of Jesus coming through other people. To grow a good life-structure we need to receive the seed of the love and acceptance of Jesus flowing through an affirming attitude from the people in authority over us and from those around us. We never outgrow our need for love.

God's pattern is for the individual to be formed in a Godly environment of love and acceptance, not just a Christian home with clean morals and firm discipline, but a family characterized by unconditional Godly love. The seed-pattern of the kingdom of God is the real love from God flowing through Godly parents, extended family, and community, from conception to maturity, always affirming the worth of the child while tenderly nurturing and training.

*Ephesians 6:4b: Amp. "...but rear them [tenderly] in the training and discipline and the counsel and admonition of the Lord."*

### THE GOOD ROOT

The seed of love sown in the soil of our heart will begin to grow the foundational **ROOT** system of our life-structure. The tap root is the reality of the **LOVE OF JESUS** in our heart. The tip of the tap root is **abundant life.** The main root of the love of Jesus along with its beautiful secondary roots will fill our heart-soil with the fullness of God. The secondary roots that branch from the main tap root are both in-working and out-working characteristics. They are things like **peace, approval, devotion, kindness, calmness, blessing, joy, gladness, goodness, satisfaction, hope, cheerfulness, and delight.**

*Ephesians 3:17-19: ...that Christ may dwell in your hearts through faith; that you, being **rooted and** **grounded in love,** may be able to comprehend with all the saints what is the width and length and depth and height - to know the **love of Christ** which passes knowledge; that you may be **filled with all the fullness of God.***

## THE ENEMY'S SCHEME

### THE BAD SEED

The bad seed is **UNLOVE.** Unlove is perceived in our hearts primarily as **REJECTION,** and is felt in the heart as **PAIN.** Seeds of **rejection, accusation, condemnation,** and **unforgiveness** flowing through a **judgmental or critical attitude** are the seeds the enemy uses to plant a bad life-structure. Unlove is the absence of the unconditional God-kind of love.

*THE BAD SEED*

Rejection may come in many forms and from many sources. Usually the rejection that produces the most severe pain comes from those closest to us, from those who should love us. Rejection is often communicated in subtle ways. The child who is severely abused, abandoned, or who suffered the trauma of parental divorce may not be the only child who feels the pain of rejection. If our parents were just too busy with their own situations to really be there for us when we needed them, <u>we</u> experience rejection, too. Apathy can be the worst kind of unlove.

*Psalm 109:2-4a, 22-23: For the mouth of the wicked and the mouth of the deceitful have opened against me; they have **spoken against me** with a lying tongue. They have also surrounded me with words of hatred, and fought against me without a cause. In return for my love they are my **accusers.** I am poor and needy and my **heart is wounded** within me. I am gone like a shadow when it lengthens; I am shaken like a locust.*

*Romans 2:1a, Amp.: Therefore you have no excuse of defense or justification, O man, whoever you are who **judges** and **condemns** another.*

*Ephesians 6:4a, Amp.: Fathers, do not irritate and provoke your children to **anger**; do not exasperate them to **resentment**...*

There is no more **painful seed** which can be planted in our heart than being judged and condemned by someone we love; especially by those who have some measure of authority in our lives. We are particularly open to parents, pastors, teachers, coaches, mates, older siblings, and close friends. The enemy knows this and will seek to cause unforgiveness and accusations from those who should love us. He wants us to feel the devastating pain of rejection and to react to it with **resentment.**

## THE BAD ROOT

The pain in our heart begins to grow the foundational ROOT structure of our life. The painful seed of rejection begins to produce anger, resentment, and bitterness. Left to its natural course, the seed of rejection will always produce a root of **BITTERNESS.** The tip of the tap root of bitterness is **death.** The secondary roots are both out-working and in-working characteristics. The out-working characteristics are things like **anger, resentment, hatred, wrath, retaliation, rage,** and an attitude of **murder.** The in-working characteristics are things like **grief, sorrow, guilt, remorse, hopelessness, depression, despair,** and an attitude of **suicide.**

Remember, the heart did not necessarily want these things. They are the natural result of the seed of unlove planted in the heart soil. The soil will grow whatever is planted.

*Hebrews 12:14-17: Pursue peace with all men, and holiness, without which no one will see the Lord: looking diligently lest anyone fall short of the grace of God; lest any **ROOT OF BITTERNESS** springing up cause trouble, and by this many become defiled.*

The Greek word translated "bitterness" also carries the meanings of "piercing, sharp, pungent, and poison". The life-structure becomes poisoned with bitterness, as the tap root of bitterness with all of its ugly, subsidiary secondary roots grows and entwines to permeate the entire heart-soil.

*Acts 8:21-23: You have neither part nor portion in this matter, for **your heart is not right** in the sight of God. Repent therefore of this your wickedness, and pray God if perhaps the thought of your heart may be forgiven you. For I see that you are **poisoned by bitterness** and **bound by iniquity**.*

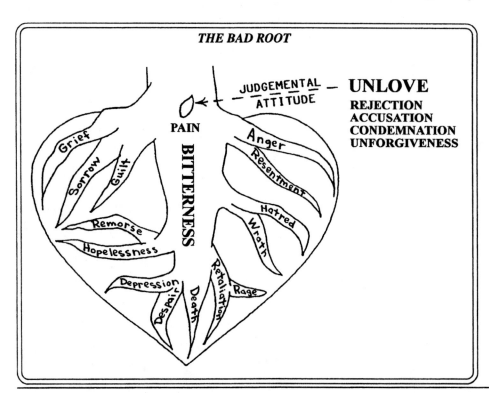

THE BAD ROOT

## THE BAD TRUNK

The root of bitterness will spring up, cause trouble, and defile many. The trunk of our life-tree that springs forth from the root of bitterness is always without exception—**REBELLION.** Rebellion (**a disobedient attitude**) is the natural outworking of bitterness, which is the natural result of inner pain from rejection. Rebellion is not usually something that we plan, or even desire for our lifes. We didn't want it. It got planted in our heart-soil, usually before we were old enough to choose. Feelings of rejection by parents, teachers, siblings, relatives, and peers planted the seeds that will produce the predominant structure of our life—a trunk of rebellion.

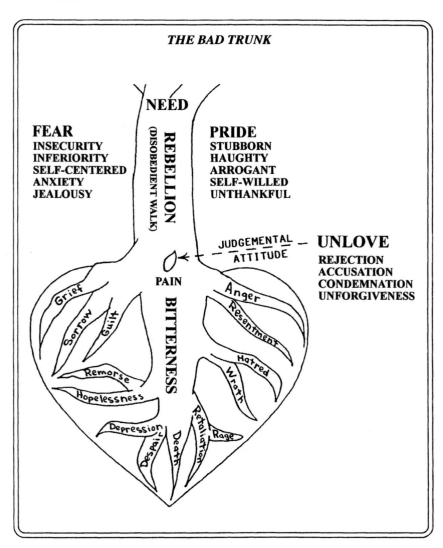

THE BAD TRUNK

NEED

REBELLION (DISOBEDIENT WALK)

FEAR
INSECURITY
INFERIORITY
SELF-CENTERED
ANXIETY
JEALOUSY

PRIDE
STUBBORN
HAUGHTY
ARROGANT
SELF-WILLED
UNTHANKFUL

JUDGEMENTAL ATTITUDE — UNLOVE
REJECTION
ACCUSATION
CONDEMNATION
UNFORGIVENESS

PAIN

BITTERNESS

Grief, Sorrow, Guilt, Remorse, Hopelessness, Depression, Despair, Death, Retaliation, Rage, Wrath, Hatred, Resentment, Anger

The trunk of rebellion is characterized by **FEAR** and **PRIDE.** The rebellion turns into fear as we feel unloved and subconsciously reasons something like this: "The authorities over me, or those around me, do not love me as much as they love themselves. Therefore, they are going to take care of themselves first and not me. And I don't feel God loves me; I'm in rebellion against Him. So, He's not going to take care of me. No one is going to take care of me. So, **I must take care of myself."** We are now self-focused, **self-centered** and have a **poor self-image.**

Then we take a look at ourselves and a look at the big, mean world, and reason something like this. "Wow! I'm not very big and the world is so big. I don't think I can do it. I can't take care of myself." **FEAR, insecurity, inferiority,** and **anxiety** enter at this point.

Then we look around and see others taking care of themselves, and we reason something like this. "If they can do it, I can too. So I'll take hold of my boot straps, double up my fist, set my jaw and start getting tough." And when we begin to succeed at taking care of ourselves, when we get that good job, new car, etc., then we're **PROUD.** "Why not? I did it all myself. God didn't do it. My authority over me or those around me didn't do it. I did it." Now we are filled with **PRIDE,** and we become **stubborn, haughty, arrogant, self-willed** and **unthankful.**

When we are winning, pride reigns, but when things don't go so well, fear rules. We will flip back and forth in fear or pride depending upon our own evaluation of our performance. We are now **performance-oriented.** We find our self worth only in our performance. Only **perfection,** which we never seem to achieve, will satisfy us.

The central characteristic of our entire life-structure is **NEED.** It does not matter how much we have; it is not enough. There is always a sense of lack; of not being good enough, not doing enough, not having enough. This continuous feeling of **need or lack becomes the primary motivational force in our life-structure.**

# THE BAD HEART TREE

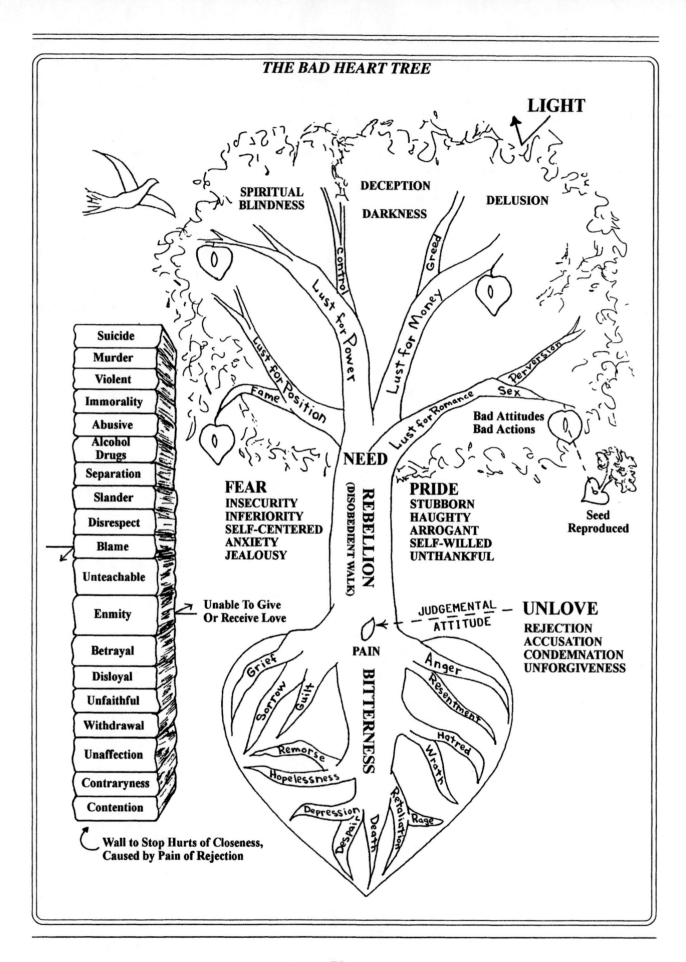

LIGHT

SPIRITUAL BLINDNESS

DECEPTION

DARKNESS

DELUSION

Control

Lust for Power

Lust for Position

Fame

Lust for Money

Greed

Perversion

Sex

Lust for Romance

Bad Attitudes
Bad Actions

Seed Reproduced

**NEED**

Suicide
Murder
Violent
Immorality
Abusive
Alcohol Drugs
Separation
Slander
Disrespect
Blame
Unteachable
Enmity
Betrayal
Disloyal
Unfaithful
Withdrawal
Unaffection
Contraryness
Contention

**Wall to Stop Hurts of Closeness,
Caused by Pain of Rejection**

**FEAR**
INSECURITY
INFERIORITY
SELF-CENTERED
ANXIETY
JEALOUSY

Unable To Give
Or Receive Love

**REBELLION**
(DISOBEDIENT WALK)

**PRIDE**
STUBBORN
HAUGHTY
ARROGANT
SELF-WILLED
UNTHANKFUL

JUDGEMENTAL
ATTITUDE

**UNLOVE**
REJECTION
ACCUSATION
CONDEMNATION
UNFORGIVENESS

PAIN

Grief

Sorrow

Guilt

Remorse

Hopelessness

**BITTERNESS**

Anger

Resentment

Hatred

Wrath

Depression

Despair

Death

Retaliation

Rage

## THE BAD LIMBS

The limbs of the bad heart-tree do not grow from a trunk of well being and abundance, but rather from a driving sense of intense need; a feeling that "I will not make it if I don't have more." From this strong sense of need, the limbs or branches of the life-structure come forth. The natural product of great need is **a strong desire to have** in order to attempt to satisfy the strong sense of need. That strong desire to have is **LUST.** We're not talking about just a spurious want, type of desire. We're talking about what seems to some people to be a life or death situation.

We subconsiously reason something like this. "I must provide for myself or I might not make it. If I'm going to provide for myself, I must have **money,** money that is mine, that I **control. Lust for money and greed** come forth in the life-structure. "If I'm going to get and keep money, I must have **power** and **position."** A **lust for power, control, position and fame** develops into the life- structure.

The greatest need we all have, what we are really searching for, is love—to be able to receive and give real love. But this type of heart does not even know what real love is. The bad-heart tree has never fully experienced real love, the unconditional God-kind of love. This type of individual does know, however, the good feelings of **romance and sex.** So, **lust for romance or sex** comes forth and promises to meet that deep inner need.

Remember, we didn't just decide to be this way. It got planted in us a long time ago as painful rejection—unlove.

The major limbs of the bad heart-tree life-structure are: **lust for money, lust for power, lust for position,** and **lust for romance or sex.** On these limbs the fruit of the life is borne.

## THE BAD FRUIT AND SEED

The fruit that will always come forth on these limbs is **BAD DEEDS.** The attitudes and actions will be **selfish** and involve **taking,** rather than giving. This type of individual may really wish in his heart that he really cared about others. He may even convince himself that he does care some. But, deep in his inner being, when he really gets honest, he just doesn't care about others like he does himself. Some of the attitudes causing his actions and words to offend and wound others are **aggression, competition, striving, high achievement, defensiveness, inconsideration,** and **hostility.** Wounding others sets up his own rejection from those he offends. When he offends and wounds others, he causes them to reject him again. This plants more pain in his own heart and starts the cycle all over again.

These offensive and wounding bad deeds are the fruit. Most fruit has a seed inside. Inside this fruit is the **SEED of unlove—rejection.** The seeds produced by this person's life are exactly the same as the seeds that were planted in his own heart-soil. The individual is helplessly unable to control his **judgemental and critical attitude** toward those he should love. **Rejection, accusation, condemnation, and unforgiveness** are sown from the person into the heart-soil of others, especially the wife or husband and children. And the **kingdom of darkness** is reproduced in the hearts of others, producing the same life-structure all over again. In a real and practical way, the sins of the fathers are passed on to the next generation. The situation tends to grow worse to third and fourth generation. *Exodus 34:7.*

## THE BAD BIRDS

Certain kinds of birds are attracted to the bad fruit of the Bad Heart Tree. The birds are BAD SPIRITS. The Bible calls these bad spirits demons. Demon spirits of darkness, blindness, deception, and delusion will come with all of their filthiness and torment to lodge in the limbs of the bad-heart tree. These spirits will shut out the light. The truth of God cannot get through to the heart, but lies, deceptions, and delusion will flow readily into it.

*2 Corinthians 4:3-4a: But even if our gospel is veiled, it is veiled to those who are perishing, whose minds the **god of this age has blinded...***

*1 John 2:11: But he who hates his brother is in darkness and walks in darkness, and does not know where he is going, because the **darkness has blinded his eyes.***

*2 Thessalonians 1:9b-11: ...according to the working of Satan, with all power, signs, and lying wonders, and with all unrighteous **deception** among those who perish, because they did not receive the love of the truth,*

79

*that they might be saved. And for this reason God will send them strong **delusion**, that they should believe the lie.*

This type of individual is now ready to receive occult interest and involvement, and seems powerless against the enticing drawing of the lying promises of the occult to meet the needs of the life-structure. Promise of excitement, power, control, peace of mind, and riches turn into hopeless bondages and addictions that imprison him and steal all hope and eventually, his very life.

Anyone involved in occult, witchcraft, or other demonic activities has the bad heart-tree as his life-structure. It is the only way to great deception. The occult activities can range from overt, satanic worship and witchcraft to church members who are deceived into practices of spirit power that look like God. Some have called this Christian witchcraft. The bad heart-tree, mixed with religion, produces false prophets.

Remember, this individual didn't plan it this way. He didn't want this at all. It was planted in him as rejection, which caused pain that grew into bitterness, and then into rebellion, with fear and pride. And then his need became lust, which produced bad deeds and bad seeds, which invited the evil spirits to lock him into bondage and torment, unable to hear God or His truth. In addition, if the enemy can cause the heart to be closed off to Godly people as well, he has this individual locked into bondage.

### THE WALL

All of this is not pretty. The individual soon learns this behavior is not acceptable and it causes him to be rejected and suffer more pain again and again. He learns that every person who gets close to him eventually hurts him. He also recognizes that every person who gets close to him gets hurt themselves as well. He then begins to build a **WALL OF DEFENSE.** The wall of defense is designed to hide what really is in the heart-tree and is created to stop the hurts of closeness caused by the pain of rejection. The wall is built of things used by the individual to try to make himself feel better by venting on others.

*Proverbs 18:19: **A brother offended is harder to win than a strong city, and contentions are like the bars of a castle.***

The person with the wall of defense says to himself: "No one is ever going to get close enough to me to hurt me again." He builds the wall as strong and as tall as necessary to keep anyone from seeing what is really in the heart, and to keep anyone from ever really getting close enough to hurt him. He usually begins building his wall with **contention** and **contrariness.** Next comes **"unaffection"**, **withdrawal,** and so on. If this doesn't work to keep everyone away, the wall is built higher with more serious resistance.

Remember, the wall is supposed to hide the pain, bitterness, rebellion, fear, pride, lust, bad fruit, and spiritual darkness of our heart tree that has grown from the seed of unlove planted in the heart-soil. One problem the person runs into is that the wall itself becomes very ugly. In order to cover its ugliness, he might white-wash the outside of the wall. This mask is temporary, but may last long enough for him to make it while in the presence of others, such as, at work or church etc. Another problem is that the limbs keep growing over the wall. He must keep adding more bricks to make the wall higher and stronger.

*Acts 23:3: Then Paul said to him, "God will strike you, you **whitewashed wall!** For you sit to judge me according to the law, and do you command me to be struck contrary to the law?"*

In the upper portion of the wall of defense, **blame** turns to **slander** to produce **separation.** If **alcohol** and **drugs** don't create enough distance to keep others away, he becomes **abusive, immoral** and **violent.** If he can't keep others out any other way, he will **murder** them. Now that the wall is strong enough and high enough to keep people out from the side, and now that the spirits of darkness keep the light of God out from above, the helpless individual has become an island. He cannot give or receive love. The feelings of **loneliness** and **hopelessness** overwhelm him. The angry, hostile attitudes begin to be focused inward on himself. **Self-rejection** now plants its own painful seeds in his own heart-soil producing the deadly cycle of **depression** and **self-hate.**

The person now must try to build a wall to separate himself from himself. He becomes two people in one body; one rejecting the other. He is actually **dying for love** and is unable to receive it or give it. Finally, he realizes it won't do any good to just murder the one who rejects him; he's got to kill the one that is hurting him from the inside. So he stacks the last brick on the wall. **Suicide** makes this statement: "You'll never touch me now; you'll never hurt me again; and I'll never hurt me again."

Remember again, this person didn't want it to be this way. It just happened—It got planted in him. The work of Satan is complete when he can cause people to reject each other long enough **to grow the seed of unlove to its final maturity—death**—which is separation from God and His kind of life.

## DEALING WITH THE BAD TREE

Most people in the world today are at some stage of this life-structure. It is the only life- structure available to those without God; and many Christians are to some degree in bondage to the bad heart-tree life-structure. We've not known fully the ministry of Jesus to set the captives free, give sight to the blind, proclaim the opening of the prison, to set at liberty the bruised, and heal the brokenhearted.

We've tried to deal with bad actions by demanding that those individuals simply stop doing those bad deeds. That's like getting a baseball bat and knocking the fruit off the tree. It may help for awhile, but not for long. The tree is still there and will soon produce the same fruit again.

Then we grew a bit wiser and decided we had to deal with the lust. Getting rid of the lust is like getting out a pruning saw and cutting off the limbs of the tree. It will help a little longer, but eventually the limbs will grow back because the "trunk of need and rebellion" is still standing.

Now we get out our chain saw and cut down the trunk of the tree. We tell them to stop their rebellion and control their fear and pride. It takes a little longer this time, but, you guessed it. The tree will grow back from the root. Even when we tell them to dig out the root of bitterness by forgiving everyone from the heart, we're still leaving them with a broken heart. The gaping hole and torn soil left after extracting the root is open and fertile for the next seed of rejection that comes by. It will be planted in their heart soil and will start the process all over again. Until the soil of the heart is healed, the ministry is not finished. That's why Jesus said, *"I am come to heal the brokenhearted."*

*Luke 4:18-22* *"'The Spirit of the Lord is upon Me, because He has anointed Me to* **preach the gospel** *to the poor. He has sent Me to* **heal the brokenhearted,** *to* **preach deliverance** *to the captives and* **recovery of sight** *to the blind, to* **set at liberty** *those who are oppressed, to* **preach the acceptable** *(favorable)* **year** *of the Lord" Then He closed the book, and gave it back to the attendant and sat down. And the eyes of all who were in the synagogue were fixed on Him. And He began to say to them,* **"Today this Scripture is fulfilled in your hearing."**

*Matthew 3:10:* *"And even now the ax is laid* **to the root of the trees.** *Therefore every tree which does not bear good fruit is* **cut down** *and thrown into the fire."*

*Matthew 15:13:* *But He answered and said, "Every plant which My heavenly Father has not planted will be* **uprooted."**

*Isaiah 61:1b:* *"He has sent me to* **heal the brokenhearted,** *to* **proclaim liberty** *to the captives, and the* **opening of the prison** *to those who are bound ..."*

The ministry of Jesus to heal the broken heart is brought forth today by the Holy Spirit to heal the inner wounds in our spirit and soul. The soul includes our mind, will, and emotions. Jesus will heal the hurting memories in our mind, our shattered emotions, crushed will, and wounded spirit.

*Isaiah 61:3-4:* *"... to console those who mourn in Zion, to give them beauty for ashes, the oil of joy for mourning, the garment of praise for the spirit of heaviness; that they may be called* **trees of righteousness,** *the planting of the Lord, that He may be glorified. And they shall rebuild the old ruins, they shall repair the ruined cities, the desolations of many generations."*

We must then replant our heart-soil with the seeds that will produce a kingdom-of-God life-structure. The good heart-tree will grow as naturally as the bad one did, and will produce beautiful fruit in our life.

The seeds of unconditional love, acceptance, mercy, grace, and forgiveness flowing through an affirming attitude will plant the root system of the love of Jesus with all its beautiful tributary roots filling our heart.

# GOD'S KINGDOM PATTERN

## THE GOOD TRUNK

Always, without exception, the trunk of the tree that will grow upon the root of the love of Jesus is **SUBMISSION**. A walk of obedience and submission to God and to the authorities that He has established over us will naturally flow from a heart filled with the love of Jesus.

Remember, this is not something we can work up by striving within ourselves. It was planted in us and grows naturally from the seed of love. It is an easy yoke of freedom. The trunk of our life structure of submission and obedience is characterized by **FAITH** and **HUMILITY**. We know that we are loved. We know that God loves us and that He is able to control those over us and around us so that His love will eventually flow through them as well. Therefore, "since God loves me and those over me and around me love me, all my needs will be met. I don't have to worry about taking care of myself by myself. It is easy for me to have faith, to trust and believe. So, I feel **secure, confident, safe, self-assured**, and **considerate** of others. I also know that God has supplied my needs, not myself. So, I feel **HUMBLE, thankful,** and **meek."** This leads to a **gentle, caring,** and **yielding** attitude toward others. The central characteristic of the good heart-tree life-structure is a sense of **ABUNDANCE,** a feeling of having all we need and more. It doesn't matter how much or how little we have, we feel no sense of lack, **no driving wants** or frustrating needs in our heart.

*Psalm 23:1: The Lord is my shepherd; I shall  **not want.***

*Psalm 37:4: Delight yourself also in the Lord, and He shall give you the **desires (or wants)** of your heart.*

*Philippians 4:19: And my **God shall supply all your need (or lack)** according to His riches in glory by Christ Jesus.*

## THE GOOD LIMBS

The limbs of our life-structure grow out of the overflowing abundance of our life. Our desire is no longer to take from others, but to give to others from our overflowing rivers of living water from within. The limbs of our tree on which our life-fruit is to be borne are: **Desire to Give, Desire to Serve, Desire to Minister,** and **Desire to Build Others.**

## THE GOOD FRUIT AND THE SEED

The attitudes, words and actions of our life-structure are **GOOD DEEDS** and **GOOD SEEDS**. We are free to do what we want to do, according to the desire of our hearts. All we do and say is giving in nature and brings blessing to those around us. Our work becomes fun as we let the love of God flow to others through the things we do.

The seeds we sow in the heart-soil of others around us through this kind of fruit are exactly the same that were sown into our own heart-soil. **Love, acceptance, mercy, grace, and forgiveness are sown through an affirming attitude, and the kingdom of God is reproduced** in the hearts of our wives, husbands, children, and others.

Remember again, the wonderful life-structure of the good heart-tree is not something we can fake, nor is it something we can make happen by trying to build ourselves up into it. No amount of human effort nor sacrifice can enable us to have faith, humility, a sense of abundance, the desire to serve and give, intimacy with God, or good actions and deeds.

We must receive the seed of the resurrected life of Jesus the Christ. A tree grows from a seed. Natural growth will occur in our heart soil when the seed is planted and maintained. There must be cleared, quality soil available in which to plant the seed. If another tree occupies the soil, there is no room for the new tree to grow. The new tree must be watered by the Spirit and fed by the Word.

## THE GOOD BIRDS

Certain kinds of birds are attracted to the good fruit of the Good Heart Tree. They are **SPIRITS** of enlightenment. **Truth, wisdom, understanding and revelation** come to dwell in the limbs of our Good Heart tree. We are open to receive the **light** of God, which flows readily into our lives. We can hear and obey the direction of God for our lives. We are able to have intimate communication with God. His truth is revealed

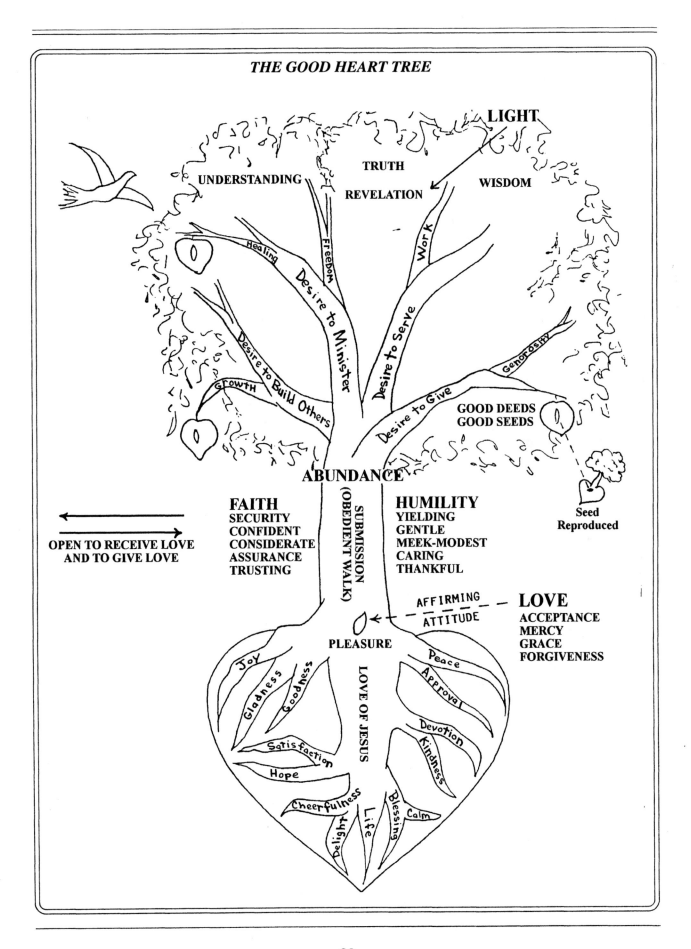

THE GOOD HEART TREE

to us from His Word by His Spirit. We can hear and understand spiritual truth with clarity. Deeper understandings are revealed to our open hearts. We have enlightened ability to discern truth from error.

*Isaiah 11:2: "The Spirit of the Lord shall rest upon Him, the Spirit of **wisdom** and **understanding,** the Spirit of counsel and might, the Spirit of **knowledge** and of the fear of the Lord."*

*Ephesians 1:17-18a: ... that the God of our Lord Jesus Christ, the Father of glory may give to you the **spirit of wisdom and revelation** in the **knowledge** of Him, the eyes of your **understanding being enlightened** ...*

*1 John 5:6b,4:6b: And it is the Spirit who bears witness, because the Spirit is **truth.** By this we know the spirit of truth and the spirit of error.*

### NO WALLS

Not only are we open toward the heavens and able to intimately relate to God, we are also able to relate intimately to others. We are open and transparent. There is **no need for a wall** of defense. We are **able to give and receive love** from others. Since we are giving and receiving love from others from the side, and relating to God openly from above, our lives are filled with life. There is no opportunity for loneliness, boredom, or depression to overpower and defeat us.

*Ephesians 2:14: For He Himself is our peace, who has made both one, and has broken down the middle **wall of division** ...*

*1 Corinthians 13:13: **And now abide faith, hope, love, these three; but the greatest of these is love.***

We may suffer persecution and enter into difficult times of darkness. Tests and trials may come, and we may again battle with the enemies of our soul. But— **love** will never fail. **Hope,** though it may grow dim, will never go out. And we will emerge from the battle with stronger **faith** than ever, more filled with the light and life of God, more solidly convinced of His love, more prepared to manifest His glory and rule and reign with Him.

# CHAPTER 16

## THE DOUBLE TREE

*James 1:8 ...he is a double-minded man, unstable in all his ways.*

Have you ever felt like your life, since becoming a Christian, was much like a roller-coaster ride? If you haven't, maybe you have known someone who was on fire for God for a season and then lower than dirt for a season. Then they would get back up to the mountain top for a while, just to slide back down again into the same old trash—only sometimes worse than before. Unfortunately this is a much too common happening among Christians. It certainly was a picture of my early years as a Christian.

There is a tendency among some Christians to accept this as normal. True, it is reality in the world to meet challenges and to sometimes feel less than living on the mountain top. But it is not needful for Christians to fall back into the pit or the ways of the pit from which Jesus redeemed them. The enemy loves to use our backsliding to beat us with guilt and to punch holes in our faith. He tells us something like, "See, your not saved; you're a rotten, stinking sinner, a hypocrite; you can't serve God."

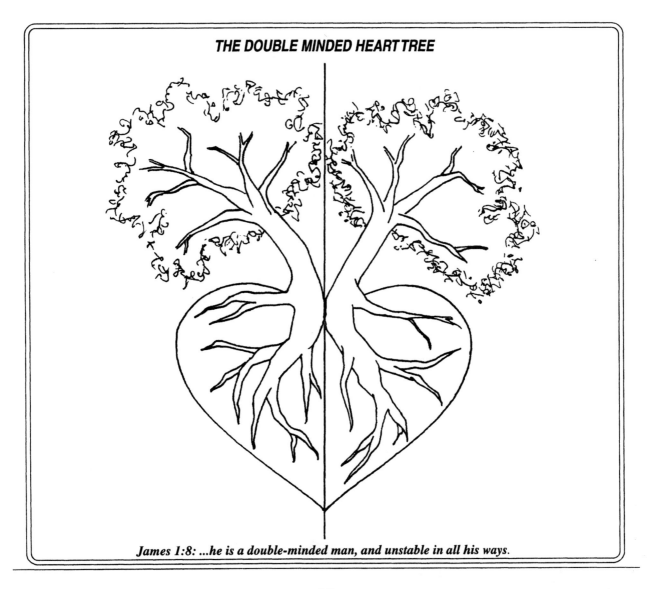

**THE DOUBLE MINDED HEART TREE**

*James 1:8: ...he is a double-minded man, and unstable in all his ways.*

85

We must be missing something somewhere. The "roller-coaster Christians" may have received Jesus as savior; committed their life to Him as much as they know how; and followed the instructions from their church as best they could. In other words, they have planted the good seed in their heart and cared for it as best they can. And they have evidenced a good measure of growth of their good tree. So, what is wrong? Why are they so double-minded and unstable?

The double-minded heart tree is one in which the good heart-tree has found enough soil to begin to grow, but **the bad heart-tree has not been cut down and uprooted.**

These Christians may function in one tree for a period of time and then suddenly switch over to the other lifestyle. They may switch to the good tree on Sunday and back to the bad tree on Monday. Or they may live in the good tree Sunday through Friday and switch to the other on Saturday night. They will live **all the way**, one way or the other, depending on which tree they are functioning in. This is not a blended mental condition. It is a sudden change from one set of life patterns to the other, much like changing channels on a TV set.

Sometimes they may be in the good tree for six months, a year, or longer, and then suddenly shift back to the old structure and surprise everyone around them, including themselves. Some event or situation may trigger a seemingly automatic shift. The individual may not have made a conscious decision to change. It just happened before they realized what was happening. When they are in one tree, it's like the other one never existed. They may wonder, "How in the world could I have thought that way?" "How could I have ever thought all that wild stuff was fun?" Or; "How could I have thought all that church stuff was so great." They are unstable in all their ways, and tossed about.

**The answer is to get the bad heart-tree forever cut down, rooted out, and the soil healed so the good tree can take over the whole heart and flourish.** When the old life-structure is gone, there is great freedom to walk continuously in the good heart-tree life-structure.

However, it is never impossible for Christians to decide to rebel and again become disobedient to God. Even those growing up surrounded by the unconditional love of God can willfully decide to become rebellious and disobey God. But it is not their normal manner, and they will have to work at it by ignoring many road blocks and strong warnings from the Holy Spirit.

# CHAPTER 17

## THE KINGDOM FAMILY PATTERN

## GOD'S KINGDOM PATTERN

We have seen God's plan and pattern for the individual and the enemy's scheme to pervert and divert it. We have seen, in part, how God builds and establishes Godly character in his children. We have also seen how the enemy goes about bringing destruction, and planting ungodly character in whomever he can.

Now we want to understand God's plan for human relations and governing. The family is the basic plan of God. God's pattern for the family is basically the same for business, church, and political governments. We also want to uncover the enemy's scheme to destroy the plan of God and install his own diabolical scheme to rule. His scheme is also basically the same for family, business, church and political governments.

### PATTERNS OF LIFE

New Jerusalem is that great pattern-city of God. The patterns of life are coming down from God to form and shape the Bride of Christ. The other great pattern-city, Babylon, has imposed its patterns of rule upon the earth. The kingdoms of this earth will become the kingdoms of our God, as New Jerusalem-patterns for life come forth and are planted into the hearts of men, and then brought forth into the world. We will view some of the New Jerusalem (Bride-of-Christ) patterns and contrast them to the Babylonian (harlot) patterns.

God's pattern for the family is the basic relational structure for all institutions in the kingdom of God. Church, business, government, and families are to be established and governed according to the pattern God has provided. No other pattern will produce successful kingdom results.

The enemy's schemes have so polluted society today that God's plan tends to seem foreign to most people. There is temptation for even the most conservative-minded people to modify the plan of God in order to conform more closely to the society in which they live. As different as God's plan may seem to some, it is the only plan that will bring the results mankind desires. In the long run, every other plan will lead to disorder and loss. The so-called alternate lifestyles and family structures will lead to poverty and eventually death. A nation, culture, or society that does not function according to the pattern God has provided will fail.

*Exodus 25:9,40: According to all that I show you, that is, the pattern of the tabernacle and the pattern of all its furnishings, just so you shall make it. And see to it that you **make them according to the pattern** which was shown you on the mountain.*

We would think a person strange who would attempt to operate a piece of complicated equipment without referring to the instruction book. Almost anything you can buy today comes with an instruction book. Many hours of training are used to prepare people to operate modern machines. College-level courses and well-written textbooks are used to prepare people in most any area of scientific or artistic endeavor. But when it comes to life, most people don't know that God has provided a textbook that answers all our major questions. The only patterns that really work are in the Bible.

The book of Genesis (the book of beginnings) is filled with patterns of New Jerusalem life. The Garden of Eden was the New Jerusalem, ruling city of God, from which the world was ruled by God through Adam. Its God-given patterns for life and for ruling are New Jerusalem patterns.

*Genesis 1:26,28, Amp.: God said, "Let Us (Father, Son, and Holy Spirit) make mankind in Our image, after Our likeness; and **let them have complete authority** over the fish of the sea, the birds of the air, the (tame) beasts, and over all of the earth, and over every thing that creeps upon the earth." And God blessed them, and said to them, "**Be fruitful, multiply, and fill the earth and subdue it** (with all its vast resources); and have dominion over the fish of the sea, the birds of the air, and over every living creature that moves upon the earth."*

The first pattern we note is that God made man after his own image and gave him dominion or authority over all the resources of the earth. God rules or reigns over all of His vast creation. God has complete authority, and nothing can ever overrule Him. God chose to delegate the rule of the earth and all its creatures to man. Please note that **God did not give man authority to rule over other men.** Mankind is not part of the resources of the earth. He is the ruler of the earth and is to be ruled over by God. God formed man from dust and made him a living spirit. God is Spirit, and He made man a spirit who dwells in an earthly body. God's pattern is for man to communicate with Him spirit-to-Spirit. Adam walked with God in the garden and had close communion with Him. Adam had an occupation. He was given the job of tending the garden and naming the animals. Adam could receive daily instruction from God in how to do his job according to God's desire or plan. Adam was to partake of the tree of life. The tree of life represents hearing God, receiving revelation of God, as opposed to reasoning things out for himself in his own mind, which is the tree of knowledge of good and evil.

*Genesis 2:7-9, Amp.: Then the Lord God formed man of the dust of the ground, and breathed into his nostrils the breath or **spirit of life**; and man became a living being. And the Lord God planted a garden toward the east in Eden (meaning delight); and there He put the man whom He had formed (framed, constituted). And out of the ground the Lord God made to grow every tree that is pleasant to the sight or to be desired, good, (suitable, pleasant) for food; **the tree of life** also in the center of the garden, and the **tree of the knowledge** of (the difference between) good and evil, and blessing and calamity.*

*Genesis 2:15-17, Amp.: And the Lord God took the man and put him in the garden of Eden **to tend and guard and keep it.** And the Lord God commanded the man, saying, "You may freely eat of every tree of the garden, except of the tree of the knowledge of good and evil and of blessing and calamity you shall not eat, for in the day that you eat of it you shall surely die."*

To this point man did not have a wife. God's pattern is that **before man has his mate** he is to: (1) have spiritual life breathed into him, (2) be walking in close communion with God daily, (3) have a good occupation and instruction (education) for doing it, and (4) depend on revelation from God for direction for his life. **God's pattern is for man to be properly related to Him and established in His purpose before marriage.**

Most of us who have been married for a number of years can only imagine how wonderful it would have been if we had known and obeyed this pattern. There would have been much less stress and a lot more opportunity to enjoy the blessings of marriage. It would have been much easier for children to grow up in security and peace. With the help of the indwelling Spirit of God we must begin to live kingdom patterns and teach them to our children.

*Genesis 2:18-25, Amp.: Now the Lord God said, "It is not good (sufficient, satisfactory) that the man **should be alone; I will make him a helper meet (suitable, adapted,** completing) for him." And out of the ground the Lord God formed every (wild) beast and living creature of the field and every bird of the air, and brought them to Adam to see what he would call them, and whatever Adam called every living creature, that was its name. And Adam gave names to all livestock, and to the birds of the air, and to every (wild) beast of the field; but for Adam there was not found a helper meet (suitable, adapted, completing) for him.*

*And the Lord God caused a deep sleep to fall upon Adam, and while he slept He took **one of his ribs - a part of his side** - and closed up the (place with) flesh instead of it; and the rib or part of his side which the Lord had taken from the man, **He built up and made into a woman** and brought her to the man. Then Adam said, "This (creature) is now bone of my bones and flesh of my flesh. She shall be called Woman, because she was taken out of a man."*

*Therefore a man shall **leave** his father and his mother and shall become united and **cleave** to his wife, and **they shall become one flesh.** And the man and his wife were both **naked,** and were **not embarrassed or ashamed** in each other's presence.*

The wife is to be formed from the man. Man and every other living creature was made from the dust of the earth. Only woman was made "built up" from another living creature (man). The husband is the source of life to the wife. He must receive life from God and bring it to the wife. The pattern for the family, direction for the family, and spiritual life for the family, comes through the husband.

Therefore, a man must leave his father and mother and cleave to his wife, and become one flesh with her. She is to become his "**helper** - meet, suitable, adapted, completing for him". He has the vision, the pattern, the life, and the occupation or business direction from God. **She is to adapt to him, not him to her.** She is to become suited to him.

Anyone involved in ministry to families can readily verify that many difficult problems arise from a husband's remaining tied to his mother's apron strings or staying overly- dependent upon his father. The position of the parents of married children is one of advice, not control. The married couple should honor their parents, but no longer be dependent on them. It is not possible for a couple to cleave together and become one until they leave their parents.

They must **leave** dependency on parents and become their own institution. They must **cleave** to each other. She must look to her husband as head, not her father or pastor or anyone else. He must look to her for intimate help and completing, not to his mother or secretary or anyone else. Only the husband should meet the wife's need for headship, and only the wife should meet the husband's intimate needs.

The man and his wife are to be naked before each other, and yet not embarrassed or ashamed. Intimacy is a part of God's pattern. Again, anyone involved in ministry to families will verify that one major problem in marriages is a lack of intimacy. Intimate communication is vital to any marriage relationship. There is great fulfillment in loving intimacy between a husband and wife, much the same as there is in a loving, intimate relationship between man and God. Intimacy can exist only with transparency in an atmosphere of unconditional love when both are naked and open to each other emotionally, physically, and spiritually. There can be no great secrets, no deception, no hidden agendas, no defensive walls, no whitewashed coverings, and no manipulation. True intimacy is a deep need for every married couple. God's pattern is that nothing exist between the couple that hinders their being one flesh. One must speak the truth in love. However, a husband or wife must lovingly consider how and when to reveal information that might be hard for the mate to bear.

You are probably already sensing the direct parallels between God's kingdom family pattern for husband and wife, and His pattern for Jesus and His bride or wife. The natural family is to be a clear picture to the world of God's relationship to His wife, the church. The husband represents Jesus who must bring life and headship to the church, represented by the wife. The children are the fruit or the production of the marriage. They are to become the image of their father, Jesus. The husband (Jesus) is to be closely related to Father God and do and say what He sees and hears the Father doing and saying. Wives, like the church, are to greatly respect and be subject to their husbands.

*Ephesians 5:22-24, Amp.: **Wives, be subject - be submissive and adapt yourselves to your own husbands** as a service to the Lord. **For the husband is the head of the wife as Christ is the Head of the church,** Himself the Savior of (His) body. As the church is subject to Christ, so let wives also be subject in everything to their husbands.*

The husband as head of the wife is God's pattern. It is the only plan that will lead to success. The enemy has devised powerful schemes to attack the plan of God. Many perversions exist as a result of the enemy's efforts. We will discuss some of the perversions and what God wants us to do about them later. There are many considerations and real-life situations that seem to say that this is an impossible, idealistic goal. The bottom line is, it is God's pattern and the only one that will really work.

Please be aware that there is a difference between talking about "man and woman" and talking about "husband and wife". Marriage and family is an institution, a structure of order for function in life on earth. "Husband and wife" are positions or offices in the institution. **These offices are _what_ we _do_, not _who_ we _are_.**

Every person on earth has the opportunity to relate to God through Jesus the Christ. Each individual is a living spirit, a real living being created by God with purpose. And each individual person must give account to God for his or her own life. Every person, male or female, is an eternal spirit with equal opportunity to know God—and enter into a spiritual, heavenly relationship with Him now—as well as enter into eternal heaven with Him after leaving this life. God is no respecter of persons.

Some perversions occur when we lose that understanding and fail to make the proper distinction between the person and the office. Men may begin to think of themselves as primary and women as secondary. There is no distinction made by God. He created man only. When he created man from the dust of the earth, He created him male and female. Both are man. One is the male man and the other is the female man. They are bone of bone and flesh of flesh. Man is the only creation. Woman was built up from man.

Marriage is an earthly institution that reflects the spiritual marriage of the bride and wife of Christ to Jesus. The institution of marriage between husband and wife does not reach into heaven. It is clearly designed by God with heavenly principles, but it is an earthly institution. Because people have such a great involvement in marriage in this life, it is mistakenly assumed by many that the marriage goes on into the heavenlies. Jesus made this clear to the Sadducees who had brought him a challenging question about whose wife a woman would be in heaven when she had had more than one husband in this life. Please do not be greatly concerned about missing "being married" in heaven. One moment of experiencing the fullness of your heavenly marriage to your husband, Jesus, will wipe away all your concern.

*Mark 12:24-25: Jesus answered and said to them, "Are you not therefore mistaken, because you do not know the Scriptures nor the power of God? For when they rise from the dead, they neither marry nor are given in marriage, but are like angels in heaven."*

## THE OFFICE OF HUSBAND

*Ephesians 5:25-32, Amp.:* **Husbands, love your wives, as Christ loved the church and gave Himself up for her, so that He might sanctify her,** *having cleansed her by the washing of water with the Word, that He might present the church to Himself in glorious splendor, without spot or wrinkle or any such things - that she might be holy and faultless. Even so husbands should love their wives as (being in a sense) their own bodies. He who loves his own wife loves himself. For no man ever hated his own flesh, but nourishes and carefully protects and cherishes it, as Christ does the church, because we are members of His body. For this reason a man shall leave his father and his mother and shall be joined to his wife, and the two shall become one flesh. This mystery is very great, but I speak concerning (the relation of) Christ and the church.*

**The first and primary function of the office of the husband is to love his wife,** just as Jesus loved the church and gave Himself up for her. In a sense, the husband is to be the savior of the wife. He must be willing to become a sacrifice for her. Self must be set aside that he might provide for her need above his own selfishness. Selfish love embraces someone because it is "good for me. It makes me feel good. It meets my own need". Selfish love will give in order to get. This is not the love Jesus had for the church, and it is not the kind of love a husband is to have for his wife.

God's pattern is for the husband to love his wife with unconditional love. That means that the love is not dependent in any way on the performance of the wife. She is not required to meet any conditions whatsoever in order to have his love.

It is a "NO MATTER WHAT" kind of love. While we were yet sinners, Jesus the Christ loved us and died for us. It does not matter if she fixes supper or not; if she meets his needs sexually or not; whether the house is clean or not; whether she gripes and complains or not; whether she is faithful or unfaithful. There is nothing we can do or fail to do that can stop God from loving us. And this is exactly the same kind of love the husband must have for the wife.

The only great problem that husbands have with this is that there is not a man alive that can do it. Oh, the husband can really love his wife when she is sweet and faithful to him. In fact, she seems like the most precious, wonderful gift from God, the fulfillment of all his dreams. There is nothing in the world he would not do for her. No sacrifice would be too great for her. He would fight wild animals for her or conquer the world and bring it to her in a basket. It is easy for him to love those that love him. But what happens to that love if she sins against him and is unfaithful to him. Or what if she nags, sags, and looks like a hag and no longer meets his needs.

There is only one source for true, unconditional love. Yes, only God can love no matter what. Therefore, **the husband's greatest responsibility is to go to God and get this love for his wife.** The husband must remain in close communion with God and be continuously filled with His agape love. All of the husbands' responsibilities are secondary to his own personal relationship and love affair with God. **God's**

# KINGDOM FAMILY PATTERN

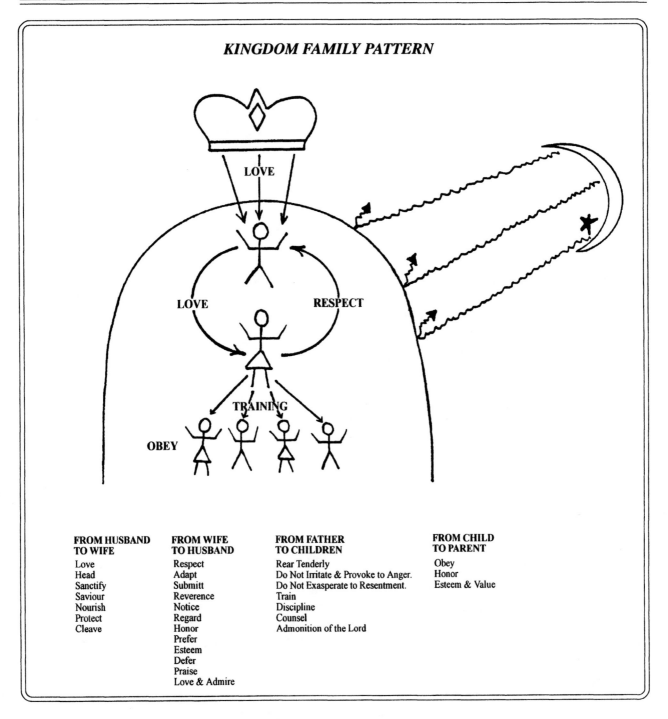

| FROM HUSBAND TO WIFE | FROM WIFE TO HUSBAND | FROM FATHER TO CHILDREN | FROM CHILD TO PARENT |
|---|---|---|---|
| Love | Respect | Rear Tenderly | Obey |
| Head | Adapt | Do Not Irritate & Provoke to Anger. | Honor |
| Sanctify | Submitt | Do Not Exasperate to Resentment. | Esteem & Value |
| Saviour | Reverence | Train | |
| Nourish | Notice | Discipline | |
| Protect | Regard | Counsel | |
| Cleave | Honor | Admonition of the Lord | |
| | Prefer | | |
| | Esteem | | |
| | Defer | | |
| | Praise | | |
| | Love & Admire | | |

**pattern is that the husband go to God and get an abundance of the overflowing, unconditional love of God and bring it to his wife.** This ministers life to the wife.

This flow of unconditional love flowing through her husband has a great affect on the wife. It can cause her to become faithful where she was unfaithful. It makes it possible for her to become sanctified. Harlotry can be changed to purity by this kind of love. The husband can present her to himself without spot or wrinkle. Just as it is with Jesus and the church, so it is with husband and wife. Yes, the wife still has the opportunity to remain rebellious and to reject the true love of her husband, but it is really hard for her. She must say "no" to the very love of God coming to her through her husband. In order to reject her husband, she must reject the love of God. If, however, that unconditional love is not there, it is easier for her to reject her husband.

Husbands, if you don't like something about your wife, you should first look at your relationship to God. Before you begin to complain about lack on her part, consider asking yourself, "Am I really consistently fulfilling my part? Am I bringing her the unconditional love of God in such a way she can really receive it?" If for some reason it is not getting through to her, it is as if it weren't there. Love must get to her in a form and a way that she can know and experience.

Isn't it amazing when you stop to think about how much effort a man may put into learning a vocation? Some put in many years of extensive study becoming a medical doctor, scientist or something else. Yet in God's pattern for a successful life, the first and most important priority, by far, is loving God with his whole heart and relating to Him in such a way that he can love his wife unconditionally. Often very little effort is applied toward the number-one priority. Husbands must learn to love God and learn how to love their wives in such a way that it gets through to the wife.

The wife who submits to this kind of love will find her greatest fulfillment in helping her husband to become great. The wife who does not receive this kind of love may have difficulty being fulfilled. Establishing a career of her own and reaching for independence can not replace the deep fulfillment of being loved by her husband and becoming the best helpmate she can be to him.

## THE OFFICE OF WIFE

We have seen the wife's part of being subject to and of submitting to her own husband as head—just as the church is subject to Jesus as head. Submitting to headship is very important in God's pattern. But it is not the most important function of the wife toward her husband. Her most important function is the same as the husband—that is to love God with her whole heart and relate to Him in such a way that she can have what she needs to fulfill her responsibility toward her husband. The thing that she must have is just as important to her husband as love is to her as the wife. But it is not exactly love; nor is it submission. As important as those things are, they are not her number-one responsibility to her husband.

The number-one responsibility of the wife is to **respect** her husband. This is relatively easy to do if he is bringing love to her and is perfect in all of his char-

acter. As long as he is a lot like Prince Charming, and she is drawn to him romantically, she might see him as perfect and have an awesome respect for him. If he does have a small flaw, it seems to be so insignificant, that it really does not matter. She probably doesn't even see it at all. It is very easy for her to respect her dream boat. But true respect is more than romantic chemistry.

God's pattern does not call for the wife to respect her husband only if he performs to her expectations. What if he won't make decisions like she thinks he should? What if he begins to look like a slob? What if he never seems to notice the things the wife does for him and the family? What if he is not providing for the family as well as her friend's husband provides for his family? What if he is not serving as spiritual head as well as some of the other men at church do for their families? What if she catches him looking too long at the young lady across the street in her bathing suit? What if he gets frustrated and shouts at one of the children? What if he is unfaithful?

Surely it must be right for the wife to clobber him with every disrespectful, contentious, complaining word she can think of. Surely God wants the wife to point out just how sorry he really is. And it must be time to call her friends at church to let them know just how bad he is so that they can pray. Certainly her mother will talk to Daddy and help her out of this mess if she can convince them that this husband is not the nice guy they think he is. Maybe those ladies at the beauty shop can give her some sympathy and advice if she shares with them how sorry this creep of a husband really is. Surely, if she nags him constantly, he will improve and be more like that handsome, friendly man at church. Surely God does not expect her to respect this husband. WRONG!

Respect is a reflection of love. **God's pattern is that unconditional love be reflected back by the wife to the husband as unconditional respect**—a "NO MATTER WHAT" kind of respect. This respect will go a long way toward moving the husband to perform better as a husband. It becomes a strong motivational force for him to correct flaws and to do better. Nagging and disrespect have exactly the opposite effect. Just as love from the husband ministers life to the wife, respect from the wife ministers life to the husband.

Husbands and wives each have different jobs to do to fulfill their respective offices. Man and woman are each designed to do their own job. God has designed woman to be an emotional-based creature, and man to be an ego-based creature. Love from the husband keeps the wife's emotions healthy. Respect from the wife keeps the husband's ego healthy.

One of the major responsibilities of the wife of God (the church) toward her husband (Jesus) is to **praise and worship** Him. Worship may be too strong a term when referring to the natural husband and wife. But the pattern is the same. The wife is to praise, praise, and praise her husband. She is to honor him, esteem him highly, and show forth her respect for him. She is to love and admire him exceedingly, just like the church does Christ.

*Ephesians 5:33: However, let each man of you (without exception) love his wife as (being in a sense) his very own self; and let the wife see that she **respects and reverences her husband - that she notices him, regards him, honors him, prefers him, venerates and esteems him; and that she defers to him, praises him, and loves and admires him exceedingly.***

God's patterns always work. Nothing else will produce the kingdom life we all desire. Our only choices are to adjust to God's pattern or to try to adjust God's pattern to us. I think you know which choice will work and which one will not. We can, if we look, always find the things that we can honestly praise. And we can always find the love and grace in God to fulfill our part.

A Godly wife is perhaps the most beautiful and valuable thing in God's earthly creation. The wife is vital to bringing forth the will and plan of God on earth. Without Godly wives, there will be no manifestation of the kingdom of God on earth. As the husband is the head of the wife, the **wife is the heart of the husband.** As it is with Jesus and the church, so it is with husband and wife.

*1 Corinthians 2:16b Amp.: ...but we have the mind of Christ, the Messiah **and do hold the thoughts (feelings and purposes) of His heart.***

The Wife has her husband's heart; he has entrusted it to her. She is very sensitive to what is going on in his heart. More than anyone else in the world, she can understand his motives, inner feelings, and needs. She can comfort and help him as no one else can. She can

also hurt him like no one else can. His heart is in her hands.

*Proverbs 18:22 Amp.: He who finds a (true) wife finds a good thing, and obtains favor of the Lord.*

*Proverbs 31:10-12,23 Amp.: A capable, intelligent and virtuous woman, who is he who can find her? She is far more precious than jewels, and her value is far above rubies or pearls. **The heart of her husband trusts in her confidently and relies on and believes in her safely,** so that he has no lack of honest gain or need of dishonest spoil. She will comfort, encourage and do him only good as long as there is life within her. Her husband is known in the city's gates, when he sits among the elders of the land.*

A Godly wife is like a fertile field receiving the seeds of love from her husband and multiplying them so that many can partake. The love of God sown in her from the husband is manifested in great service and many are blessed. The children, the neighbors, everyone who is near, receives acts of the love of God from her. As it is with the wife, so it is with the church. Read *Proverbs 31:13-31*, for a clear picture of part of God's pattern for both.

There is no more fulfilling, joyful, exciting, happy and rewarding life for a woman than living in God's pattern of the office of wife. All the careers and professional achievements in the world cannot replace it.

## THE CHILDREN

God's kingdom pattern for family produces Godly children. Everything is provided that is needed for the children, and their primary responsibility is to **obey**, honor, and esteem their parents.

*Ephesians 6: 1-3: Children, **obey** your parents in the Lord (as His representatives), for this is just and right. Honor (esteem and value as precious) your father and your mother; this is the first commandment with a promise: that all may be well with you, and that you may live long on the earth.*

God's pattern is for the children to be **obedient** and **honor** their parents. It will be easy for children growing up in God's kingdom-family pattern to know God. They see Him demonstrated in their parents. They see a clear picture of God's love in the love their father has for their mother. They are trained in how to reflect God's love as they see their mother respect and praise her husband, their father. It is easy for them to understand God's love and to know how to respond to it with loving respect and submission.

**In God's pattern, the father is responsible for training the children,** not the mother. Certainly the mother has a vital part in training the children. Her part is especially important to the very young. She is especially equipped to nurture them with gentleness. But she is to be "flowing" the love from her husband to them. The father is the source of **training** and **discipline** for the children. The mother will help to train the children as directed by the father.

*Ephesians 6:4: **Fathers,** do not irritate and provoke your children to anger, do not exasperate them to resentment, but **rear them tenderly in the training and discipline and the counsel and admonition of the Lord.***

The children feel extremely secure under the care and protection of a strong, loving father and a tender, loving mother. Fathers have a strength that instills the feelings of safety in a child. That same loving firmness gives them great assurance that firm boundaries exist for their protection. Only the special strength of a father can provide the security of discipline and protection. Small children are very sensitive to their mother's feelings and attitudes. Because she feels safe with her husband, the children feel safe. Fathers are warned to be very careful with their strength in regard to the children.

The wife and children are secure because the husband is being instructed and empowered by God to direct the family. The presence of God is throughout the family. The whole family is under a dome of protection, and the enemy can find no place to plant stress and torment. There is no opportunity for his perverted ways and diabolical schemes to enter. The family is protected from the spiritual harlotry of Babylon. Darkness is turned away by the protective covering of God. And the presence of God reigns throughout the family.

All of this allows the world to see a clear picture of God's love and how He works with mankind. This is God's pattern message to the world. All can see what Jesus is like in the husband, and what the bride church is like in the wife and in the maturing process of the children. This may be the only way some will understand the sacrifice of love, the pleasure of respect and submission, and the security of obedience.

## KINGDOM BUSINESS PATTERN

The Word of God is filled with principles, patterns, and specific information instructing His people as to how to have good success in business. We will take a look at some of the major principles later in the work.

Unfortunately, we've not always looked to God's plan for patterns for our business or work life. Most of our training may have come from the existing world system which is heavily infested with the enemy's schemes. The patterns and principles that we've learned from the world's system can temporarily produce high levels of success in segments of our life-structure. But they cannot produce total success in our whole life. The enemy's schemes always produce loss, and eventually death. The lack of success in one area will eventually erode the success we may have gained in another.

*Joshua 1:8: "This book of the law shall not depart from your mouth, but you shall meditate in it day and night, that you may observe to do according to all that is written in it. For then you will **make your way prosperous, and then you will have good success."***

God's success (good success) encompasses every area of our life. Family, church, business, recreation, education, and all other areas of our lives are to be in proper, functioning order in God's good success plan.

Because most people have been so programmed in the enemy's schemes and perversions, the pattern of God may seem strange to them. God's New-Jerusalem patterns are still the only ones that will ever really work to produce real success, peace, and joy in the world.

The pattern for a kingdom business is exactly the same as the kingdom-family pattern. The husband (president, entrepreneur, chief executive officer) must go to God and get the **love** and **vision** which is brought back to the wife (second-level management). The second-level management must **respect** the executive and **submit** to him. Like the wife, this management must carry out the care and training of the employees (children) as directed by the executive (husband, father).

The husband (entrepreneur) receives vision, ideas, understanding, and direction from God. A union similar to the marriage union is made with second-level management (the wife). The vision or idea is a seed planted in the wife from the husband. The wife nurtures and grows the idea or vision and brings it forth. The employees are trained in the vision or idea and production occurs.

The vision from God will always lead to serving God by serving mankind. The purpose of the business is to **provide for** the needs of people, not to **get from** people so the businessmen can be richer.

The union of marriage between the husband (entrepreneur, C.E.O.) and wife (second-level management) is just as **permanent** as marriage between the natural husband and wife. The C.E.O. must bring unconditional **love** to the management, and the management must have unconditional **respect** for the C.E.O. The employees must **obey** and **honor** management (mother) and the C.E.O.(father).

Stress, fear, strife, and competition are eliminated, and production increased in God's pattern.

## KINGDOM CHURCH PATTERN

Yes, you guessed it. All the same structures exist in God's pattern for the local church as the kingdom family, or business. We will look at more of the specifics of the local church and its role in the kingdom later in this work.

God has given only one plan for government. Whether it is family, church, business, state, nation, or world—the same kingdom (New Jerusalem) patterns must eventually rule. No other substitute plan or perversion will ever bring peace, joy, and righteousness.

The spiritual universal church has one husband. His name is Jesus. The husband (Jesus) has a wife and children, the universal or spiritual church. This is the great family of God. The Israel of God (the children), is mothered by New Jerusalem (the wife), the mother of us all.

*Galatians 4:28-29, 6-16:  There is neither Jew nor Greek, there is neither slave nor free, there is neither male nor female;  for you are all one in Christ Jesus. And if you are Christ's, then you are Abraham's seed,* *and heirs according to the promise. And as many as walk according to this rule, peace and mercy be upon them, and upon the Israel of God.*

*Galatians 4:26:  the Jerusalem above is free, which is the mother of us all.*

The local churches are cells of the universal church and are to reflect the spiritual church-structure. A local church usually begins with a chief elder (husband) who receives the vision from God for the local church. Other elders or leaders, whatever we might call them, serve as the wife in God's pattern.

All of the kingdom-family pattern principles apply to the local church just as they do for kingdom business. In a church, the chief elder (husband) must relate to God properly, get the **love** and **vision,** bring it to the elders or leaders (whatever they may be called). The leaders must **respect** the chief elder and **submit** to him. The leaders (wife mother) are to carry out the training and care of the congregation (children) under the direction of the chief elder (husband, father).

**The fivefold ministry of apostle, prophet, evangelist, pastor, and teacher will function within the pattern in church or business**. The gift of apostle is identified with the position of chief elder. The chief elder may be an apostle, or he may be appointed by and closely involved with an apostle. If the chief elder is a prophet, evangelist, pastor, or teacher, the local church will predominantly bear the characteristics of his respective gift. If the chief elder (husband) is an apostle, and the other four gifts are present in the elders (wife), the church will have a balance of characteristics.

There can never be more than one head. The final authority must always rest in the "husband".  He must be willing to accept and maintain the responsibility to represent what God is doing and saying to the local church. **It is not a husband's or wife's part to make decisions**—but to find out and represent what the **true** head has already decided about a matter and not substitute man's idea. Though the chief elder is always accountable, he is not required to hear every word on his own, alone. The chief elder must hear from the other gifts in the wife. He must hear and evaluate wisely all recommendations and appeals from the wife. She will usually have insight that will bring balance.

The kingdom patterns of government for families, businesses, churches, and every Godly human institution are New Jerusalem patterns coming down from God to form and shape the Bride of Christ. The enemy's patterns are harlot patterns from "Mystery Babylon".

# CHAPTER 18

## HARLOTRY OF BABYLON

### THE ENEMY'S SCHEME

There are two great ruling cities from which mankind can receive patterns for life. We have talked about the great ruling city of God, New Jerusalem, the Bride-of-Christ City. The other great ruling city is Babylon, the Harlot of the devil. The great ruling city of Babylon has planted its harlot patterns throughout the current world system. Babylon's patterns have produced much riches for some. She is extremely enticing and beautifully clothed in wealth. Yet inside, she is full of filth and abominations, a habitation of demons.

Babylon must fall. The great religious, and political system with all its patterns of life is judged of God and is coming down. Before the patterns of New Jerusalem can rule, the patterns of Babylon must be destroyed. The person seeking to enter the city-of-God lifestyle must have the Babylonian patterns and ways broken and removed from their life. The Babylonian system has been very deadly to the saints of God. Many have fallen and many are in captivity in Babylonian ways. God's people are warned to come out of Babylon, lest they share in her sin and receive of her plagues.

*Revelation 17:1-6: Then one of the seven angels who had the seven bowls came to me, "Come, I will show you the judgment of the **great harlot** who sits on **many waters,** with whom **the kings of the earth committed fornication, and the inhabitants of the earth were made drunk with the wine of her fornication."** So he carried me away in the Spirit into the wilderness. And I saw a woman sitting on a scarlet beast which was full of names of blasphemy, having seven heads and ten horns. **The woman was arrayed in purple and scarlet, and adorned with gold and precious stones and pearls,** having in her hand a golden cup **full of abominations and the filthiness** of her fornication. And on her forehead a name was written: "MYSTERY BABYLON THE GREAT MOTHER OF HARLOTS AND ABOMINATIONS OF THE EARTH." And I saw the woman drunk with the blood of the saints and with the blood of martyrs of Jesus. And when I saw her, I marveled with great amazement.*

*Revelation 17:15,18: And he said to me, "**The waters which you saw, where the harlot sits, are peoples, multitudes, nations, and tongues.**" And the woman whom you saw is the **great city** which reigns over the **kings of the earth.***

*Revelation 18:2-4: And he cried mightily with a loud voice, saying, "Babylon the great is fallen, is fallen, and has become **a habitation of demons, a prison** for every foul spirit, and a cage for every unclean and hated bird. For all the nations have drunk of the wine of the wrath of her fornication, the kings of the earth have committed fornication with her, and **the merchants of the earth have become rich through the abundance of her luxury."** And I heard another voice from heaven saying, "Come out of her, my people lest you share in her sins, and lest you receive of her plagues."*

What a great contrast between the harlot city of Babylon described in the book of Revelation (chapters seventeen to nineteen), and the beautiful Bride-City of God, New Jerusalem described in Revelation (chapters twenty one and twenty two). The beautiful Bride-of-Christ lifestyle is filled with the glory of God—God abiding with man and man living in His very presence—partaking of a pure river of water of life, clear as crystal, proceeding from the throne of God and the Lamb. Tears are wiped away and curses broken. Men and women are thankfully serving God and joyfully praising Him.

Just as there is a natural Jerusalem and now a spiritual New Jerusalem coming forth, there was a natural Babylon that was destroyed and now a Mystery Babylon that is being destroyed. Many patterns that began thousands of years ago in old Babylon are traceable throughout ancient history and up to the present time. Ancient Babylon was the first great-walled city after the flood. It was built by Noah's great grandson, Nimrod. Noah beget Ham; Ham beget Cush; and Cush begot Nimrod.

Babylon became the birth place of idolatry that was spread throughout the ancient world and passed to empires and civilizations throughout history. Nimrod and his wife, Semiramis, were the first people to be worshipped as gods. Although many different names were used in different cultures, they were worshipped similarly in much of the world, and can still be easily recognized in many religions today. These patterns were subversively planted into the Christian religion, and churches today are still affected by them. This nation, the good old U.S.A., and much of the world is primarily ruled by the patterns of ancient Babylon. The patterns seen in Nimrod and Semiramis of ancient Babylon are very similar to the dynamics of worldly families, businesses, churches, and political governments of today.

*Genesis 10:8-12a: Cush begot Nimrod; he began to be a mighty one on the earth. He was a mighty hunter before the Lord; therefore it is said, "Like Nimrod the mighty hunter before the Lord." And the beginning of his kingdom was Babel, Erech, Accad, and Calneh, in the land of Shinar. From that land he went to Assyria and built Nineveh, Rehoboth Ir, Calah, and Resen.*

The word **"before"** in the statement, "He was a mighty hunter before the Lord", could be translated **"against"**. Nimrod was a mighty man "against" the Lord. He and Semiramis some way tapped into the darkness of mystical and occult powers. A departure from the patriarchal faith had occurred. It is represented by some profane history that Cush had become a ringleader of apostasy. Nimrod added mystical, demonic powers and knowledge to his natural strength and became a powerful force on the earth, conquering all those around him.

Nimrod was the first to wage war upon his neighbors, the first to train troops with exercise and hardship, the first to build towers and walled cities for battle. Nimrod exercised strong control over men. They were enticed with unbridled self-gratification. Everywhere Nimrod went, there were extravagant parties with orgies, dancing girls, music, games, and anything that would bring self-gratification. Nimrod also controlled by locking up the mysteries of science and sorcery that he had discovered and releasing them to men only when they were under his control. He used confession of sins and faults to control. When he had enough information on someone, and when they were awestruck by his great display of magic, he could easily control them.

Nimrod was **suddenly cut off** in the midst of his career of glory. Mystery surrounds his disappearance. But it is believed that he met with a violent **death** while on one of his expeditions. Semiramis, whose **feminine beauty** covered her **immoral, manipulative, deceitful** self, had **usurped** the attributes of her husband before his death. At his death, she **took over** her husband's place.

Semiramis, in her **licentious ways,** gave birth to a son after Nimrod was gone. She told people that Nimrod had reappeared in the person of a posthumous son. She held the son up as God and the people worshipped him. They worshipped her as the mother of God. Eventually she became the predominant goddess overshadowing the son. Thus through **deception** and **manipulation** she **took over** the assets and attributes of Nimrod and continued her lavish lifestyle.

Semiramis was seen as both the mother and wife of her husband. Nimrod was seen as the husband and the son of his wife. She was revered as the mother of god. The image of the mother of god with the child in her arms spread to all the idolatrous world. Semiramis is said to have finished the wall of Babylon and thus became the goddess of fortress and towers. The Diana of the Ephesians mentioned in the New Testament with her crown of towers is identified with Semiramis.

Babylon became known as a great center of extravagant wealth and revelry—a monument of glamour to the accomplishments of man—a place of harlotry and sorcery—a place of great wizardry, human knowledge and discovery—a place of competition and contention. But the primary characteristic was spiritual harlotry.

**Spiritual harlotry is the seeking of our own needs and desires apart from God.** God is our provider. He desires to meet our needs in every area of life. If we look to anything or anyone else to meet our needs, we are looking to another god and are involved in spiritual harlotry. Harlotry and idolatry are very closely related. Harlotry is looking to **an idol (another god) for what our Heavenly Father should provide for us. Spiritual harlotry is selling our purity to meet our needs.** It is **self-seeking** and **self-serving.**

It's easy to see how the bad heart-tree is a harlot tree. Spiritual harlotry is seeking to meet the needs of our life-structure on our own, instead of trusting God

Babylon is a harlot system, a means of meeting human needs and selfish wants apart from God. Babylon is ruled by a spirit of **harlotry** and is characterized by **competition, immorality, and sorcery.**

**HARLOTRY** IS **SELF-SEEKING** AND **SELF-SERVING:**
It is seeking to meet my own needs and desires apart from God.

**COMPETITION** IS SEEKING **POSITION** OR **CONTROL:**
Contention, Strife, Thieving (taking), Lying, Deceit, Manipulation, Seduction, Control, Dominance, War (fighting), Overlord, Tyrant, Back-Biting, Murder, Greed, Covetousness.

**IMMORALITY** IS SEEKING **PLEASURE** OR **ENTERTAINMENT:**
Lust, Fantasy Lust, Fornication, Sexual Perversion, Unclean, Overeating, Overplaying, Overworking, Overresting, Reveling (partying).

**SORCERY** IS SEEKING **POWER** OR **DIRECTION:**
Occult, Witchcraft, Hypnosis, Mind Control, Mind Power, P.M.A., Humanism, Intellectualism, Astrology, Psychics, New Age Junk.

to take care of us. The good heart-tree is a bride tree, in which we are able to trust God to meet all of our needs and satisfy our wants.

Much of the world has taken giant steps into Babylonian harlotry in recent decades. Games and "playing" have become a major part of the U.S.A. Gambling lotteries and casinos are spreading widely across the land. Sexual perversion and recreational immorality are accepted as normal behavior. Psychics now openly advertise their "Psychic Hotline" numbers on daytime TV and are being looked to by many as a valid source of direction for their lives. Competition has intensified as people struggle for control in families, businesses, governments, tribes and nations. Computer and video games, gambling, spectator sports, recreational drugs and alcohol, entertainment, and other recreational industries probably already represent the largest segment of production in the U.S.A.

**Are we seeking from another god what our true God desires to supply?**

# CHAPTER 19

## BABYLONIAN FAMILY PATTERN

### THE ENEMY'S SCHEME

The family life patterns of Nimrod and Semiramis as seen through the profane history of ancient Babylon are functioning today as a scheme of the enemy to destroy God's plan for the family. This same Babylonian pattern is seen in Queen Jezebel and King Ahab in the Bible.

Ahab was king of Israel. Like Nimrod, he **departed from faith in the true God** and did evil in the sight of the Lord. He even married a Sidonian woman, Jezebel. Jezebel brought the licentious worship of the Cannanite cults into Israel. The Sidonites worshiped Baal and Ashtoreth. Ahab entered into idolatry. He worshipped Baal and built a temple and altar to Baal and set up a wooden image to Asherah, a Cannanite goddess.

*1 Kings 16:31-33: And it came to pass, as though it had been a trivial thing for him to walk in the sins of Jeroboam the son of Nebat, that he took as wife Jezebel the daughter of Ethbaal, king of the Sidonians; and he went and served Baal and worshipped him. Then he set up an altar for Baal in the temple of Baal, which he had built in Samaria. And Ahab made a wooden image. Ahab did more to provoke the Lord God of Israel to anger than all the kings of Israel who were before him.*

Jezebel was obsessed with **destroying the prophets of God.** Had it not been for a Godly servant who hid one hundred of the prophets of God, Jezebel would have killed all the prophets of God in Israel. Apparently Ahab did not, or could not, restrain her. At one point, she even threatened the great prophet, Elijah, and he ran to the wilderness in fear.

*1 Kings 18:4: For so it was, while Jezebel massacred the prophets of the Lord, that Obadiah had taken one hundred prophets and hidden them, fifty to a cave, and had fed them with bread and water.*

We see this same pattern carried out in the New Testament in Herodias and Herod the tetrarch. The **immoral wife,** Herodias, stirred up King Herod to put John the Baptist (the last Old Testament type prophet) into prison. She **manipulated** Herod into killing John by using her daughter as an enticement.

*Matthew 14:3-4,6-8,9a,10: For Herod had laid hold of John and bound him, and put him in prison **for the sake of Herodias,** his brother Philip's wife. For John had said to him, "It is not lawful for you to have her." But when Herod's birthday was celebrated, the daughter of Herodias danced before them and pleased Herod. Therefore he promised with an oath to give her whatever she might ask. So she, having been prompted by her mother, said, "Give me John the Baptist's head here on a platter." And the king was sorry; nevertheless, — he sent and had John beheaded in prison.*

The ancient queen of Babylon Semiramis, though **sensuously** beautiful, was **abandoned by her husband,** Nimrod, first by his many escapades and expeditions, and then by his **sudden death.** The **sensuously** beautiful Jezebel was **abandoned** by Ahab by his **apathy, passivity, deep depression, and finally by his sudden death.** Also like Semiramis, Jezebel was **usurping** her husband's authority and position. Both felt they should **take over** and rule. Clearly each woman had more respect for her own cunning and ability to rule, than she had **respect** for her husband.

Ahab's **apathy** and **passivity** showed itself clearly when Ahab would not fight to protect his wives and children. Ben-Hadad, the king of Syria, had gathered forces against Ahab and sent a message to him.

*1 Kings 20:2-4: Then he sent messengers into the city to Ahab King of Israel, and said to him, 'Thus says Ben-Hadad: "Your silver and you gold are mine; your loveliest wives and children are mine." And the king of Israel answered and said, "My lord, O king, just as you say, I and all that I have are yours."*

Suddenly a prophet showed up and caused Ahab to stand up and defeat the Syrian armies, but Ben-Hadad escaped. He gathered more armies and returned in the spring to make war against Israel again. And again God gave Israel complete victory over them. But Ahab, in his **toleration** and **passivity**, spared Ben-Hadad, called him his brother, and made a treaty with him. The prophet showed up again and told Ahab that his life and his family's life would go in place of Ben-Hadad's because he had let him go. Ahab became very **"sullen and displeased"**.

The sullen Ahab went back to his palace and asked one of his subjects to sell him a piece of land, a vineyard next to the palace so he could have it for a garden. Naboth refused to sell the land to Ahab, because it was not lawful for him to sell the inheritance of his fathers. Ahab became very **depressed** and laid in bed with his face to the wall and **Jezebel took over.**

*1 Kings 21:4,7-8a: So Ahab went into his house sullen and displeased because of the word which Naboth the Jezreelite had spoken to him; for he said, "I will not give you the inheritance of my fathers." And he lay down on his bed, and turned away his face, and would eat no food. Then Jezebel his wife came to him, and said, "You now exercise authority over Israel! Arise and eat food, and let your heart be cheerful; **I will give you the vineyard** of Naboth the Jezreelite." So she wrote letters in Ahab's name, sealed them with his seal, and sent letters to the elders and nobles.*

Jezebel had knowingly usurped her husband's authority and devised a diabolical plot to have the elders and nobles of the city place Naboth in a seat of honor and then bring **false witnesses** with **false accusations** against him. They accused Naboth, a good and innocent man, of blaspheming God and the king. Then they took him outside the city and stoned him to **death.**

When Ahab got up and went to the vineyard to possess it, the prophet Elijah was there to meet him. Elijah prophesied that because Ahab had sold himself to do evil, that he and all his posterity would be cut off, and that Jezebel would be eaten by dogs by the wall of Jezreel. All of the prophesy later came to pass. In the ninth and tenth chapters of 2nd Kings, after Ahab was killed, his seventy sons and forty-two brothers were killed along with all the rest of Ahab's family. Jezebel was trampled under foot and eaten by dogs. The end of the enemy's scheme for the family is death. Ahab had **abandoned** his position as Godly husband and allowed Jezebel to incite him to wickedness.

*1 Kings 21:25: But there was no one like Ahab **who sold himself** to do **wickedness** in the sight of the Lord, because Jezebel his wife stirred him up.*

*2 Kings 9:22b: (Jehu) "What peace, as long as the **harlotries** of your mother Jezebel and her **witchcraft** are so many?"*

The Babylonian family pattern is an attack on God's plan for the family, business, church, or government. It is ruled by a spirit of harlotry, working through a network of spirits to simultaneously attack every member of the family group.

We have seen this same pattern in ancient Babylon, in Old Testament Israel, in New Testament Israel, and we can see it in history right up to today. It is the enemy's primary scheme for tearing down God's rule and replacing it with his rule. Isn't it interesting that through thousands of years in many different lands and cultures, this attack is so consistently the same? It is carried out by the same demon spirits today that carried it out thousands of years ago. The demons didn't die; nor have they left the earth.

The enemy fervently continues to try to keep Christians from realizing that they are under attack. He wants Christians to believe that because Christ defeated him, he is no longer able to attack Christians. Certainly the enemy is not able to do anything that Christians do not allow him to do. But because of blindness, most Christians do not know **to resist**, nor do they know **how to resist.** Many do not even want to believe that they are in a war. So they fail to show up for the battle and the enemy wins by default!

The fact that this is an attack of the enemy does not in any way relieve the individual of responsibility. Just to say "the devil made me do it" is not an excuse. The enemy cannot make a child of God do anything that the child of God does not allow him to. We must repent and make adjustments ourselves. Remember, deception is the enemy's only tool. But once we are deceived, the enemy can trick us into many bad decisions and inner feelings. The important thing for us at this point is to uncover the enemy's scheme and see clearly what is being done, so that we can know exactly how to zero in on the enemy's work — bring forth the anointing of Jesus to destroy the work of the enemy.

## THE ATTACK ON THE HUSBAND

The enemy's attack on the husband is designed to cause **abandonment** and\or **death**. The object is to get the husband (the life-source of the family) out of position. The enemy knows he can destroy the whole family if he can cause the husband to abandon his position as Godly head of the wife. The object is to cut off the life-giving flow of unconditional love coming from God through the husband. God is the only source of this kind of love. The husband must be properly related to God to receive it before he can "flow" it to the wife. Therefore, the enemy will entice the husband to abandon his closeness with God in favor of some other idol.

His number one goal is to cause the man's **death**—to **suddenly cut him off** and leave the wife and children uncovered and unprotected. If he cannot cause the husband's death, he will try for **incapacitation**. If that doesn't work, he will try to **get the man to abandon his position** as head over the wife. As long as the husband is in proper relation to God and in proper position as head of the wife, a protective covering is in place that will not allow the enemy's attack on the family to get through to them. Once the man moves out of position and is entrapped into disobedience to God, the hedge of protection is lifted, and the enemy can attack the wife and children.

The enemy will use anything he can to bring **death, incapacitation**, or **preoccupation** to keep the husband from relating to God as he should. **Alcohol, drugs, spectator sports, participation sports, TV, gambling, computer and video games, other women, business, ministry**, and **overworking** are some of the husband's favorite idols and the enemy's favorite tools. The husband's abandonment ministers unlove (death, and not life) to the wife.

## THE ATTACK ON THE WIFE

When the wife senses that her husband is not in position, she feels uncovered. She may go through a series of emotional responses and spiritual attacks. After the initial **shock, trauma, panic, and fear, anger** sets in. She may become very angry at her "stupid" husband for abandoning his position. Finally, she **accepts the situation, loses all respect** for her husband, and decides she's going to have **to be her own head.**

She is attacked by a spirit of **takeover**, or **usurper**. She is driven to takeover, to usurp authority, and to **control** as the head of the family. She may feel if she doesn't get control of the money, it will not be managed well, and the children will suffer. This **disrespect** from the wife joins the attack already coming against the husband and further drives him out of his position as head.

When the wife cannot openly rule, she may begin to **manipulate**. **Lying, deception**, and **deceit** begin to do their work of **rebellion** in her. She knows her husband well and may develop many ways to get him to do what she wants, without his knowing what is really going on. She learns how to pump up his ego or to deflate his ego to cause him to do her will. She learns to use sex, either by giving it or by withholding it, to control him. She knows when to turn on the tears or when to have a screaming fit. She may even use the kids and what they will think of their father to manipulate him. She may "finagle" the checkbook and the cookie jar to get what she wants. She might even learn to misrepresent things to authorities over her husband to get them to pressure him and influence him in her behalf. She is driven to **control** one way or another.

She becomes **dominant** and **contentious.** No matter what her "stupid" husband does, it is not right or is not good enough. If he brings her flowers, he has done it for the wrong reason and wasted precious money the family needed. If he does not bring her flowers, he is insensitive and does not love her anymore. If he does not work extra hours, he is slothful and does not provide well enough for the family. If he does work extra hours, he doesn't care about being with his family and is neglecting them.

At some point the husband will often give up, **abandon** his position, and give up the battle for position as head. He may become very **tolerant and passive** toward the wife and family. He looks to the wife as Mom to make decisions and tell him what to do. In this **toleration** and **passivity** mode his ego is shattered and **masculinity is weakened.** He may experience **depression, rejection, sexual lust,** and/or lack of sexual potency. He may become **sullen** and **withdrawn** and have thoughts of **suicide.**

She experiences loss of confidence in her husband and begins to feel she must be a **mother** to her husband. Now she has five children instead of four.

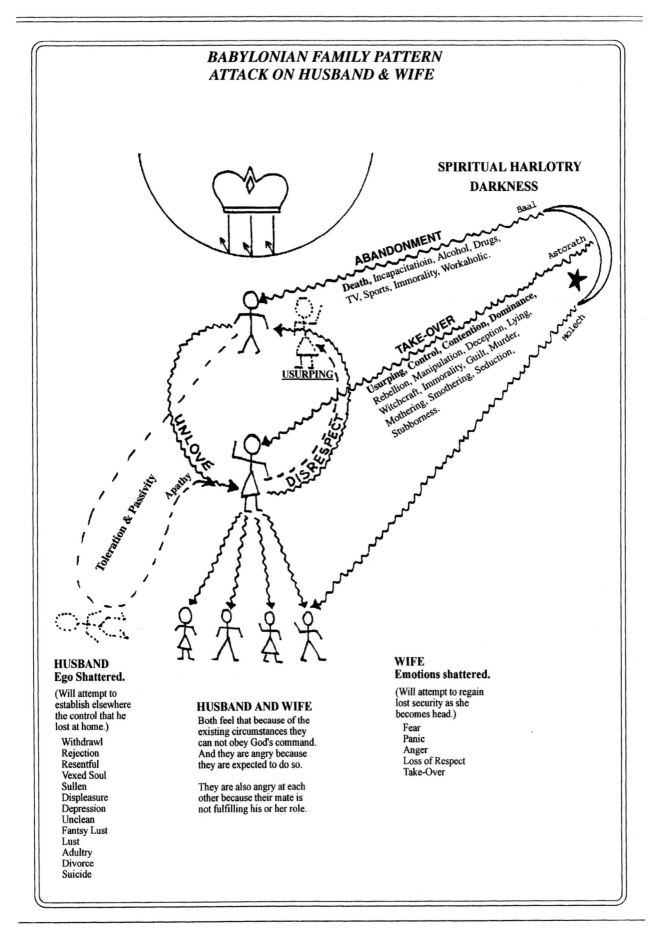

# BABYLONIAN FAMILY PATTERN
## ATTACK ON HUSBAND & WIFE

SPIRITUAL HARLOTRY

DARKNESS

Baal

Astorath

ABANDONMENT
Death, Incapacitatioin, Alcohol, Drugs, TV, Sports, Immorality, Workaholic.

Molech

TAKE-OVER
Usurping, Control, Contention, Dominance, Rebellion, Manipulation, Deception, Lying, Witchcraft, Immorality, Guilt, Murder, Mothering, Smothering, Seduction, Stubborness.

USURPING

UNLOVE

DISRESPECT

Toleration & Passivity

Apathy

**HUSBAND**
**Ego Shattered.**

(Will attempt to
establish elsewhere
the control that he
lost at home.)

Withdrawl
Rejection
Resentful
Vexed Soul
Sullen
Displeasure
Depression
Unclean
Fantsy Lust
Lust
Adultry
Divorce
Suicide

**HUSBAND AND WIFE**

Both feel that because of the
existing circumstances they
can not obey God's command.
And they are angry because
they are expected to do so.

They are also angry at each
other because their mate is
not fulfilling his or her role.

**WIFE**
**Emotions shattered.**

(Will attempt to regain
lost security as she
becomes head.)

Fear
Panic
Anger
Loss of Respect
Take-Over

She is now the mother and the wife of her husband. He is her husband and her son. Remember the old pattern.

She has such lack of respect for her husband, that other men, especially those with some authority, begin to be very attractive to her. Her respect and adoration need some place to go. She is now very open to immorality and may begin to develop a **fantasy-lust** love life. She may be drawn to romance novels, soaps, etc. Or she may have an affair. She may feel she is in love with someone she respects, even though she probably doesn't really know him.

## THE POWER STRUGGLE

The husband is knocked out of position by all of this and may be overcome by a spirit of **toleration** and **passivity,** which ministers **apathy** to the wife. "Here is the checkbook. Do whatever you want to do; it makes no difference to me. I don't care what you do or how you do it, just do whatever you want to do. Don't bother me with it; you take care of it. I'm sure you will think of something. I don't know what to do about it. I've got to go now. I'll late for bowling with the guys. By the way I've got to work late tomorrow evening."

More than ever, she feels she must take over and run the family. So she rises up and fights against her husband even stronger. This often does serious damage to the husband. The husband's **ego is shattered**, he loses **masculinity**, and will often try to establish, somewhere else, the control and respect that he has lost at home. He may become more involved in **work** or **hobbies** and is very open to **adultery.**

"My wife doesn't respect me, but my secretary really thinks I'm somebody. She is such a sweet thing. She really makes me feel so good and looks out for my needs at work so well. And I never noticed before what a cute figure she has. Boy! The way she looks deep into my eyes and smiles just warms me all over. She really understands me."

The husband feels the loss of control at home and does not know how to get it back. He may hear a sermon on husbands' being the head of the wife. Or the guys at work may talk about how they rule the roost at their house and might even start calling him henpecked. However it happens, when he realizes his control is lost and that he  is supposed to be the head of the wife, he may react through the flesh and open himself to spir-

its of **overlord, tyrant, abuser,** and **anger** as he tries with **violent aggression** to beat his way back into leadership. "Give me that checkbook and do what I say. When I say "jump," you say, "how high? I'm the man!" This is where wife-abusers often come from. Sometimes the cause is a very frustrated attempt to be in control. She may be able to outtalk him, outsmart him with manipulation, and outdo him in almost every way, but he is physically stronger than she and may resort to his last strength greater than hers and attempt to beat her into his control. Guess what? If he beats hard enough and long enough, he will beat her down and retake the throne. He may beat her down in some way other than physically. But however he does it, she goes down when he takes control. He feels strong again, but she feels very down.

We're now in an all-out **power struggle.** The husband may shift from his role of "toleration and passivity" and of giving up control to his usurping, takeover wife, to his role of "aggression", fighting against the wife to take back control.

When the husband is up in his "aggression role", he ministers **unlove** to his **wife** in the form of **abuse.** When he is "down in his toleration and passivity role", he ministers **unlove** to the wife in the form of **apathy.** Remember, love is what the wife needs.

When the husband is down in "toleration and passivity", the wife is up in her "takeover, controlling" mode. When the husband is up in his "aggression, tyrant, overlord" mode the wife may be knocked down to her "defeated loss of control" mode.

The wife believes she and the children will not make it if she does not control. So, as long as she's winning and in control, she feels good, but the husband is down in his toleration and passivity mode. When he rises up and tries to retake the throne by aggression, if he beats her down enough to cause her to give up control, he feels good; but her self esteem is lower than dirt; she is emotionally **shattered** and feels **defeated, worthless, unworthy, weak, depressed, hopeless,** and **deeply bitter.** So it's an up-and-down power struggle. Just as soon as one is up, the other is down. Now, they cannot even get within shouting distance of each other without fighting. The really sad thing is: they really love each other.

# BABYLONIAN FAMILY PATTERN
## POWER STRUGGLE

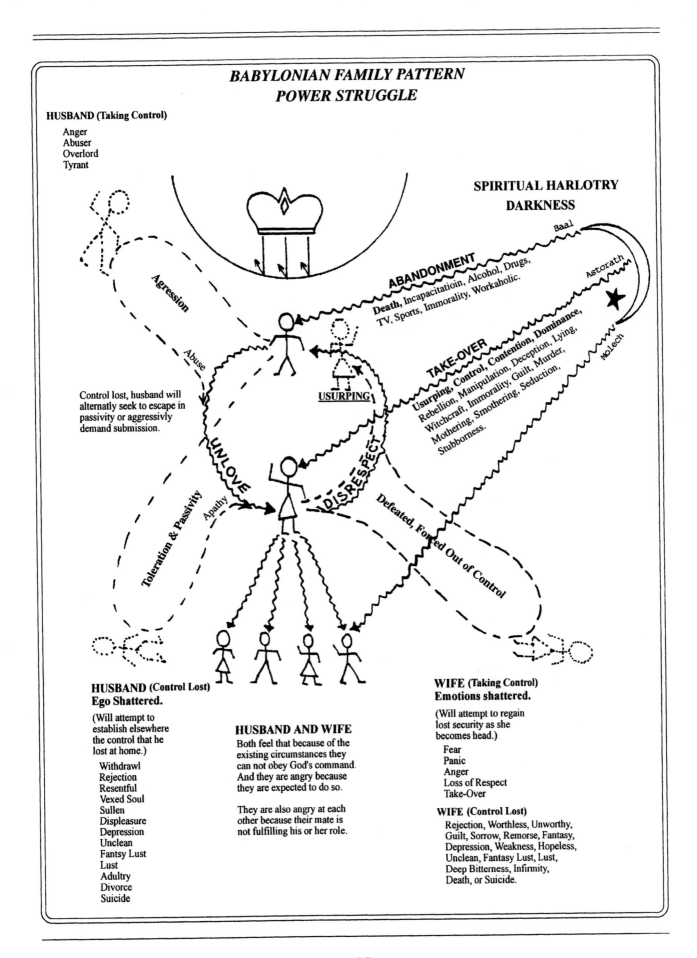

**HUSBAND (Taking Control)**

Anger
Abuser
Overlord
Tyrant

**SPIRITUAL HARLOTRY**

**DARKNESS**

Baal

*Agression*

*Abuse*

Control lost, husband will alternally seek to escape in passivity or aggressivly demand submission.

**ABANDONMENT**

Death, Incapacitatioin, Alcohol, Drugs, TV, Sports, Immorality, Workaholic.

Astorath

**TAKE-OVER**

Usurping, Control, Contention, Dominance, Rebellion, Manipulation, Deception, Lying, Witchcraft, Immorality, Guilt, Murder, Mothering, Smothering, Seduction, Stubborness.

Molech

**USURPING**

*UNLOVE*

*DISRESPECT*

*Toleration & Passivity*

*Apathy*

*Defeated, Forced Out of Control*

**HUSBAND (Control Lost)**
**Ego Shattered.**

(Will attempt to establish elsewhere the control that he lost at home.)

Withdrawl
Rejection
Resentful
Vexed Soul
Sullen
Displeasure
Depression
Unclean
Fantsy Lust
Lust
Adultry
Divorce
Suicide

**HUSBAND AND WIFE**

Both feel that because of the existing circumstances they can not obey God's command. And they are angry because they are expected to do so.

They are also angry at each other because their mate is not fulfilling his or her role.

**WIFE (Taking Control)**
**Emotions shattered.**

(Will attempt to regain lost security as she becomes head.)

Fear
Panic
Anger
Loss of Respect
Take-Over

**WIFE (Control Lost)**

Rejection, Worthless, Unworthy, Guilt, Sorrow, Remorse, Fantasy, Depression, Weakness, Hopeless, Unclean, Fantasy Lust, Lust, Deep Bitterness, Infirmity, Death, or Suicide.

The wife, in herself, does not want to be head. She wants to be protected, loved, and cared for. But she is driven to **take over** at all costs.

Communication is further destroyed by the enemy working between the couple, twisting what one says before the other hears it, so that no one really knows what the other one said. The husband may say, "I love you," and never be able to understand why he got the reply, "What on earth are you trying to pull now?" The enemy will set each one of them up and cause them to expect something bad from the other to the point that every word will be misunderstood and used to cause more painful wounds.

After they are apart for a while, they remember the good things about each other again and would really like to make up and start over. They forget to some degree just how ugly and painful it was the last time they were together. So the husband calls and says he will be home in a while and is looking forward to seeing her. He says he is sorry things weren't so good when he left, but he would like to make up. It all sounds good so far.

On the way driving home, he begins to hear these thoughts like his own voice talking to him. "Boy! Are you a sap. She is going to cut you to pieces with that sharp tongue. Remember all those ugly, hurting things she said last time. Well it's going to be worse tonight. How can you be so stupid? Those things she said were really mean and still hurt. What!? Are you going back for more!? You had better stop and get a little pain killer. This will be much easier to face with a couple of beers under the belt. You know she is never going to change. She's just using you for your money. She's probably got someone else that she really cares about. Here is the beer store; you'd better get a whole case." So the husband is all set up and primed to battle and run."

Meanwhile at the house, she begins to hear thoughts that sound a lot like her own voice talking to her. "Yea! He wants to make up. Bahh! He _is_ up to something or he's been up to something. Probably been out drinking and messing with some chick. That dirty so-'n so. Remember how he lied about that fishing trip. You can never trust him. He just uses you for a housemaid, baby sitter, and sex. He doesn't care anything about you. Yes! I'm so sick and tired of housework all the time. Never going anywhere, while that "so-'n-so" is out having a good time in the world. That's right! If

he really wanted to make up, he would bring you something nice like flowers or maybe jewelry. We'll see. And if you smell beer on his breath, you'll know what he's been up to." So the wife is all set and primed to fight and dig in.

The enemy is familiar with things about us and knows how to work between people to set up miscommunication. Spirits are able to twist the meaning of words so that what is heard is not what was said. So the response to what was heard is totally off-base and can be frustrating or wounding. This may cause one person to raise the level of his voice slightly, which will be heard as shouting by the other person. "Well, you don't have to shout at me!" "I'm not shouting and why are we arguing." "We are not arguing!" Now they are arguing about whether are not they are arguing!

Remember, this is a scheme of the enemy to destroy the kingdom-family pattern in families, churches, businesses and governments. All these same attacks come against the "husband and wife offices" in all of these institutions.

The problems within each individual (The Bad Heart-Tree) causes them to be easy prey for the enemy's scheme. And what about the children in all this?

## THE ATTACK ON THE CHILDREN

The children are devastated by all of this. The primary attack on the children is **perversion.** Their view of God is greatly perverted; subsequently their view of life is perverted. It is very hard for children growing up in this pattern to know God. They cannot see a true picture of what God is like by looking up at their parents. Children tend to see God as they see their natural father. If their father is not present or is apathetic toward the family, the children will tend to see God as distant and not really there, or not interested in them. If the father is sometimes violent and aggressive, they will tend to see God as very judgmental and not loving. They may feel that God is looking for opportunities to whack them with a big stick of authority.

If their mother has little respect for their father and treats him like a child, the children tend to feel God is not an authority for their life. They may feel that they are in charge of their own lives, and it may be difficult for them to submit to God or any authority. They are **cursed** children, and will be **disobedient** and

# BABYLONIAN FAMILY PATTERN
## ATTACK ON THE CHILDREN

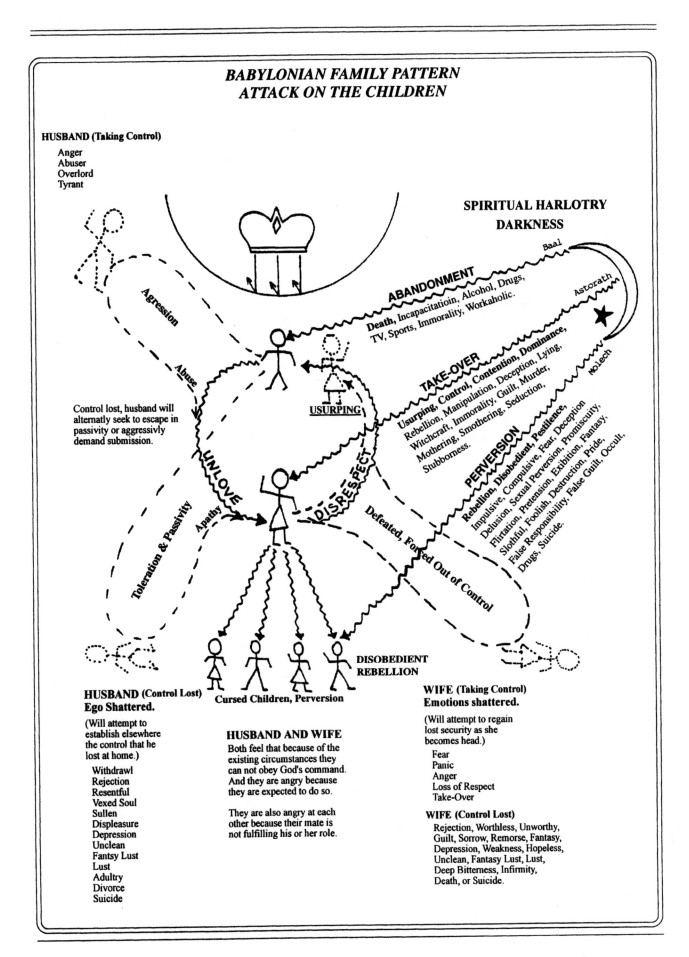

**HUSBAND (Taking Control)**

Anger
Abuser
Overlord
Tyrant

**SPIRITUAL HARLOTRY**

**DARKNESS**

Baal

Astorath

**ABANDONMENT**

Death, Incapacitatioin, Alcohol, Drugs, TV, Sports, Immorality, Workaholic.

**TAKE-OVER**

Usurping, Control, Contention, Dominance, Rebellion, Manipulation, Deception, Lying, Witchcraft, Immorality, Guilt, Murder, Mothering, Smothering, Seduction, Stubborness.

Molech

**PERVERSION**

Rebellion, Disobedient, Pestilence, Impulsive, Compulsive, Fear, Deception Delusion, Sexual Perversion, Promiscuity, Flirtation, Pretension, Exibition, Fantasy, Slothful, Foolish, Destruction, Pride, False Responsibility, False Guilt, Occult, Drugs, Suicide.

Agression

Abuse

USURPING

Control lost, husband will alternately seek to escape in passivity or aggressivly demand submission.

UNLOVE

DISRESPECT

Toleration & Passivity

Apathy

Defeated, Forced Out of Control

**DISOBEDIENT REBELLION**

**HUSBAND (Control Lost) Ego Shattered.**

(Will attempt to establish elsewhere the control that he lost at home.)

Withdrawl
Rejection
Resentful
Vexed Soul
Sullen
Displeasure
Depression
Unclean
Fantsy Lust
Lust
Adultry
Divorce
Suicide

**Cursed Children, Perversion**

**HUSBAND AND WIFE**

Both feel that because of the existing circumstances they can not obey God's command. And they are angry because they are expected to do so.

They are also angry at each other because their mate is not fulfilling his or her role.

**WIFE (Taking Control) Emotions shattered.**

(Will attempt to regain lost security as she becomes head.)

Fear
Panic
Anger
Loss of Respect
Take-Over

**WIFE (Control Lost)**

Rejection, Worthless, Unworthy, Guilt, Sorrow, Remorse, Fantasy, Depression, Weakness, Hopeless, Unclean, Fantasy Lust, Lust, Deep Bitterness, Infirmity, Death, or Suicide.

**rebellious.** They also may be attacked by **pestilence** and be vulnerable to deadly diseases. **Rebellion** is a product of Babylon.

Many different perversions will develop in these children including **sexual perversion.** The girls will often become **like their mother,** living out the same, dominating patterns, disrespecting men, and seeking to be their own head. They may not be able to relate intimately to a man; and may find they prefer relating intimately to other women. They may become tomboyish and relate to men competitively, more like another man than as a woman. **Lesbianism** is a product of Babylon.

Or some may relate better to men than women because they learn to **control** men rather than compete with them. The girls will often become very manipulative. They may enjoy using their sexuality to control men. They may be **flirtatious** and have a tendency toward **exhibition** and **promiscuity.** They learn to handle men, but other women see through their manipulation and are therefore more difficult for the girls to relate to. **Promiscuity** is a product of Babylon.

A husband who is down in his toleration and passivity mode and is disrespected and "mothered" by his wife is behaving at the same level as the children. He may develop incestuous lust and respond to his daughter's or stepdaughter's flirting. This type of incest is just as likely to happen to an upstanding and moral-appearing man as a more promiscuous man. A promiscuous man is more likely to just go out and find someone to meet his pent-up desires. A moral and upstanding-appearing man does not feel that he has that option. He is more likely, therefore, to slip gradually into more intimacy and eventually incest. **Incest** is a product of Babylon.

When the father is cut off from the family either by death, divorce, apathetic abandonment, or by dominance from the wife, the son is left without a strong male role model. Because his dominant mother is the strongest parental influence around, he may begin to be trained subconsciously by her and begin to emulate her feminine ways. In addition, the mother may transfer affection that should have been for her husband toward a son, usually the eldest son. This sexually-laden affection may be uncomfortable to the son. He may feel that it is too much, and begin to resist that affection, which could lead to resisting affection from all women. **Homosexuality** is a product of Babylon.

The mother in this pattern may also transfer responsibility for what her husband should have provided to a son, again usually the oldest son (or occasionally a daughter). She may tend to lean on him for emotional strength. "Well you're Mama's big man now. You have to take care of Mommy, since Daddy isn't here any more. You're the only one I've got. You're so big and strong; you can do it even if you are only five years old." "Please don't cry Mommy. I'll take care of you. I'll always be here for you. I can take care of things. There, doesn't it feel all better when I hug you."

The responsibility placed on the son to meet his mother's needs is **false responsibility** and produces **false guilt** when he is unable to meet her needs for a husband. He becomes like the savior (Jesus, husband) to his mother, and may be lifted up by her as savior of the world. (Remember the old pattern of Semiramis lifting up her son as God and husband after Nimrod was cut off.) The son may begin to see himself as **savior** and god. The weight of the world is upon him, and the world revolves around him. **False pride, deception,** and **grandiose delusion** set him up to become as a god within himself. Since he sees himself as final authority, he will despise all other authority. He will be **presumptuous, self-willed,** and **quick to bring accusation against authority.** Not only does he act and think like he is God, the center of the universe, in cases of severe delusion, he may actually believe that he is the Christ. The **"I am God"** syndrome is a product of Babylon.

*2 Peter 2:10-14: "...those who walk according to the flesh in the lust of uncleanness and **despise authority.** They are **presumptuous, self-willed;** they are not afraid to **speak evil of dignitaries;** whereas angels, who are greater in power and might, do not bring a reviling accusation against them before the Lord. "*

*"But these, like natural brute beasts made to be caught and destroyed, speak evil of the things they do not understand, and will **utterly perish** in their own corruption, and will receive the wages of unrighteousness, as those who count it **pleasure to carouse** in the daytime. They are spots and blemishes, **carousing in their own deceptions** while they feast with you, having eves full of **adultery** and that cannot cease from sin, **beguiling unstable** souls. They have a **heart trained in covetous practices, and are <u>cursed children</u>."***

As the children in this pattern grow up and become the parents, the situation gets worse. The chil-

come the parents, the situation gets worse. The children that they produce are more perverted and further from the plan of God. If nothing happens to change the pattern, such as the father's getting born again in Christ and being redeemed, the children will deteriorate further in each generation. The Bible says that the sins of the father are passed on to the third and fourth generation. Why does the Scripture stop at three or four generations? Is it perhaps, that it is as bad as it gets, and the lineage will probably not continue, because premature deaths and reproductive system diseases will end the posterity of the fathers? It only takes about three generations to produce homosexuality. Or, perhaps, due to these fiery judgments there will be true repentance and the redemptive healing work of Christ will end the generational degradation and begin generational regeneration.

*Exodus 34:7:* *"...keeping mercy for thousands, forgiving iniquity and transgression and sin, by no means clearing the guilty,* ***visiting the iniquity of the fathers upon the children and the children's children to the third and the fourth generation."***

*Lamentations 5:7:* ***Our fathers sinned*** *and are no more, but* ***we bear their iniquities****.*

*Numbers 14:33:* *"And* ***your sons shall be shepherds*** *in the wilderness forty years, and* ***bear the brunt of your infidelity,*** *until your carcasses are consumed in the wilderness."*

*Isaiah 14:21:* ***"Prepare slaughter for his children because of the iniquity of their fathers,*** *lest they rise up and possess the land, and fill the face of the world with cities."*

*Nehemiah 9:2:* *Then those of Israelite lineage separated themselves from all foreigners; and they stood and* ***confessed their sins and the iniquities of their fathers.***

Without redemption they will become deceived carousers and beguiling unstable souls. "Beguiling" means to "deceive by craftiness". "Carousing" means "hard drinking and reveling". Children in later generations of this pattern are often **intensely unfulfilled**. They feel like a big empty hole is in their inner being. The simple mundane recreational practices of healthy young people are not enough to even start to fill their emptiness. Hard reveling, hard drinking and drugs fill their empty place for a season. Eventually, the games grow wilder and may begin to involve **demonic activities** and **satanic practices.** Every sordid ,evil violent practice is play to them, including **murder.**

These enemy schemes and the kingdom patterns for the individual and family will have a direct affect on the local Church and community. The local Church will reflect to some degree the beliefs and the practices of the individuals and families.

# CHAPTER 20

## THE BRIDE CHURCH  AND  THE HARLOT CHURCH

( GOD'S KINGDOM PATTERN )      THE ENEMY'S SCHEME

Just as there were two trees in the garden and two great ruling cities, there are two churches—the glorified, beautiful, purified Bride of Christ (New Jerusalem Church) and the glamorous, gaudy, impure harlot (Babylon Church).

**The Bride Church** is an assembly of "called-out ones" and is characterized by truth and spiritual life. It is a joyous, spiritual meeting of God and man, of heavenly beings and earthly beings, joining together in festive worship, praise, and fellowship. The potential for the joining of the heavenly and earthly is in Jesus, the God Man, the mediator of the covenant between God and man. Man, standing on earth and looking toward heaven, sees Jesus as heaven's representative to earth, the head of the church from heaven. God, looking toward earth from heaven, sees Jesus as the representative of earth, the advocate of man to the Father in heaven.

*Hebrews 12:22-24a: But you have come to **Mount Zion** and to the **city of the living God, the heavenly Jerusalem,** to an **innumerable company of angels,** to the **general assembly (festal gathering)** and church of the firstborn who are registered in heaven, to **God the Judge of all,** to the **spirits of just men made perfect,** to **Jesus the Mediator of the new covenant**.*

The Bride church is always **God-seeking** and **God-serving**. As a faithful and pure bride, she seeks to intimately know and serve her Husband, Jesus. She knows that she is loved by her Husband, and was selected and called by Him. She respects, reverences and praises Him exceedingly. She feels very secure and comfortable in His presence and provision. She knows that He will protect her and meet her every need. She has no sense of lack or need in her heart. She is **free** to **obediently** carry out the wishes of her Husband.

**The Harlot church** is **self-seeking** and **self-serving**. She does not trust God to meet her needs. She has sought other lovers, and she trades her purity to meet her needs. In the "harlot church", preachers in the pulpit do not bring the pure message from God to the

**THE BRIDE CHURCH**
*BRIDE OF CHRIST, NEW JERUSALEM*

**THE HARLOT CHURCH**
*ADULTRESS OF BABYLON*

people. Instead, they substitute a sermon that they believe will be more acceptable to the people, one that causes them to "feel good", without causing them to change. They preach a message that attracts people and does not offend them, so that the people will continue to put money into the offering plate. They may overemphasize the "great spiritual significance" of giving generous offerings to their own church or ministry. Then they will make other sacrifices of spiritual purity in order to accommodate the big givers.

The harlot church is not comfortable and feels very insecure in the presence and provision of God. She cannot truly praise God, but heaps flattery on her lovers. She gives them what their "flesh" wants and tells them what they want to hear. The true presence of the Spirit of God may not be evident in the services. The leadership may not allow the gifts and flowing of the Spirit because they don't want to chance offending someone. Superb quality, soulish music may replace true spiritual praise and worship. Leaders may give much attention to acknowledging people and may hand out compliments generously to stroke the egos of the people.

The harlot church feels she must take care of herself and reason matters out for herself. She is bound by her lust, and is not free to hear and obey God. She goes her own way and is in rebellion against God. She pretends obedience to God, but yields herself to the rule of the spirit of harlotry and antichrist.

*Hosea 2:5: "For their mother has played the harlot; she who conceived them has done shamefully. For she said, ' I will go after my lovers, who give me bread and my water, my wool and my linen, my oil and my drink.'"*

The harlot church is very religious with many rules, restraints, and demands. She is characterized by deception and manipulation. She is a "communion" between the powers of darkness and man. The darkness may appear as light, the ministers having transformed themselves as angels of light. A hierarchical system of a few men controls many. Using control by manipulation, and often through fear, the leadership keeps the church in bondage. They hand out rewards of acceptance to those who obey the system and rewards of rejection to those who show differences or "independent thinking." This rejection causes some to fear losing their sense of belonging and well-being, and sometimes to even fear losing their eternal salvation.

## THE CHILDREN

One of the major functions of a natural bride or wife is reproduction, giving birth to and nurturing children. As it is in the natural, so it is in the spiritual. The Bride Church, the wife of Jesus, is God's only provision for reproducing Himself into the earth.

The Bride Church is formed as God's love draws man to submit to Him willingly and totally. In the inti-macy of this relationship, the word (seed of God), Jesus, is planted in faith by the Holy Spirit in the heart of man. The Bride Church then nurtures the new creation in her inner parts, protecting, caring for, and feeding the child with tender, loving care.

The obedient wife labors and travails to give birth and then tenderly cares for the child. She provides all of the child's needs at **her breast** and with **her hand**. She feeds it, cleans it, disciplines it, trains it, and firmly directs it until it becomes a mature person and is like its Father, Jesus. Thus, the kingdom of God on earth is carried forth as the resurrected life of Jesus is manifested in the hearts and lives of God's children.

*Isaiah 66:10-14: "Rejoice with Jerusalem, and be glad with her, all you who love her; rejoice for joy with her, all you who mourn for her; that **you may feed and be satisfied with the consolation of her breasts**, that you may drink deeply and be delighted with the abundance of her glory. For thus says the Lord: 'Behold, I will extend peace to her like a river, and the glory of the Gentiles like a flowing stream. Then you shall feed; on her sides shall you be carried, and be dandled on her knees. As one whom his mother comforts, so I will comfort you; and you shall be comforted in Jerusalem.' When you see this, your heart shall rejoice, and your bones shall flourish like grass; the hand of the Lord shall be known to His servants, and His indignation to His enemies."*

*Isaiah 29:23-24: "But when he sees his **children, the work of My hands**, in his midst, they will hallow My name, and hallow the Holy One of Jacob, and fear the God of Israel. **These also who erred in spirit will come to understanding, and those who murmured will learn doctrine.**"*

In the Bride Church, the Holy Spirit, through the hand of God, (God's gifted servants), brings forth true spiritual teachings to bring the church to understanding as they learn doctrine.

## THE HAND OF GOD

God extends His loving hand to and through the Bride Church that she might grow up and come to perfection as mature sons and daughters, walking in love. God provides equipment—spiritual gifts of apostles, prophets, evangelists, pastors, and teachers who edify the body, bring truth, unity and love— **to grow up** the church.

*Ephesians 4:11-16:   And He Himself gave some to be **apostles**, some **prophets**, some **evangelists**, and some **pastors,** and **teachers**, for the equipping of the saints for the work of ministry, for the edifying of the body of Christ, till we all come to the unity of the faith and the knowledge of the Son of God, to a perfect man, to the measure of the stature of the fullness of Christ; that we should **no longer be children**, tossed to and fro and carried about with every wind of doctrine, by the trickery of men, in the cunning craftiness by which they lie in wait to deceive, but, speaking the truth in love, may grow up in all things into Him who is the head - Christ - from whom the whole body, joined and knit together by what every joint supplies, according to the effective working by which every part does its share, **causes growth** of the body for the **edifying of itself in love.***

In the Bride Church, the hand of God is always ready and attentive to meet the needs of the children, to build up the body with **loving firmness.** The gifted **rulers are servants and never lord it over the people or exercise authority** over them. The hand of God in the Bride church does not place heavy burdens on the body. There is a sense of freedom and release to fully exercise spiritual gifts and callings, and thereby, be trained.

*Matthew 11:28-30:   "Come to Me, all you who labor and are heavy laden, and I will give you rest. Take my yoke upon you and learn from Me, for I am gentle and lowly in heart, and you will find rest for your souls. For **My yoke is easy and My burden is light**."*

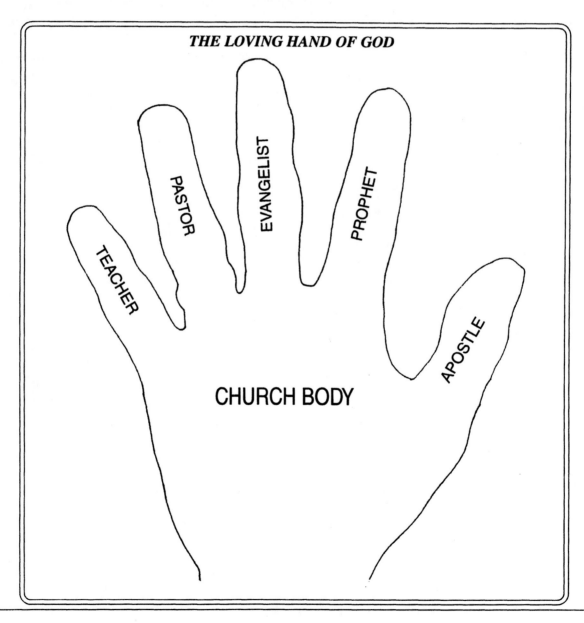

THE LOVING HAND OF GOD

TEACHER · PASTOR · EVANGELIST · PROPHET · APOSTLE

CHURCH BODY

*Matthew 20:25-26: But Jesus called them to Himself and said, "You know that the rulers of the Gentiles **lord it over them**, and those who are great **exercise authority** over them. **Yet it shall not be so among you; but whoever desires to become great among you, let him be your servant."***

Please note that the Lord **did not say** that they "did not have authority"; but He did say that they **"will not exercise authority."** In the New Jerusalem Bride Church, leaders come to understand the difference between **having authority** and **exercising authority. God is the one who establishes authority and the one who exercises authority.** He is also the one who sustains the authority He establishes.

No Old Testament character had more authority from God than Moses. Yet in the sixteenth chapter of Numbers, when Korah led a rebellion against Moses, Moses did not try to squelch it by exercising his own authority. He **did** exercise his authority toward God to represent the people as he petitioned God to refrain from destroying all the people for the rebellion of a few. God exercised authority and caused the earth to open up and swallow the guilty ones with all their families and belongings. Then the next day, the people themselves raised up against Moses and accused him of killing God's men. God again exercised authority and began an instant plague among the people. Moses sent Aaron into the congregation to stand between the dead and the living to make atonement for the people and to stop the plague.

In the New Testament, James and John were rebuked by the Lord when they asked if they could call down fire from heaven on a village of Samaritans who had not received Jesus and His party. Jesus told them they did not know what kind of spirit they were of. He told them He had come to save men's lives, not to destroy them. The spirit of a servant in the leaders of the New Jerusalem Bride Church saves lives. The spirit of "overlord" destroys men's lives.

*Hosea 11:3-4: "I taught Ephraim to walk, taking them by their arms; but they did not know that I healed them. I drew them with gentle cords, with bands of love, and I was to them as those **who take the yoke from their neck**. I stooped and fed them."*

*Isaiah 49:15-16: "Can a woman forget her nursing child, and not have compassion on the son of her womb?*

*Surely they may forget, yet I will not forget you. See, I have inscribed you on the **palms of My hands**; your walls are continually before Me."*

*Job 10:8a: "Your **hands** have made me and fashioned me."*

Isn't it wonderful how God can use simple figurative language and natural things we all understand to explain great complex spiritual works. Everyone is familiar with a hand. We can sit and look at it, move it about, and watch how it works. If we meditate the design of the hand, we are impressed with the marvel of it. How perfectly it functions to carry out so many complex works.

God speaks of His Church and its servant leaders as His "hands". Just as a natural hand could do nothing except as it is attached to a source of life, strength, and direction; so the hand of God, the Bride Church, must remain attached to God for life, strength, and direction.

The general assembly of His church is spoken of as "inscribed on the palm of His hand". Out of the palm area or general assembly, the fingers and thumb extend, and can be thought of as symbolizing the five special servant gifts.. The thumb represents the apostle, the one who is always sticking up from the extended open hand. Extend your open hand as though you were going to give a hand shake, and then observe it. The thumb (apostle) is sticking up so as to see what is going on. The pointer finger next to the thumb represents the prophet, the one that is always pointing things out and pointing the way. The longest finger that reaches out the farthest is the middle finger which represents the evangelist, the outreach of the church. The ring finger represents the pastor, the one who is married to the local church and shepherds the flock. The little finger represents the teacher, the one who is very picky about the details of the finer points of the Word.

Now fold your four fingers toward the palm of your hand. Notice that all four fingers though different lengths reach the palm at the same time and all can massage the palm equally well. The prophet, evangelist, pastor, and teacher all minister to the general assembly very well. Now attempt to massage the palm with the thumb. It doesn't reach the palm very well. But now notice how well the thumb reaches each of the fingers and works with each of them very well. The apostle ministers to the prophet, evangelist, pastor, and teacher very well—and they, in turn, minister to the general assembly very well. The apostle works with the prophet, evangelist, pastor, and teacher individually or collectively to pick things up, move them about, and do many marvelous works.

Now make a fist of your hand. When trouble comes, men double up their fists which become a formidable weapon against an enemy. Notice that the palm, the general assembly, is completely protected by the fingers, the leadership of the church. Notice also that the apostle, (the thumb), is outside over the fingers, adding protection to the prophet, evangelist, pastor, teacher, and subsequently to the general assembly (the palm).

*Isaiah 64:8: But now, O Lord, You are our Father; we are the clay, and You our potter; and all **we are the work of Your hand**.*

*Jeremiah 18:6: "O house of Israel, can I not do with you as this potter?" says the Lord. "Look, as the clay is in the potter's hand, **so are you in My hand**, O house of Israel!"*

*Isaiah 25:10a-11: For on this mountain the hand of Lord will rest ... and He will spread out His hands in their midst as he who swims spreads out his hands to swim, and He will bring down their pride together with the trickery of their hands.*

The gifted leaders of the hand of God literally flow the anointings of Christ as head of the church. They are not lords, but must reflect the Lord Jesus the Anointed One. They are not to exercise authority, but must be the "servant of all" as they represent the Lord, the head of the church, who came "not to be served, but to serve".

*Mark 10: 42-45: But Jesus called them to Himself and said to them, "You know that those who are considered rulers over the Gentiles **lord it over them**, and their great ones **exercise authority** over them. **Yet it shall not be so among you; but whoever desires to become great among you shall be your servant. And whoever of you desires to be first shall be servant of all. For even the Son of Man did not come to be served, but to serve, and to give His life a ransom for many."***

The end of the Harlot church, unless she repents and is delivered and healed, is destruction. Both the harlot mother and the children will be destroyed together unless repentance, deliverance and healing come forth in her. Babylon, the mother of harlots, is being destroyed, and all who are with her will perish with her.

All local churches and their leaders are under attack by the spirit of harlotry. Anyone at any level of church leadership is a potential target. Few, if any, local churches are completely free from the penetration of the attacking spirit of harlotry. Any leader, at any level with unhealed wounds in the heart, from anywhere in their past, is vulnerable, and at sometime, may loose a battle with the spirit of harlotry. We must be healed by the anointed ministry of Jesus "to heal the brokenhearted" — before we can ever walk consistently in **freedom.**

Perhaps the most common and most pitiful local church of today is neither the Bride Church nor the Harlot Church. It is an **adulterous church**—a church that has a Husband, is married to Jesus—yet is still entertaining other lovers to meet some of her needs or desires. Because many leaders are not yet fully healed and have needs remaining in their lives that are not fulfilled by God, they can be deceived by the spirit of harlotry and enticed into practices outside of God's direction, creating a powerful, but deadly mixture.

# CHAPTER 21

## THE DIVIDED HEART TREE
### (SPIRITUAL ADULTERY)

This is another heart tree different from those we've seen. This is not the purified-bride-heart tree; nor is it the impure-harlot heart-tree. It is not the double-minded heart tree, which operates all the way, one way or the other, at any given time. **The Divided Heart-Tree is a hybrid, <u>impure-wife</u>, heart tree.** It is the **adulteress** heart-tree. This person is married to Jesus, and one side of his heart is producing good fruit to Jesus. But because he is not completely healed, one side of his heart is still affected by the harlotry of Babylon.

It's like two streams coming together; one muddy and one pure. It's like a wife riding in the front seat of the car with her husband, and reaching back in the back seat to hold hands with her old lover.

Spiritual adultery is both **GOD-SEEKING** and **SELF- SEEKING** at the same time.

*Psalm 12:2: They speak idly everyone with his neighbor; with flattering lips and a **double (divided) heart** they speak.*

*Hosea 10:2: Their **heart is divided;** now they are held guilty. He will break down their altars; He will ruin their sacred pillars.*

*2 Chronicles 25:2: And **he did what was right** in the sight of the Lord, **but not with a loyal heart.***

*James 3:10-14: Out of the same mouth proceed blessing and cursing. My brethren, **these things ought not to be so.** Does a spring send forth fresh water and bitter from the same opening? Can a fig tree, my brethren, bear olives, or a grapevine bear figs? Thus no spring can yield both salt water and fresh.*

Adultery, both spiritual and natural, is one of the most hideous sins of man. Perhaps no other sin brings as much loss and destruction in this life. Adultery in the natural realm can cost a person his office or position and respect in the community, all his wealth, every good thing he has accomplished in his life—and perhaps his very life.

Spiritual adultery in God's called-out people is a horrible thing

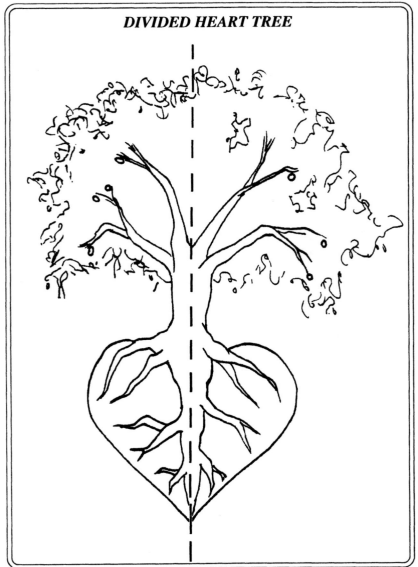

*DIVIDED HEART TREE*

and never goes unnoticed by God. The adulteress, unlike the harlot, sincerely loves, respects, and honors her husband (Jesus) with part of her heart. She really knows Him and partially obeys Him; and **pretends obedience** with the rest of her heart. But she is still in bondage to some Babylonian harlot ways. While genuinely seeking to serve God, at the same time she is seeking to serve herself and get the position, money, security, fame, or whatever she needs or wants.

The man of God with an adulterated heart will often be among the most highly-esteemed by the church, at least for a season. He has double motivation—both a sincere desire to serve God and a desire to accomplish something for himself at the same time. Therefore, he will be among the most zealous, the first to arrive, the last to leave, eager to volunteer, the best at keeping the rules, always willing to help, and generally very busy. This makes him the most likely to be promoted or ordained in the church. Whatever he is doing will usually grow rapidly and, suddenly, at some point, come crashing down. Spiritual wisdom and discernment will be required to distinguish the truly dedicated, totally sold out, dynamic servant of God, filled with vision and compassion of the Spirit—from the doubly-motivated, divided-heart adulteress.

Some Christians can become very confused if they see only one side of the divided-heart person. They view the godly side and are convinced that he is truly a man who sincerely desires to serve God. He truly loves God with one side of his heart and life. Some good fruit will really be there. But if and when these Christians are exposed to the **other** side of this person, they may be quite shocked, disappointed, and confused. Much failure may result, and much damage may occur to the Christians. Adulterated men of God bring a curse to the church and the people.

*Jeremiah 23:14: "Also I have seen a horrible thing in the prophets of Jerusalem: they commit adultery and walk in lies; they also strengthen the hands of evildoers, so that no one turns back from his wickedness. All of them are like Sodom to Me, and her inhabitants like Gomorrah."*

*Jeremiah 23:10: For the land is full of adulterers; for because of a curse, the land mourns. The pleasant places of the wilderness are dried up. Their course of life is evil, and their might is not right.*

All of us have been greatly affected by and trained in Babylonian ways. The study of old Babylon and old Jerusalem in the Old Testament gives us clear insight into the Mystery Babylon and New Jerusalem of today. Most of the world, the church, and each of us individually have been or are now ruled by the patterns of Babylon. In a very real sense, the church and world have been taken captive to Babylon. We've all been held captive in Babylon for a long season. We've had to be trained in the ways of Babylon in order to survive there. We had to learn to live and prosper in Babylon while we were captive there. Now, God is saying, "Your captivity is over; come out of Babylon, my people; come into New Jerusalem." It is time now for God's people to fully lay aside the ways of life in Babylon and walk in God's ways only.

*Jeremiah 29;4-15,28: Thus says the Lord of hosts, the God of Israel, to all who were **carried away captive**, whom I have caused to be carried away **from Jerusalem to Babylon**: "Build houses and dwell in them; plant gardens and eat their fruit. Take wives and beget sons and daughters; and take wives for your sons and give your daughters to husbands, so that they may bear sons and daughters - that you may be increased there, and not diminished. And seek the peace of the city where I have caused you to be carried away captive and pray to the Lord for it; for in its peace, you will have peace."*

*For thus says the Lord of hosts, the God of Israel: "Do not let your prophets and your diviners who are in your midst deceive you, nor listen to your dreams which you cause to be dreamed. For they prophesy falsely to you in My name; I have not sent them," says the Lord.*

*For thus says the Lord: "After seventy years are completed at Babylon, I will visit you and perform My good word toward you, and cause you to return to this place. For I know the thoughts that I think toward you," says the Lord, "thoughts of peace and not of evil, to give you a future and a hope. Then you will call upon me and go and pray to Me, and I will listen to you. And you will **seek Me and find Me, when you search for Me with all your heart**. I will be found by you," says the Lord, "and I will bring you back from your captivity; I will gather you from all the nations and from all the places where I have driven you," says the Lord, "and I will bring you to the place from which I caused you to be carried away captive."*

*"Because you have said, 'The Lord has raised up prophets for us in Babylon. For He has sent to us in Babylon,*

*saying, "This captivity is long; build houses and dwell in them, and plant gardens and eat their fruit"'."*

*Jeremiah 51:44-45, 49-5: "I will punish Bel in Babylon, and I will bring out of his mouth what he has swallowed; and the nations shall not stream to him anymore. Yes, the wall of Babylon shall fall. **My people, go out of the midst of her!** And let everyone deliver himself from the fierce anger of the Lord. As Babylon has caused the slain of Israel to fall, so at Babylon the slain of all the earth shall fall. You who have escaped the sword, get away! **Do not stand still! Remember the Lord afar off, and let Jerusalem come to your mind."***

It is time for us to be set free from our Babylonian ways that have become ingrained in our lives. Much of the Babylonian thinking has become so much a part of us that it may be difficult to realize we need to be changed. In Babylon, it was commendable to strive to get fame and fortune. Striving to get more and be better than others was normal, good behavior. Getting the most you could for the least you could get by with giving, was considered good business. If the other guy got the short end of the deal, so what? That was "good horse-trading". After all, if you didn't outsmart him and "get him first", he would get you. We have been infiltrated with this same kind of thinking. But in New Jerusalem, competition has no place, either in the church, or in business. In New Jerusalem, we seek to serve God by serving mankind. A job or business is something we do **to serve**, not something we do **to get—but to give.** A ministry is no different—it is something we do **to serve**, not what we do to get something we need: such as money or position.

If we stop to really consider why we do what we do, we might find that our motives are mixed with self-seeking, along with our desires to be God-serving. If we examine our methods of relating in our family, business, or church, we may find some of the practices of Babylon.

God said that we would find Him and be delivered from our captivity of Babylonian ways when we seek Him with our **whole hearts.** We have paid a very great price for our adulterated ways. Our divided hearts have caused us broken lives and broken families. It has split up churches, wrecked our finances, and turned many against the church. The sick and needy are left to suffer and die for lack of power to effectively minister to their needs. The lost wander on in darkness be-cause we are too busy seeking to meet our own needs to effectively minister to their needs.

*Proverbs 5:14: I was on the verge of total ruin, in the midst of the congregation and assembly.*

*Proverbs 6:26, 32-33: For by means of a harlot a man is reduced to a crust of bread; and an adulteress will prey upon his precious life. Whoever commits adultery with a woman lacks understanding; he who does so, destroys his own soul. Wounds and dishonor he will get, and his reproach will not be wiped away.*

*Proverbs 7:23, 17-18: I have perfumed my bed with myrrh, aloes, and cinnamon. Come, let us take our fill of love until morning; let us delight ourselves with love. Till an arrow struck his liver, as a bird hastens to the snare, he did not know it would take his life.*

**We must give up seeking our own profit (self-seeking).**

Only as the Bride is completely faithful to her husband, can the kingdom-of-God lifestyle rule our lives, our local churches, our businesses, our nation, and eventually the planet. Our mixture of self-serving and God-serving will never bring forth the kingdom in our life. We will continue to strive and fail after a measure of success for a season. People will continue to suffer needlessly for lack of purified, powerful ministry. Only a pure-heart motivation to serve God only, no matter what happens to ourselves, will do. Whether we are personally blessed, accepted to a place of leadership, or rejected and stoned by those we serve, we must give our whole heart, our whole life to our husband, Jesus. We must stop trying to protect and take care of ourselves, while at the same time, trying to serve God. We must seek the kingdom of God first (above all else), and not seek to take care of ourselves.

It is time for all of us to come out of Babylon. It is time for us to be released from the spirit of harlotry and all that works with it that has caused us to be spiritual adulterers (**self**-seeking and **God**-seeking). The price we've paid, because of our adultery, is too great.

*1 Corinthians 10:33: ...just as I also please all men in all things, **not seeking my own profit**, but the profit of many, that they may be saved.*

*Luke 12:29-33: "And **do not seek what you should eat or what you should drink**, nor have an anxious* *mind. For all these things the nations of the world seek after, and your Father knows that you need these things. But seek the kingdom of God , and all these things shall be added to you. Do not fear, little flock, for it is your Father's good pleasure to give you the kingdom. Sell what you have and give alms; provide yourselves money bags which do not grow old, a treasure in the heavens that does not fail, where no thief approaches nor moth destroys."*

*Hebrews 13:4-5: Marriage is honorable among all, and the bed undefiled; but fornicators and **adulterers** God will judge. Let your conduct be without **covetousness**, and be content with such things as you have. For He Himself has said, "I will never leave you nor forsake you."*

**We must serve God only,** no longer serving God mostly and ourselves a little—no longer living according to the old ways. God is our source. He will provide all we need as we seek to serve Him and follow His direction.

*Matthew 4:10: Then Jesus said to him, **"Away with you, Satan!** For it is written, 'You shall worship the Lord your God, and **Him only you shall serve.'"***

**We are an adulterous generation.** We are trying to serve almighty God with our self-seeking, Babylonian, harlot ways mingled with the purity and power of Holy God. And we wonder why so little is accomplished, and why so many are wounded and destroyed within their own church and family—the very places where they should be built up and protected. The God-seeking side of our heart starts a good work and draws people to trust us; but the self-seeking side causes devastation and mistrust. Eventually failure will occur, and whatever was gained is lost.

We are then always looking for a miracle from God to bail us out of the corruption we have created with our adultery. We pray for a miracle to get us out of debt. God didn't get us into debt, and He probably isn't going to bail us out if we do not change our self-serving ways. We do not hear the voice of God clearly because we do not want to change just now. So we look for a miraculous sign to help us.

*Matthew 12:39a Amp.: "... An evil and adulterous generation [that is, a generation morally unfaithful to God] seeks or demands a sign..."*

*Matthew 16:3-4,6: "... Hypocrites! You know how to discern the face of the sky, but you cannot discern the signs of the times. A wicked and adulterous generation seeks after a sign, and no sign shall be given to it except the sign of the prophet Jonah." Then Jesus said to them, "Take heed and beware of the leaven of the Pharisees and the Sadducees."*

We become like the Pharisee who makes a great show of "being a Christian", yet we are mixed with uncleanness in our own heart. This always causes the Pharisee to become legally-minded as we attempt to justify our self-seeking sin with legal loop holes and focus on the lawbreaking of others. Or, since we are not experiencing the abundant, spiritual resurrection life of Christ in ourselves now, we deny it in others. Thus we are Sadducees, denying the resurrection life now—denying spiritual gifts and experiences. Because we are not experiencing them, we believe others are not as well.

We tend to look at those that are experiencing the resurrection life of God and judge them from our own heart. Since they are outspoken and dynamic, bringing the Word of God boldly, we assume they must have the same mixed motivation we have and are therefore trying to make a name or place for themselves. So we resist and fight against God's purified people, thinking they are great self-seekers. The rejection of those who are experiencing God leads to rejection of the Word coming through them, which robs us of God's provision.

**We must stop looking at others and allow the Holy Spirit to reveal what is really in our own heart.** Friends, it is not them we must be concerned about. It is us. Am I a minister in part because I need and like the attention and applause of others? Is the position of authority something that I need to make me feel better? Am I a Christian to some degree because it is acceptable in the circles I move in? Am I a Christian businessman in part because I want to meet the wants and needs of my family and those in my own heart? Am I doing what I do for a paycheck? Am I concerned about the amount of the paycheck? Or am I concerned about what the work I am doing does to serve God by serving mankind?

Am I more drawn to minister to the pretty girls, (or handsome guys for the ladies), than to those unattractive needy folks? Is it easier for me to hear the call to minister in Hawaii than to Africa? Am I willing to go out of my way to see that the wealthy man is taken care of and minister to him ahead of the poor man? Do I get up and go to work in the morning to get a paycheck to take care of me and my family; or do I go to work to serve God with what I do, and trust Him to provide for me and my family? Will I leave a field because there is little acceptance, but great need, to go to one where they believe like I do and like me better?

Hypocrites! Do we think the preacher should not serve for money but think that we should serve (work) for money? The truth is, that when we serve or work for money, we are in harlotry. When we truly serve God with a pure heart, no matter what the pay, we will be abundantly supplied. But if we serve (do what we do), for money or anything else, we have another god and are serving it. God is not just concerned with what we do, but **why we do it.** Two men might work side-by-side, one working to get money, and the other working to serve God by what the job does for mankind. One has pure motivation, and the other is a harlot, selling himself for money. The one serving God will continue to serve as long as he can, even if the paycheck stops. The harlot will usually stop the moment the paycheck stops.

*2 Chronicles 25:2: And* **he did what was right** *in the sight of the Lord,* **but not with a loyal heart.**

As we begin to search our own heart as to why we really do what we do, we need to recognize that we usually have two reasons for doing anything: one that sounds good to us and to others—and one that is true. We must look deeper into our heart and see through our reasons that sound good and get to the real truth.

**Jesus will forgive our adultery.** We are not stuck in bondage to Babylonian ways. Repentance is the key; it is agreeing with God about our sin and turning from it. Jesus has also provided for our deliverance from the spirit of harlotry which attacks our life. We must repent and allow Jesus to set us free. Then we must work at renewing our mind to the New-Jerusalem ways of life.

*John 8;3-4, 10-12: Then the scribes and Pharisees brought to Him a woman caught in adultery. And when they set her in the midst, they said to Him, "Teacher, this woman was* **caught in adultery,** *in the very act."*

*When Jesus had raised Himself up and saw no one but the woman, He said to her, "Woman, where are those accusers of yours? Has no one condemned you?" She said, "No one, Lord." And Jesus said to her,* **"Neither do I condemn you;** *go and sin no more." Then Jesus spoke to them again, saying, "I am the light of the world. He who follows Me shall not walk in darkness, but have the light of life."*

*John 1:12-17,29b: But as many as received Him, to them He gave the right to become* **children of God,** *even to those who believe in His name: who were* **born,** *not of blood,* **nor of the will of the flesh, nor of the will of man, but** **of God.** *And* **the Word became flesh and dwelt among us,** *and* **we beheld His glory,** *the glory as of the only begotten of the Father, full of grace and truth. John bore witness of Him and cried out, saying, "This was He of whom I said,* **'He who comes after me** *is preferred before me, for He was before me.'"* **And of His fullness we have all received,** *and* **grace for grace.** *For the law was given through Moses, but* **grace and truth came through Jesus Christ** *...*

**Behold! The Lamb of God who takes away the sin of the world!**

*Matthew 18:9: "And if your eye causes you to sin, pluck it out and cast it from you. It is better for you to enter life with one eye, rather than having two eyes, to be cast into hell fire (Gehenna)." Luke 13:3: ...but unless you repent you will all likewise perish.*

*Luke 12:31: But seek the kingdom of God, and all these things shall be added to you.*

We must not continue to deceive ourselves about the reality of our mixed inner motives. The cost for our mixed inner motives is the lack of the kingdom of God lifestyle and its attributes. The benefits and blessings that we desire will only be added to us when we no longer desire anything above the kingdom of God. When we turn from our mixed inner motives and seek first the kingdom of God, the other things, which we no longer need to be satisfied, will be added to us.

Often people are astonished at the peace and joy they find in the presence of God as they give up their whole life to seek the kingdom of God and His righteousness with their whole heart. Whatever loss they feel from laying down part of their life is hardly noticeable in the beautiful presence of God. Things they had striven so hard for in the past are of little significance. Only intimately experiencing God's presence really matters. Understanding "The Good Heart-Tree" and the "New Jerusalem Family Pattern" begins to enable us to see normal kingdom-of-God living. As we contrast kingdom-of-God living with our current lifestyle, we can recognize that the life we have been living is, at best, a mixture. Knowing that we are missing the mark of the kingdom-of-God lifestyle, leads us first to true repentance. Repentance is a decision to stop going the way we have been going and turn around to pursue another way.

It may be disturbing and even traumatic to realize that much of our life has been far off the mark. In my own experience, it was somewhat like a death to realize that most of my life, even as a Christian, was far from the kingdom-of-God life. My motives, though acceptable in the church, were mixed with Babylonian desires. Turning from much of what I believed and stood for, was a lot like dying. The thing that makes it worthwhile is knowing that there really is a wonderful, totally fulfilling, kingdom-of-God life **now** that is worth dying for. There is resurrection life now after the tears of death.

We may have convinced ourselves that our motives are pure, when in reality they may yet be mingled with self-seeking desires. We may be like the young man who really thought his reason for choosing a certain Bible college was to prepare for a certain ministry in order to serve God. The fact that the young lady of his dreams had previously chosen the same school and type of ministry was only a bonus and perhaps a confirmation from God.

When the young lady fell in love with and married someone else, the young man no longer wanted to go to school, nor to serve God. His secret, self-seeking desire was painfully revealed to him.

If we will now allow God to reveal our secret, self-seeking desires that may be hidden even from us, and give them up now, we will avoid the future disappointments and heartaches that they will eventually cause.

It is now time to step off the treadmill of busy life, quiet ourselves, and be still before God. Allow the Holy Spirit to reveal the mixture of our motives. We will not know and experience the wonderful at-hand, kingdom-of-God lifestyle until after we identify the self-seeking desires mixed with our God-seeking motives, repent of them, and put them to death.

Before reading on in this work, please stop and search your heart. Ask God to reveal all self-seeking desires mixed with your God-seeking desires and repent.

"REPENT, FOR THE KINGDOM OF GOD IS AT HAND."

# CHAPTER 22

## BEYOND REPENTANCE

Beyond the decision of repentance is the reality of actually dealing with the life-structures we have built through the years. There must come a total destruction of the existing ways and a rebuilding of the new structure. God has provided our place of repentance in Jesus. He has also provided all that we will need to destroy the old and rebuild the new in Christ. His provision is not lacking in any area.

Much of the devastating disorders we have faced and are facing are no more than the burning of the old way. In Isaiah 61:3, God did not promise that there would be no fire; but he promised to give us **beauty for ashes.** One thing is certain, if you have ashes, you have had a fire. We cannot build anything back from ashes. If the structure had been blown down by a storm, we might have been able to have gathered up some fragments and rebuilt something of the ruins. But when a fire has totally destroyed the building, man cannot rebuild from the pieces. If your life seems to be ablaze, and is being destroyed, take hope; God will truly give you beauty for the ashes—if you continue to move toward the kingdom-of-God life.

Seeing the New Jerusalem, kingdom-of-God life, motivates us to turn and to persist until the goal is achieved. Seeing the enemy's schemes in the Bad Heart-Tree, and the Babylonian Family Pattern, begins to give us understanding of the enemy's position, strength, and methods. Beyond repentance, there is a war to be fought and won. Before we turned and started moving, we were not meeting the enemy head on. We were unknowingly going the same way. Now that the turn around is made, we will meet the enemy head on and overcome him in the strength of our Lord, the victorious one.

Every army commander knows that an army must be motivated to fight. They must see something significant enough to be achieved to risk losing their lives. If the enemy can continue to prevent God's people from seeing the kingdom of God now, he will be successful in preventing them from standing up and fighting. If he can keep Christians focusing all their hopes in heaven someday, he will keep them from fighting now.

An alien force occupying a land would like for the people to believe that their life is good enough now and that it would not be worth trying to drive the aliens from the land. The alien government wants the people to believe that the aliens own the land, and that they are too strong for the people to resist. The people growing up in this bondage may come to think of their life as normal. They depend on their captors for food and well-being. They take the hard labor, abuse, and lack of freedom as normal for them. Until they begin to see what freedom is and how good life really can be, they have no will or motivation to fight. But once they taste freedom, (once we taste the joy and peace of the kingdom-of-God lifestyle), nothing else will do. It is well worth fighting for.

After the long Egyptian captivity, the children of Israel had lost the will to resist and accepted their life as slaves of the Egyptians. When the Egyptians greatly increased the abuse and hard labor, the enslaved nation was ready to accept deliverance. But not long after leaving Egypt, when they began to face the hardships of the journey, they wished they were back in bondage where at least they were assured spicy food to eat. Then when it was time to enter the promised land of God's provision, they would not fight to drive the aliens from the land. They chose, instead, to continue in the wilderness. Only after all the "slave-minded" people had died, did their children enter into the promised land of God's provision. **God gives the victory, but we must fight the war.**

Once the will and motivation to fight is there, the next step is to learn how to defeat the enemy. A good general wants to know his enemy as well as he knows his own army. Where are the enemy positions? What is his strength? What weapons does he possess? How does he fight? What are his battle strategies? Where are his weaknesses? Then how can the strength of his army be best applied to rout the enemy out, defeat him, and retake the land?

Looking at the enemy's schemes in the Bad Heart-Tree, the Babylonian Family Pattern and other schemes enables us to know just where the enemy is and to set our weapon sights to make direct hits on his positions.

Knowing these schemes or strategies allows us to know what the enemy will probably do next and to be prepared to resist his attacks. **The kingdom of heaven <u>does</u> suffer violence and the violent <u>do</u> take it by force.**

This is not a war in the flesh; it is a spiritual warfare against spirit powers which affect our natural lives. The Word of God not only gives us instruction for fighting, but it also is our weapon. Christ Jesus is our strength —only in His name do we have power to overcome the alien army.

Spiritual warfare is fought with **faith in God** and **His word:** believing the Word of God. Praying the Word of God. Saying the Word of God. Proclaiming and preaching the Word of God by the power of the indwelling Spirit of Christ Jesus. Walking in the Spirit and not in the lust of the flesh. Believing what God says above any other word. Standing in the Spirit and Word of God. Speaking the truth of the Word in love at all times. Taking the authority given to us to rule and reign with Christ. Doing the will of God by the power of the indwelling Spirit of God.

*Ephesians 6:12: For we do not wrestle against flesh and blood, but against **principalities**, against **powers**, against the **rulers of the darkness** of this age, against **spiritual hosts of wickedness in the heavenly places.***

*Ephesians 6:17b-18a: ...and the **sword** of the Spirit which is **the word of God; praying always** with all prayer and supplication **in the Spirit...***

## APPROPRIATING GOD'S PROVISION
### (THE MINISTRY OF JESUS)

Just because God has provided all we need to walk in kingdom-of-God freedom does not mean we automatically have those provisions manifest in our lives. We have a part to fulfill. The enemy does not want us to know how to receive the provisions of God. **Our battle is for faith, knowing and believing the Word of God.** The ministry of Jesus, the Anointed One, provides salvation, healing of our broken spirit, mind, will, and emotions; deliverance from spiritual captivity; recovery of spiritual sight to the spiritually blind; liberty from downtrodden bondage of wounding oppression; and the favor or spiritual prosperity of God, **if we have faith**. The provisions of God are activated in our own life when we believe in our heart and confess with our mouth.

*Luke 4:18-19: (And Jesus said), The **Spirit** of the Lord is upon Me, Because **He has anointed** Me to **preach the gospel** to the poor. He has sent Me to **heal the brokenhearted** to preach **deliverance** to the captives and **recovery of sight** to the blind, to **set at liberty** those who are oppressed (bruised), to preach the **acceptable (favorable)** year of the Lord."*

*Romans 10:8-10: But what does it say? "The word is near you, even in your mouth and in your heart" (that is, the word of faith which we preach): that if you **confess with your mouth** the Lord Jesus and **believe in your heart** that God has raised Him from the dead, you will be saved. For with the heart one believes to righteousness, and with the mouth confession is made to salvation."*

We know that Christ Jesus has provided salvation for all men, yet we also are aware that not all are saved. What makes the difference? God's provision is for all. Why are some receiving the provision and some are not? Only those who **believe in their heart** and **confess with their mouth** are saved. He has also provided kingdom-of-God freedom for all believers to walk in now. But all believers are not walking in kingdom-freedom now. The provision of Christ must be appropriated into the individual's life by believing in the heart and speaking with the mouth.

Every ministry of Jesus must be appropriated in similar manner. It is the way of the universal laws of God. The spiritual realm is accessed and activated by believing in the heart, praying in the Spirit, and speaking with the mouth. If we are to be changed, we must hear the Word of God by the Spirit of God, believe it in our heart, and begin to pray and speak the will of God.

Those of us who have been around in the world for a lot of years would probably testify that according to our personal observation, most people in the world never really change. They may experience some changes in status, education, location, etc., but the basic life-structure generally remains primarily the same, regardless of what happens. If they were stinkers when young, they were still stinkers when they got old. If they have a bad heart-tree, it may get worse and the wall get bigger, but it will not really be changed apart from a spiritual work of the ministry of Jesus.

Jesus is the "life-changer". The ministry of Jesus the Anointed One, by the Holy Spirit can make deep, permanent inner changes in the life-structure. Jesus will, without discrimination, change anyone who will meet the necessary conditions of believing in the heart and confessing with the mouth the resurrected Christ.

The bad heart-tree can be completely dealt with and the good heart-tree grown in the healed soil of the heart. The Babylonian patterns and demonic attacks can be completely dealt with by appropriating the ministry of Jesus the Anointed One. However, some people may require specific help to push back the darkness of the enemy while their faith is developing. Agreement in prayer with a righteous man or woman can be powerful in routing the enemy and getting the light into the heart.

*James 5:16:* ***Confess your trespasses to one another, and pray for one another, that you may be healed. The effective, fervent prayer of a righteous man avails much.***

True repentance for one's part in the bad heart-tree and lack of living in the kingdom lifestyle must be the attitude of the heart. Sin must be revealed to a person by the Holy Spirit. If we try to do the Holy Spirit's work for Him by attempting to point out and convince a person of his sin, we've made ourselves like a god.

**Intercessory prayer** may be required to release the anointing of Christ to break through the canopy of spiritual blindness, deception, and delusion of the enemy before the light of God can enter to expose sin. Once the enemy is pushed back, and the light enters by the hearing of the Word by the Spirit, the person can and must decide to repent of exposed sin and not justify or defend it. He must agree with God that sin is sin and be willing to turn from it toward **Jesus as Lord.**

Seeking to make Jesus Lord of our life in a practical and real way means receiving Him as King. The sovereign master of our total being and every aspect of our lives. It means becoming His servant, carrying out His instruction, and ordering our lives by His righteous ways. It is truly seeking the kingdom of God. *"But seek first the kingdom of God and His righteousness and all these things shall be added to you."*

The powerful ministry of Jesus the Anointed One, by the Holy Spirit, **appropriated by faith** and **executed by prayer,** can tear down the old life-structure and create a new heart. The work of enemy spirits and negative character qualities can be eliminated, and the true victory of overcoming can be established in the life. The kingdom of God is **righteousness, peace**, and **joy** in the Holy Spirit.

The objective of confessing our trespasses to one another and praying for one another is to get the person to Jesus to be fully healed and delivered by the power of God. The one praying for another person, though important to the process, becomes very secondary as the person being prayed for, focuses on Jesus the savior, healer, and deliverer, and not on the person praying. The person being prayed for must develop his own faith in Jesus. In the final analysis, only the person's own faith can keep him in freedom to walk in the kingdom-of-God lifestyle. However when the person in need is too weak in faith to walk on his own to Jesus, the faith of another can be employed to bring the person to Christ Jesus.

The story in Mark, chapter two, of a man carried by others to Jesus can help to kindle or renew hope in the person who feels hopeless, because he does not yet have faith to make it to Jesus for his freedom on his own. Jesus did not just look at the faith of the man on the cot. He was perhaps too weak, too far gone to have much faith. But Jesus saw the faith of those letting him down through the roof, as well as the lame man's faith.

*Mark 2:5-12: When Jesus saw **their faith**, He said to the paralytic, "Son, your sins are forgiven you." But some of the scribes were sitting there and reasoning in their hearts, 'why does this Man speak blasphemies like this? Who can forgive sins but God alone?" And immediately, when Jesus perceived in His spirit that they reasoned thus within themselves, He said to them, "Why do you reason about these things in your hearts? Which is easier, to **say** to the paralytic, your sins are forgiven you, or to **say**, arise, take up your bed and walk? But that you may know that the Son of Man has power on earth to forgive sins"— He said to the paralytic, **"I say to you,** arise, take up your bed, and go your way to your house." And immediately he arose, took up the bed, and went out in the presence of them all, so that all were amazed and glorified God, saying, "We never saw anything like this!"*

What we **say** in faith according to the Word of God, particularly with two in agreement, has great impact in the spiritual realm to bring forth the will of God into the natural realm. The principalities and powers of darkness in the spiritual realm must respond to what we believe and what we say when we pray in the name of Jesus. The conditions and character qualities of our heart must also respond to the Word of God as we speak according to the Word in the name of Jesus the Anointed One.

*Mark 11:23-24:* *"For assuredly, I say to you, whoever **says to this mountain,** 'Be removed and be cast into the sea,' and does not doubt in his heart, but **believes** that those things he **says** will come to pass, he will have whatever he **says**. Therefore I say to you, whatever things **you ask** when you **pray, believe** that you receive them, and **you will have them."***

*Matthew 17:20:* So Jesus said to them, "Because of your unbelief; for assuredly, I say to you, if you have **faith** as a mustard **seed,** <u>you</u> will <u>say</u> <u>to</u> this mountain, 'Move from here to there,' and it will move; and nothing will be impossible for you."

*Matthew 18:16b:* *"... by the **mouth of two or three** witnesses every word may be established."*

*Proverbs 18:21:* **Death and life are in the power of the tongue,** And those who love it will eat its fruit.

*Matthew 8:8:* The centurion answered and said, "Lord, I am not worthy that You should come under my roof. But only **speak a word,** and my servant will be healed."

*Matthew 8:16:* When evening had come, they brought to Him many who were demon-possessed. And **He cast out the spirits with a <u>word</u>,** and healed all who were sick.

*Matthew 18:18-20:* *"Assuredly, I say to you, whatever **you bind** on earth will be bound in heaven, and whatever **you loose** on earth will be loosed in heaven. Again **I say to you that if <u>two of you agree</u> on earth concerning anything that they ask, it will be done for them by My Father in heaven.** For where two or three are gathered together in My name, I am there in the midst of them."*

The scripture says that we are to "bind on earth" and that things are changed in the spiritual realm when we do. What is "binding and loosing"? How do we bind or loose according to the Word of God? Binding and loosing might be compared respectively to either tying up a subject with ropes—or cutting the ropes and letting that subject go free. We bind or loose with our words. As we ask (speak) in agreement on earth, the power of God in the spiritual realm is activated to restrain, or to set free. What we say and pray has a restraining or a releasing affect in the spiritual realm. It is as if our words are the ropes that go out from our mouth and wrap around something to bind it and stop its activity. Or, our words are the power that unties the ropes of the subject and allows it to become active.

When we pray for a person in severe need, we may need to bind the powers of darkness that are keeping the light out. Until their power and work is stopped, the person's spiritual sight is impaired. Binding is the releasing of spiritual power by prayer that can temporarily stop the enemy's activity. We may also need to loose spiritual enlightenment, so the Word can flow into the person's heart allowing repentance, cleansing, and strengthening to take place. The Word of God must be built into the life. And Jesus must truly become Lord of the life.

One of Jesus' primary instructions to us is to pray. In the "model prayer", *(Matthew 6:10-15),* he showed us how to pray and taught us to forgive others. According to these Scriptures forgiving is and important factor in seeking the kingdom of God. Unforgiveness can be a serious hinderance to the kingdom of God coming on earth, in our lives. One of the most important aspects of being restored by Christ to the kingdom of God lifestyle is forgiving.

# CHAPTER 23

## FORGIVENESS & BEYOND

Our source of forgiveness is Jesus; if He had not forgiven us, we would not have the potential to forgive. But we have the potential to forgive any and all wrongs, no matter how severe or how terrible. We must, for our own good, choose from the heart to forgive. **It is a choice, an act of the will, which we can choose over our feelings.** Forgiving is a decision. We will make a decision to forgive or not to forgive. Making no decision is a decision to remain in unforgiveness.

Choosing to forgive does not mean that we agree with what has been done. We are not saying that what has been done was right, but we are releasing the judgment of the situation to God. We must pray for the blessing of the person involved; until we can do this we have not fully forgiven the person. We are not forgiving the person for their sake as much as for our own sake. We are the ones who receive the torment, sickness, and stress if we do not forgive.

Not only must we forgive every person, but we must also forgive ourselves for anything that we have done to hurt ourselves or others; and we must forgive God for anytime that we feel that He let us down. We also may need to forgive organizations or institutions, as we would a person. The tormentors do not care who or what the unforgiveness is against; any unforgiveness gives them the license to do their deadly, painful work.

*Matthew 18: 21-35: Then Peter came to Him and said, "Lord, how often shall my brother sin against me, and I forgive him? Up to seven times?" Jesus said to him, "I do not say to you, up to seven times, but up to seventy times seven. Therefore the kingdom of heaven is like a certain king who wanted to settle accounts with his servants. And when he had begun to settle accounts, one was brought to him who owed him ten thousand talents. But as he was not able to pay, his master commanded that he be sold, with his wife and children and all that he had, and that payment be made. The servant therefore fell down before him, saying, 'Master, have patience with me, and I will pay you all.'*

*"Then the master of that servant was moved with compassion, released him, and forgave him the debt. But that servant went out and found one of his fellow servants who owed him a hundred denarii; and he laid hands on him and took him by the throat, saying, 'Pay me what you owe!' So his fellow servant fell down at his feet and begged him, saying, 'Have patience with me, and I will pay you all.' And he would not, but went and threw him into prison till he should pay the debt. So when his fellow servants saw what had been done, they were very grieved, and came and told their master all that had been done. Then his master, after he had called him, said to him, 'You wicked servant! I forgave you all that debt because you begged me. Should you not also have had compassion on your fellow servant, just as I had pity on you?' And his master was angry, and delivered him to the torturers until he should pay all that was due to him. So My heavenly Father also will do to you if each of you, from his heart, does not forgive his brother his trespasses."*

*Matthew 6: 9-15: "Our Father in heaven, hallowed be Your name. Your kingdom come. Your will be done on earth as it is in heaven. Give us this day our daily bread. And forgive us our debts, as we forgive our debtors. And do not lead us into temptation, but deliver us from the evil one. For Yours is the kingdom and the power and the glory forever. Amen. For if you forgive men their trespasses, your heavenly Father will also forgive you. But if you do not forgive men their trespasses, neither will your Father forgive your trespasses."*

*Mark 11:22-26: So Jesus answered and said to them, "Have faith in God. For assuredly, I say to you, whoever says to this mountain, 'Be removed and be cast into the sea', and does not doubt in his heart, but believes that those things he says will come to pass, he will have whatever he says. Therefore I say to you, whatever things you ask when you pray, believe that you receive them, and you will have them. And whenever you stand praying, if you have anything against anyone, forgive him, that your Father in heaven may also forgive you your trespasses. But if you do not forgive, neither will your Father in heaven forgive your trespasses."*

The torment promised to those who do not forgive does not just refer to hell someday. The word "torturers" in the Greek means, "jailers who inflict pain". If we choose not to forgive, we give the enemy legal right to hold us in painful bondage now.

We may not feel like forgiving. On the contrary, the flesh may be screaming for vengeance. In the heat of the situation, everything in us may want to do great harm to the offender. Our natural fleshly drive to destroy the offending person is there for our protection in the natural world. If an offender is attempting to rape or murder my child, I will stop at nothing to prevent that from happening. The fatherly rage that would cause me to do great harm to the offender to stop or prevent the attack is natural. The problem develops after the offense is committed, and my rage can do nothing to stop or prevent it. That natural desire now becomes a desire to become like God and do His work for Him by taking vengeance on the offender.

*Hebrews 10: 30-31: For we know Him who said, "Vengeance is Mine: I will repay," says the Lord. And again. "The Lord will judge His people." It is a fearful thing to fall into the hands of the living God.*

We must get out of the way and allow God to be God. We must make the decision to forgive, no matter what. I personally have felt rage and even hatred in my heart, and yet, made the decision to forgive regardless of my feelings. A wonderful thing often happens. As we begin to make the decision to forgive, and begin to pray, strong feelings of love and forgiveness may begin to flow into our heart.

God wants to change the pain of the offense into love—that wonderful, peaceful "love-flow" of God Himself moving upon our heart. The more painful the offense is, the more sweet the love will be that manifests by forgiveness. Personally, I am not sure we can ever really know the overwhelming, pure, sweet love of God apart from experiencing deep pain and the beautiful love that forgiving produces.

If, however, a person chooses to hold on to the anger and resentment caused by the pain, deep bitterness will be rooted in the heart and poison the entire soul and body. Many diseases that seem to have no medical cause are the result of bitterness in the soul. Much depression and severe mental illness also have their roots in the bitterness of unforgiveness.

The choice is ours. Because Jesus has forgiven us while we were yet sinners, we have the potential, by His power, to forgive. Are you ready to be set free from the torment of unforgiveness, and forgive no matter what? Jesus said, *"whenever you stand **praying**, if you have anything against anyone, **forgive** him".* When you are ready to make the decision to forgive pray something like the following prayer from your heart.

"I repent of all unforgiveness in my life. In the name of Jesus, by the power of the Holy Spirit, as an act of my will, I choose to forgive from my heart anyone and everyone who has ever hurt me or harmed me in any way, in my entire life. I specifically choose to forgive _____, _____, and _____.

I release them, in Jesus' name. I say it's all right if they never make it right. I hold nothing against them, and in the name of Jesus, I ask You, Father, to bless them, to meet their needs in all areas of their lives.

"Father, I forgive myself for all I've done to hurt or harm myself and others; and, Father, I forgive You for anytime I felt that You let me down. I say, You are good, God, and I trust You with my life. Father, I thank You that I am forgiven—and have forgiven.

I command all powers of darkness, in the name of Jesus, you may never again use any of this unforgiveness to bring torment or stress of any form into my life.

Father, I thank you that I have forgiven and that I am forgiven. Thank you Father, in the name of Jesus.

Forgiving and releasing the offender is a tremendous step and may start emotional healing, but the memory is not automatically healed when we forgive. Until the healing of the memory, by Jesus the Anointed One, is appropriated in our heart, the painful memory may still be there, and recalling it may cause unforgiveness to return. One may find himself forgiving the same situation again and again.

## HEALING THE HEART
### (BEYOND FORGIVING)

Forgiving from the heart, and releasing everyone who has ever harmed us, can remove the root of bitterness from our heart. Yet, the heart must be healed to prevent the bitterness from returning. Remember, when we speak of the heart, we are referring to the inner man, our spirit (the part that relates to God) and our soul (mind, will, and emotions).

The painful experiences of our lives are locked into the permanent memory section of our minds. Painful memories, either conscious or **subconscious**, have affected our spirit and may have wounded it. These painful memories also may have crushed our will and shattered our emotions. These negative, painful experiences stored in our heart cause us to see and understand life according to our experiences. They serve to control us by affecting our behavior. We are bound into negative patterns by the stored pains of the past. The patterns must be changed for us to walk in kingdom freedom.

The ministry of Jesus the Christ includes healing the brokenhearted. God has provided all that we need in Jesus to heal our wounded spirit and soul. We need only to appropriate the ministry of Jesus to heal the broken heart to be set free from the bondage of our wounds. When the negative experiences stored in our memory are healed, they will no longer cause bitterness to return.

*Psalm 25: 17-19: The troubles of my **heart** have enlarged; Oh, bring me out of my distresses! Look on my **affliction** and my **pain,** and forgive all my sins. Consider my **enemies,** for they are many; and they **hate me with cruel hatred.***

*Psalm 147: 9-3: The Lord builds up Jerusalem; He gathers together the outcasts of Israel. **He heals the brokenhearted and binds up their wounds.***

*Isaiah 6l: 1-4: "The Spirit of the Lord God is upon Me, because the Lord has anointed Me to preach good tidings to the poor; He has sent Me **to heal the brokenhearted, to proclaim liberty to the captives,** and **the opening of the prison to those who are bound;** to proclaim the acceptable year of the Lord, and the day of vengeance of our God; to comfort all who mourn, to*

*console those who mourn in Zion, to give them beauty for ashes, the oil of joy for mourning, the garment of praise for the spirit of heaviness; that they may be called trees of righteousness, the planting of the Lord, that He may be glorified. And they shall rebuild the old ruins, they shall raise up the former desolations, and they shall repair the ruined cities, the desolations of many generations."*

*Luke 4:18-1 9a: "The Spirit of the Lord is upon Me, because He has anointed Me to preach the gospel to the poor. He has sent Me **to heal the brokenhearted, to preach deliverance to the captives** and recovery of sight to the blind, **to set at liberty those who are oppressed (bruised),** to preach the acceptable year of the Lord."*

Imagine that our heart, as God made us, was like a brand new, shiny car. Let's further suppose a big strong man with a big sledge hammer walks up to the car and smashes the hood, leaving a huge ugly dent. Satan is like that strong man, working through people to inflict painful damage. That big, ugly dent will not go away with time. The old saying, "time heals all wounds", is a lie. Until something is done to repair that dent, it will remain stored within us to mar and disfigure our spirit, and our life.

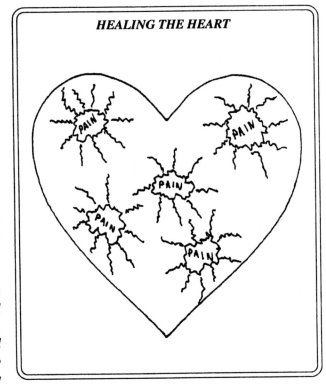

**HEALING THE HEART**

Next, the heavy hammer smashes the windshield and windows. The car windows are like our emotions; they are shattered by the blows of stressful experiences. Finally, the big hammer begins to repeatedly smash into the motor, until that which makes the car go is destroyed—just like our will is crushed by the repeated blows of negative wounding experiences. Our inner man has become a battered and shattered wreck with no power or motivation to drive down the road of life.

Our outer man may look strong, intelligent, and handsome; but our wrecked inner man causes us to have a very poor self-image, low self-esteem, lack of confidence, and lack of motivation. We would rather withdraw to a dark garage than get out on the busy streets of life. We fear others will see our shameful condition. If we do venture out of the garage, we must find some way to **cover** our dents and broken parts. We also must **defend** ourselves against any more painful blows; therefore, we often defend ourselves by **attacking** others.

Jesus the Anointed One is the healer that can knock out the dents and repair all damage, making our heart brand new again. Like a bright, shiny, new car with new windows and a powerful new motor, we're ready for Jesus to get into the driver's seat and steer us out into the beautiful highways of life.

Not only can our past wounds cause us to have a **poor self-image, low self-esteem, lack of confidence, and lack of motivation**; they can also cause us to have **unreasonable fear** that cripples us. Unreasonable fear causes us to avoid relationships and situations of life that God desires for us. Fear can cause us to act and react in such a way that we may miss entering into some of the good things God desires for us.

Our actions and reactions are affected by our stored, painful memories. We often think we are reacting to circumstances, but we may be reacting from an attitude created by our past, hurting memories. Let me illustrate this with a story about a little black dog:

A man walked out to his mail box beside the road. As he reached in to get his mail, he was painfully bitten by a little black dog. He ran limping to the house, treated his wounds, and went to the doctor for further treatment. The episode was painful and costly. The next day he was afraid to go to the mail box, but after looking very carefully, he decided no dog was in sight. He limped to the mail box, nervously looking all around.

As he opened the mail box and looked in to get his mail, suddenly, the little black dog seemed to come from nowhere and bit him again, even more viciously than before.

The man screamed out in pain and fear. He began running, limping and screaming toward his house. In his haste, he tripped and fell, headlong onto the rough driveway, injuring his knees and hands. The mail was scattered and left as the man scrambled to his feet again and continued his hysterical run to his house limping and bleeding.

This poor guy is never going to the mail box again, no matter what. He now has a great fear of little black dogs and mail boxes. He absolutely refused to go to the mail box again and devised all kinds of schemes to keep from going. He did not want his family to know how badly he feared going to the mail box; so he made all kinds of unreasonable excuses for not going. If we find ourselves searching for a reason not to do something, we may have some dog-bite memories that need to be healed.

Well, after many months of not going to the mail box, there came a time when he really needed to go. He was quite sure the check that he was waiting for was in the box, and he needed to get it in the bank. He had gained confidence as he had observed others safely getting the mail; so, he decided to try it. He carried a gun, a big stick and a teargas protection device. And, just in case all else might fail, he wore heavy, tall leather boots and two pairs of heavy pants.

Do some of us ever walk around emotionally "armed and ready" to defend ourselves like this man?

He watched anxiously as he nervously got his mail from the box and walked rapidly home. He breathed a big sigh of relief as he stepped safely into his house and leaned back against the door to catch his breath. The successful trip gave him confidence to start going daily to the mail box again. As months passed, he became less fearful and more confident with each successful journey.

One day, several months later, as he was getting his mail, a very friendly, little black puppy came toward the man. The puppy was happily bouncing along, wagging his tail, hoping to make a new friend and maybe get a few loving pats.

When the man saw the friendly, little puppy; he screamed, kicked the puppy as hard as he could, and ran in terror toward his house.

This man was not reacting to the reality of the circumstances, but was reacting from wounds of the past stored in his memory. Hurting memories caused him to be unable to receive affection from the puppy or to be able to give affection. He hurt the little puppy, and may have planted seeds in the puppy that someday could cause it to bite him, just as he feared.

## THE PROCESS OF HEALING

Healing does not automatically and completely take place when we receive Jesus as savior and Lord. However, the potential for healing and the process of healing does begin at this point. Healing may continue to occur gradually through the normal ministry of the church.

The ministry of Jesus, by the Holy Spirit, flowing through other people can bring healing to the heart, as unconditional love, acceptance, mercy, grace, and forgiveness are supplied. However, if something other than these attitudes exist within the people of the local church, more wounding can occur as we begin to let down our defenses and open ourselves to others in the church.

Healing the heart must occur in an atmosphere of acceptance, free of any form of condemnation and hostility. We cannot have the proper attitude toward those in need of healing if we are not being healed ourselves. **Only healed people can help heal people. Hurting people always hurt people.**

Appropriating the ministry of Jesus to heal the brokenhearted is one of the most potent experiences for improving our quality of life. Nothing is more valuable to kingdom living, but so often misunderstood by the church. As with every ministry of Christ provided by God, our part is to believe with the heart and confess with the mouth. The resurrected Christ is within to fulfill the Word of God. Healing our wounded heart is a provision of the Word of God. We have only to ask in prayer believing in the heart and confessing with the mouth, and it is done.

For some with severe experiences in our past it may be helpful to pray specifically for healing of our wounded heart. It may also be helpful to pray with another godly person.

*James 5:16: **Confess your trespasses (faults) to one another, and pray for one another, that you may be healed ...***

If we can recognize areas of painful memories in our heart, God wants to heal them. We must release the memories to God for healing. Holding on to a negative past can hinder a godly future. Attaining the resurrection life of Christ now involves forgetting those things which are behind and reaching forward to those things which are ahead. *(Philippians 3:11-14)*. We must choose by an act of our will to stop relating to stress from past memories. It is our decision but it is Christ that does the work.

It is important to ask God for His provision. *James 4:2 KJV*, says: *"Ye have not because ye ask not"*. Asking specifically is an important principle of prayer. If we ask God to heal our hurting memories **now**, and believe in our heart that we have what we ask, it is done. We must confess with our mouth it is done, and thank Him for healing the memory now. *(Mark 11:23)*. **We must not continue to meditate the memory and pray for God to heal us someday.**

When you recognize negative memories pray something like the following prayer from the heart.

Heavenly Father, in the name of Jesus, by the power of the Holy Spirit, I release to you for healing all the wounded, hurting, or negative memories of my entire life, whether conscious or subconscious, from my conception, through my birth, the first few years of my life, my childhood, all my adult life, and to this present moment. I specifically release to you for healing the memory of_____, _____, _____, and_____ ----

I release all these memories to you. Heal me now, give me release of all the stress. I choose by an act of my will never again to receive stress from these memories. Thank you, for healing me. I say that I am healed of all these memories, in Jesus' name. Thank you Father for healing me.

I command all powers of darkness, in the name of Jesus, you may never again use any of these memories to bring stress into my life or affect my life in any negative way, in Jesus' name.

Continue to repeat this process as long as the Holy Spirit directs, or as long as memories are coming forth. All memories do not have to be healed in one season. Many memories may come forth in rapid order, or there may be one at a time. No memory that the Father brings up should be treated as insignificant. Ask the Holy Spirit to bring forth the memories that are to be healed at this time.

We must daily walk in the process of repentance, forgiveness, and healing; repentance for every adulterated motive as we recognize them; forgiveness for every offense as they occur, and healing for every painful experience. If we are wounded during the course of the day we can be completely healed before bedtime.

Personally I have found that some severe situations may take me a few days to fully appropriate the ministry of Jesus to heal. This is my own shortcoming.

I think perhaps my soul sometimes wants to be angry for a while and gets in the way of forgiveness and healing. Subconsciously, I may be thinking something like, "don't heal me right now God, I'm not through being angry". Surely, I am the only one with this problem. Seriously, it is truly wonderful to begin each day with a clean slate. The kingdom of God is righteousness, **peace**, and joy in the Holy Spirit.

Having a healed heart free of need driven desires and fears prepares us to continue to seek the kingdom of God. A pure and unadulterated heart will seek only to serve God with the knowledge of the powerful mysteries of the kingdom. Being aligned with God and His universal laws opens the eyes of our understanding that the spirit of wisdom and revelation may enlighten us to know the exceeding greatness of His mighty power. *(Ephesians 1:17-19).*

# CHAPTER 24

## UNIVERSAL LAWS

> **God has established unchanging laws that govern all of His creation.**
>
> **The effects of these laws are predictable, do not vary, and are the same for everyone.**
>
> **Only God who made the universal laws can change or overrule them.**

Men study the effects of these laws and refer to them as laws of **science** or **nature**. The laws less understood by man, and not definable as science or nature, may be referred to as mysteries or **mystical laws.**

Secular education is the study of the effects of the universal laws. We call these studies "physics, biology, botany, chemistry, psychology," etc. Men combine and arrange this knowledge into logical systems of study to accomplish specific goals or works. These systems of study may be called "engineering, agriculture, medicine, electronics", etc.

If we are to succeed in our life, and walk in the kingdom-of-God lifestyle, we must work with the universal laws of God. Our every endeavor must be aligned with and in accord with these laws, or they will come to failure. Being aligned with universal laws and in accord with God's plan assures good success in our life experience.

Natural man seeks to achieve success by using his intellect to devise systems for working with the universal laws of God. To the degree that he is able to understand and align with these universal laws, he succeeds. However, because natural man's understanding of the universal laws is always incomplete, especially of the "mystery" laws, he never totally succeeds, and is always searching.

The laws, themselves, cannot be seen, for they are spirit. They originate in God, who is spirit, and emanate from Him as spiritual energy. In John 3:8, Jesus compares spiritual things to wind. You can hear and see its effects, but you can't see the wind and can't tell where it comes from or where it goes to. All true science researched to its deepest origin disappears into the spiritual and can be investigated no further by natural man. It becomes a mystery and can be understood only by spiritual revelation from God. Things that appear supernatural may be very natural according to the mystery or spiritual laws.

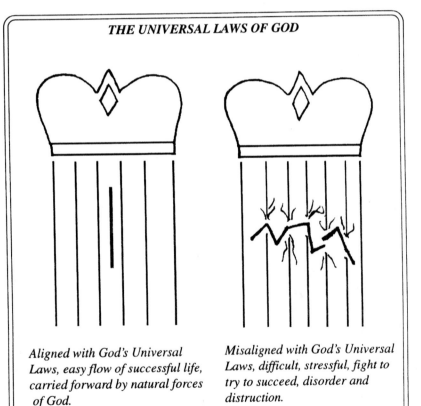

*THE UNIVERSAL LAWS OF GOD*

*Aligned with God's Universal Laws, easy flow of successful life, carried forward by natural forces of God.*

*Misaligned with God's Universal Laws, difficult, stressful, fight to try to succeed, disorder and distruction.*

An example of one of these mysteries is the "seed". How the living pattern of an oak tree—with all its limbs, life systems, bark and leaf definitions and majestic shape—is stored up in the simple light-brown matter of an acorn, is more than intellect can fathom.

Another example is found in the basic function of cell multiplication. A recent biology textbook might say something like, "The cells decide to divide and do so," which simply means "we don't have the foggiest idea why cells divide and multiply". Let's look at the atom as another example. Energy somehow changes form and becomes matter. How does energy get changed into electrons, protons, and neutrons? Where did the energy come from, and who gave the command for it to change its form?

The universal laws were spoken forth by, and continue to emanate from, the Spirit, Almighty God. All creation came into being and continues to exist by the intelligent design and released power of the spiritual, triune God.

*Hebrews 11:3: By faith we understand that **the worlds were framed by the word of God,** so that the **things which are seen were not made of things which are visible.***

*Colossians 1:16-19: For **by Him (Jesus) all things were created** that are in heaven and that are on earth, visible and invisible, whether thrones or dominions or principalities or powers. **All things were created through Him** and for Him. And He is before all things, and **in Him all things consist.** And He is the head of the body, the church, who is the beginning, the firstborn from the dead, that in all things He might have preeminence. For it pleased the Father that in Him all the fullness should dwell.*

*Hebrews 1:2-3: ...has in these last days spoken to us by His Son, whom He has appointed heir of all things, **through whom also He made the worlds;** who being the brightness of His glory and the express image of His person, and **upholding all things by the word of His power...***

Jesus fully understands the universal laws, including the mystery laws, and has complete power over them. We have potential access to Jesus and His understanding and power through the Holy Spirit. As Jesus lives in us, and we are led by the Spirit, we can prosper accordingly. Jesus demonstrated His authority over universal law as He raised the dead, healed the deformed, healed the sick and the blind with a word or a touch. How many laws of science and nature bowed to the Master as He walked on the churning sea, or, with a word, quieted the raging storm?

Jesus demonstrated His understanding of all things as He spoke forth fathomless, wisdom-of-kingdom principles, and the unraveling of mysteries in simple stories about ordinary things. The riches and the depths of wisdom are yet being revealed from these simple parables. Unlocking this wisdom and applying it in our life can be very productive.

God, unlike man, has perfect understanding of all His universal laws. He has given us **rules or instruction,** which, if followed or obeyed, will cause us to be aligned with His universal laws, even if we don't understand the universal law. Specific rules are usually given for children or those who, for lack of wisdom, cannot yet understand the greater principles. And therefore, they cannot, by reason, apply them to their decision-making processes. In the Old Testament, rules or instructional laws were given, which, if obeyed, caused the people to be successful and to prosper in their lives.

For example, the old testament people of God were told not to eat the fat of the meat. They knew nothing of cholesterol or any of the other potential health hazards of eating fat. But if they obeyed the instruction, they prospered. They were also told to rest the land every seventh year, which allowed it to replenish itself. Again, they may not have understood all about fertilizers, etc. But if they adhered to the instructional law, they were more prosperous. They were also instructed not to closely intermarry. Surely they did not understand genetics, but God did.

*Joshua 1:7: "Only be strong and very courageous, that you may observe to **do according to all the law** which Moses My servant commanded you; do not turn from it to the right hand or to the left, **that you may prosper** wherever you go."*

The instructions from God are not for the purpose of limiting our fun or preventing us from gaining wealth. On the contrary, the rules of God are the key to our success. They will bring us into alignment with the universal laws and enable us to really enjoy life. The life of obeying God is a most exciting and prosperous adventure, characterized by inner peace, real joy, and the fruits of righteousness.

In the New Testament, Jesus explains the instructions more clearly. He gives more in-depth understanding of the intent of the rules. He teaches principles which, if understood and obeyed, will bring us to real success and prosperity in all areas of life. He speaks of a purity, a righteousness that exceeds rule-keeping and flows naturally from a power source of inner love for God and man. He speaks clearly of a self-sacrificing lifestyle and a deeper level of commitment, which leads to abundant life. He also speaks clearly, as He directly commands us to love one another, love our enemies and love God with all our heart. He also speaks plainly of the hatred of the world coming against us.

Yet the deep and great mysteries regarding the rule and dominion of earth are spoken figuratively and in parables that can be received only by spiritual revelation. The great understanding of how to flow and work with God's universal laws, some of the most valuable instructions of the kingdom of God, are veiled in symbolic language and appear as foolishness to the natural man.

By the gift of the Holy Spirit, the spiritual man can receive the revelation of Jesus the Christ and His kingdom principles which will align him with universal law and produce good success in his life.

*Ephesians 1:17-19: ...that the God of our Lord Jesus Christ, the Father of glory, may give to you **the spirit of wisdom and revelation** in the knowledge of Him, **the eyes of your understanding being enlightened; that you may know** what is the hope of His calling, what are the riches of the glory of His inheritance in the saints, and what is the **exceeding greatness of His power toward us who believe,** according to the workings of **His mighty power.***

Our receiving Jesus' revelation of the kingdom of God can bring us practical keys and principles. These keys and principles can help us determine every situation in such a way as to bring us to an abundant, victorious, overcoming, and successful life. Few men, if any, have fully tapped into the revelation of kingdom living, but all who have come close find that all things are becoming possible to them, and success is their normal way of life. They also find that they are misunderstood and misjudged by those who have not yet begun to hear and apply kingdom principles.

We are about to attempt to reach into and touch the ancient wisdom of God—the deeper, hidden mysteries of the kingdom of God. It is the knowledge of this wisdom that makes the difference between the extraordinary and the ordinary. Probably all of us have wondered at some time why some men achieve great success and higher levels of accomplishment than we can even think—while others with equal or perhaps even greater natural ability, struggle desperately for very meager prosperity. Not everyone will hear the kingdom principles that can transform their lives from the ordinary to the extraordinary, that can bring them to levels of prosperity they have not even dreamed of.

**"He who has ears to hear, let him hear!"**

# CHAPTER 25

## THE GREATEST MYSTERY

There are many great understandings from the Word of God. There is wisdom beyond man's knowledge or ability to comprehend, thoughts that are simply too great for our minds to think. There are mysteries too deep for our mentality to embrace, and revelations too high to fit into words. Yet the Spirit of God relates to the spirit of man things hard to be understood, and even harder to be spoken. Sometimes they are more **felt** in the depth of our inner being than understood by our mind. They are spiritual things, communicated from the Spirit to the spirit in spiritual ways, comparing spiritual things to spiritual things.

*1 Corinthians 2:6-10,12-13: However, we speak wisdom among those who are mature, yet not the wisdom of this age, nor of the rulers of this age, who are coming to nothing. But we speak the **wisdom of God in a mystery**, the **hidden wisdom** which God ordained before the ages of glory, which none of the rulers of this age knew; for had they known, they would not have crucified the Lord of glory.*

*But as it is written: "Eye has not seen, nor ear heard, nor have entered into the heart of man the things which God has prepared for those who love Him." **But God has revealed them to us through His Spirit.** For the Spirit searches all things, yes, **the <u>deep</u> things of God.***

*Now we have received, not the spirit of the world, but the spirit who is from God, that we might know the things that have been freely given to us by God. These things we also speak not in words which man's wisdom teaches, but which the Holy Spirit teaches, **comparing spiritual things with spiritual.***

Sometimes the best we can do to communicate spiritual things in natural language is to speak of a parallel natural thing. Jesus taught the greatest concept of the Bible, (the kingdom of God, from heaven, on earth), with many parables of natural things. **The kingdom is the greatest doctrine in the Word of God.** All other teachings and understandings in the Bible relate to and are in some way a part of the great concept of the kingdom of God - kingdom of heaven.

Within the kingdom, there is one greatest of all kingdom principles—one greatest spiritual mystery law, one greatest of all kingdom concepts that saturates the entire kingdom, and every other principle or law of the kingdom. It is the force that draws and holds the kingdom together, the glue that bonds the kingdom into unity. It is the motivation for every work in the kingdom. It is the power that causes all other kingdom principles to work. It is the root of righteousness, obedience, peace, and joy, the reason for the cross, the resurrection, and Pentecost. It causes purity, purpose, production, prosperity, contentment, and faithfulness. It causes men to become faithful servants, and stewards. It can change the harlot or adulteress into a purified bride. It is the source of grace, mercy and forgiveness.

This greatest thing in the kingdom can be easily named, but cannot, with man's words, be explained. It must be experienced and felt, Spirit-to-spirit. The most passionate, intense, and pleasurable natural experience cannot equal it. We can see and say what it does. But, what it is, or why it is, goes beyond human natural understanding.

**The greatest mystery law, principle, concept, understanding, of the kingdom—the predominate force and most significant factor in the kingdom of God is:**

## THE LOVE OF GOD.

Without the love of God, there would be no salvation for mankind. Jesus would not have come to earth. There would be no cross, no resurrection, no indwelling Holy Spirit, no righteousness, no peace or joy on earth, no forgiveness, no deliverance, no healing of the heart, no reason for living, no relationship between man and the living God, no drawing force establishing God's kingdom on earth. Apart from the love of God, there is no kingdom of God, from heaven, on earth. Yet, who can describe what the love of God is?

*John 3:16: "**For God so loved** the world that He gave His only begotten Son, that whoever believes in Him should not perish but have everlasting life."*

*Matthew 22:36-40: "Teacher, which is the **great commandment** in the law?" Jesus said to him, "**You shall love the Lord your God with all your heart, with all your soul, and with all your mind.** This is the first and great commandment. And the second is like it: **You shall love your neighbor as yourself.** On these two commandments hang all the Law and the Prophets."*

Many people know of the love of God, but there may be few who really know the love of God in a personal way. Many may be heard to voice a desire to know God and to know Him better. To know God is to know love. "God is love". The spiritual union and intimacy of knowing (experiencing) the love of God is the greatest fulfillment in life. Earthly accomplishments and human desires all fade into the distance. The highest highs of life pale in the rapture of experiencing His love. There is nothing one would not do, nothing one would not give, to please Him. The only fear is the fear of disappointing Him. The heart's greatest desire is to hear His voice and to do His bidding; to be pleasing in His sight.

The intense love between a man and a woman is a natural parallel to the love of God. In the Bible, the Song of Solomon is an expression of spiritual love in natural terms. Anyone who has ever really been in love with someone knows to some degree the feelings of loving God. A man in love will do anything to be with the one he loves. When they are apart, a deep aching and longing fills his chest. Only embracing her and pressing her against his chest will stop the ache and fill the longing. Her every characteristic, even her flaws, seem intensely beautiful and desirable to him. He will look deep into her eyes and say, "I will change the whole world for you. I will climb the highest mountain, defeat the fiercest enemy for you." They kiss and she melts in his arms and replies, "I am yours forever. I will serve you with my whole heart; only, please, never leave me nor forsake me." He promises, "I will never leave you nor forsake you."

The world may have difficulty in understanding why one in love with God will leave the activities and things of the world to be with Jesus. Religious people, with their rules and strife, may demand for the person in love with Jesus to be more involved with their religious activity. They may never understand why their ceremonies mean so little to the one who is personally experiencing the loving presence of God.

We love God because he first loved us. **But, why does he love us so!?**

The love of God is **love from God** and **love for God.** The love of God flows toward us from God through Jesus. The Holy Spirit in us produces love from within us that flows toward God through Jesus. We feel intense love <u>from</u> Jesus, and we feel intense love <u>for</u> Jesus. We are passionately and desperately in love with Jesus.

This **love motivates us to purity.** Our desires are to be, to have, and to do, according to His will. No other needs drive us. He is all we need. His will and ways are always righteous obedience to the Father.

## LOVE PURIFIES

**This greatest mystery of love changes harlotry to purity. Love Purifies - Unlove Putrefies.** The love of Jesus can change a rebellious, adulterous bride into a faithful, purified bride without spot or blemish. Jesus, by the love relationship, becomes one flesh with His bride and is manifest in her so that His life becomes flesh on the earth. As His presence appears within us and is revealed through us, we become like Him; we are purified.

*Ephesians 5:25-27,29-32: Husbands, **love** your wives, just as **Christ also loved the church and gave Himself for it that He might sanctify and cleanse it** with the washing of water by the word, that He might present it to Himself a glorious church, not having spot or wrinkle or any such thing, but that it should be **holy and without blemish** .*

*For no one ever hated **his own flesh**, but nourishes and cherishes it, **just as the Lord does the church. For we are members of His body,** of His flesh and of His bones. For this reason a man shall leave his father and mother and be joined to his wife, and **the two shall become one flesh.** This is a **great mystery**, but I speak concerning Christ and the church.*

*1 John 4:7-9: Beloved let us love one another, for love is of God; and everyone who loves is born of God and knows God. He who does not love does not know God, for **God is love.** In this the love of God was manifested toward us, that God has sent His only begotten Son into the world, that we might live through Him.*

*1 John 4:12b-13,16,19: If **we love one another**, God abides in us, and His love has been perfected in us. By this we know that we abide in Him. and He in us, because He has given us of His Spirit. And we have known and believed the love that God has for us. **God is love, and he who abides in love abides in God, and God in him. We love Him because He first loved us.***

*1 John 3:7-8: Little children, let no one deceive you, He who practices righteousness is righteous, just as He is righteous. He who sins is of the devil, for the devil has sinned from the beginning. **For this purpose the Son of God was manifested, that He might destroy the works of the devil.***

We practice righteousness as Jesus is manifested in us to destroy the works of the devil. The intense feelings of love empower us to turn from sin, and the works of the enemy are destroyed, as we produce the righteousness of God. We love our brother as Jesus' love is manifested in us. The love for our brother causes us to seek his betterment. We become his servant. This love draws together those who are of Jesus; but it may cause those who are of the world to despise us.

### LOVE SERVES

The love of Jesus will manifest in us—in deed, and not just in words. We will lay down our lives for our brothers. We will **seek to provide** for our brothers' needs. The love of Jesus coming forth in us will cause us to **serve one another.** We become humble servants and not proud rulers. We keep His commandments to love God and love one another.

*Galatians 5:13-14: For you brethren, have been called to liberty; only do not use liberty as an opportunity for the flesh, but **through love - serve one another.** For all the law is fulfilled in one word, even in this: You shall love your neighbor as yourself.*

### LOVE ORDERS

Love is the greatest motivational force. By the law of love, all things work together and are held together in unity. **Love produces unity; unity produces order.** Order causes increase in the **production** of life as the energies of life are focused in one direction, working together and leading to **prosperity.** Cooperation increases production. Competition decreases production.

*Ephesians 4:2-3: ...with all lowliness and gentleness, with longsuffering, **bearing with one another in love, endeavoring to keep the unity** of the Spirit in the bond of peace.*

*Colossians 2:2-3: ...that their hearts may be encouraged, being knit together in love, and **attaining to all riches** of the full assurance of understanding, to the knowledge of the **mystery of God**, both of the Father and of Christ, in whom are hidden all the **treasures** of **wisdom** and **knowledge**.*

*Colossians 2:5b: ...rejoicing to see your good order and the steadfastness of your faith in Christ.*

*Galatians 5:14-15: For all the law is fulfilled in one word, even in this: You shall love your neighbor as yourself. **But if you bite and devour one another, beware lest you be <u>consumed</u> by one another!***

Unlove produces disunity-disorder-no production-then poverty. Disunity always leads to poverty and death. The energies of life are consumed as competition causes energies to be applied toward each other—either pushing against, or resisting the push. Energy cannot be applied in a positive direction when it is being applied toward another and neutralized by the resisting force. It would be much like two cars facing each other with their front bumpers pushing against each other. Each car might produce two-hundred horse power of energy. The net result of their combined energy would be zero. Each one would neutralize the power of the other one. The cars would soon destroy themselves. A house divided against itself cannot stand. If, however, they both turned in one direction, the result would be four-hundred horse power of production.

If we have love for the brethren, both in **deed** and in truth, then our **hearts are assured** within us and do not condemn us. We have great confidence or **faith** toward God, and we will have what we ask of Him. We are truly born of God and overcome the world by our faith. The love of God, in deed and truth, provides an atmosphere of assurance, in which **faith works. Even faith, which is the second greatest kingdom law, works by love.**

*Ephesians 23:18-19,21-29a: My little Children, let us not love in word or in tongue, but in **deed** and in truth. And by this we know that we are of the truth, and shall assure our hearts before Him. Beloved, if our heart*

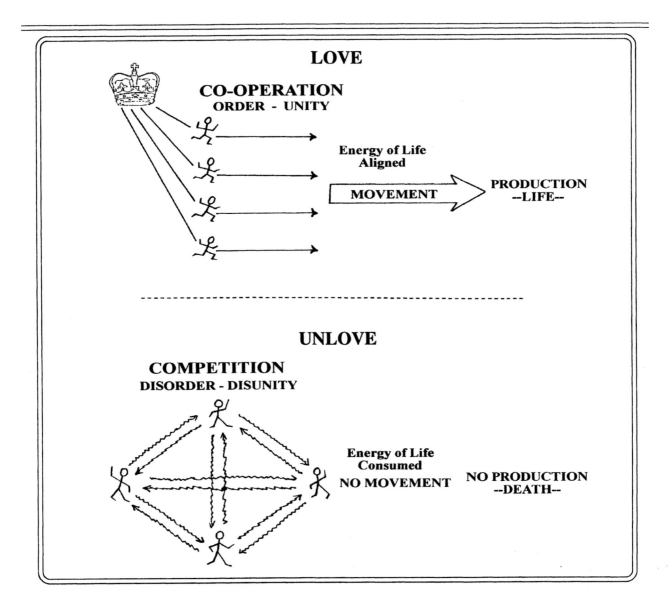

**LOVE**

**CO-OPERATION**
ORDER - UNITY

Energy of Life
Aligned

MOVEMENT

PRODUCTION
--LIFE--

**UNLOVE**

**COMPETITION**
DISORDER - DISUNITY

Energy of Life
Consumed

NO MOVEMENT

NO PRODUCTION
--DEATH--

*does not condemn us, we have confidence (faith) toward God. And whatever we ask, we receive from Him.*

*Galatians 5:6 Amp.: For [if we are] in Christ Jesus, neither circumcision nor uncircumcision counts for anything, but only faith activated and energized and expressed and working through love. (Faith worketh by love.)*

### LOVE PROVIDES

Love causes us to desire to serve others. We serve Jesus as we serve mankind by providing for peoples' needs. We are able to do a good job of providing because love has ordered our lives, and cooperation enables greater production.

In the parable of the sheep and the goats, the only factor considered by the Lord in making the division is whether or not the people had provided for the needs of the brethren. *Matthew 25:31-46.* Those who had were told to come inherit the kingdom. Those who had not, did not enter the kingdom but were sent away into punishment. Because they were providing for others' needs, Jesus could know that the love of God was in them.

No one can provide food for the hungry or clothes for the naked unless they have first acquired food and clothing. We cannot supply what we do not have. One must grow and process food; one must obtain fiber, process it into cloth, and then sew it into clothing. Or, one must, through production of some sort, obtain the money to pay others to do the work by buying the food and clothing from them. Obviously, the sheep in this parable were involved in industry, the production and distribution of goods and services.

## LOVE PROSPERS

The kingdom principle here is greater than just giving away some of our surplus to the needy. The principle is that, because of the love of God, we desire to serve, and thus our lives become productive in providing for others. The more our love leads us to provide, the more we will reap. The law of sowing and reaping never fails. The more we provide, the more we will have. Our needs will be provided for, and we will have more to provide to the brethren. The more we are producing and providing for the brethren, the more people will be required to help. This means gainful employment for more people. Jobs are created as the love of God creates a desire to serve others by providing for their needs.

The sheep who serve by meeting the needs of the brethren inherit the kingdom-of-God quality of life (true prosperity). The goats who do not serve by meeting the needs of the brethren have only punishment (real poverty).

The thing that divides the sheep from the goats is not just their belief in Jesus. The sheep inherited the kingdom of God because they produced. They met the needs of the brethren. **Love motivated them** to cooperate with and serve the brethren. The goats were motivated by unlove to use what they had only for themselves.

The goats exist in everlasting punishment **now** and **later.** The sheep live in eternal life **now** and **forever.** Remember, eternal life is not just length of existence; it is a quality of life; even the goats exist forever. **Death is separation from God. Life is the presence of God.** The kingdom-of-God lifestyle is abundant life, eternal life, now and forever.

**Am I a servant?**

**How do I serve God?**

**How much do I serve God?**

## LOVE RULES

*Matthew 24:45-47:* *"Who then is a **faithful and wise servant,** whom his master made **ruler over his household,** to give them food in due season? Blessed is that servant whom his master, when he comes, will find so doing. Assuredly, I say to you that he will make him **ruler over all his goods."***

A faithful and wise servant who does a good job of providing for the needs of other servants will be made ruler over his Master's goods. His Master's goods include things like money, houses, farms, businesses, ministries, etc.

A faithful servant becomes ruler of his Master's household to give them food at the proper time. **Love** motivates the faithful servant to rule with kindness and to see that needs are met promptly.

*Matthew 20:95-28:* *But Jesus called them to Himself and said, "You know that the rulers of the Gentiles lord it over them, and those who are great exercise authority over them. Yet it Shall not be so among, you; but whoever desires to become **great** among you, let him be your **servant.** And whoever desires to he first among you, let him be your servant - just as the Son of Man did not come to be served, but to serve, and to give His life a ransom for many."*

Rulers are servants in the sense that they provide service to others. They must give more of their strength, time, and talent, to meet the needs of others. They must shoulder more responsiblilty. They must carry the heavy burdens of meeting others needs. The more we serve, the more we rule. The more needs we meet, the more authority and responsibility we will be given, and the more prosperous we will become.

When we hear the term servant, we may tend to think of a fawning, cringing, subservient person, performing the most menial insignificant task. A servant is a person who provides service. A great servant is one who provides a great service. The kingdom principle is that the one who provides the greatest service is the ruler. Jesus provided the greatest service that could ever be provided for mankind. He gave His live a ransom for many. Jesus is the ruler of all God's creation. He is the greatest person of all creation, the greatest servant of all time and eternity.

Which of these two provides the greatest service: a businessman who builds a chain of hospitals, or a nurse's aid who comforts patients in one of the hospitals? Both are very necessary services, but who is really doing the greater service to mankind? The Lord will not forget any service; even a cup of cool water will not go unrewarded by Him. Yet, which will receive the greater reaping from his service? Which paid the greater price? Which of the two has given the most? Which must have the greater wisdom and understanding? Which bears the greater load of responsibility? Which then is providing the most service to mankind?

The businessman who saw the need of many people for a local hospital and **invested what he had** to meet that need is providing more service to more people and subsequently will reap more. **Our prosperity begins with feeling the hunger of the hungry and the nakedness of the naked and doing something about it.** The more authority we have, the more potential we have to do something about it. Thus, "to him who has, more will be given."

$$\text{(Service)} = \text{(Gain)} \quad - \quad S = G \quad - \quad 10S = 10G$$
$$- \quad 100S = 100G$$

Should we then serve to gain, or should we serve to give? If we are serving to get or gain, we will be ready to receive our wages and could become frustrated or demanding if they are delayed. If however, we are truly serving as unto the Lord, we can leave the gain up to Him. Can we trust Him enough to serve Him and leave the gain (the pay) to Him? If we can, we are God-serving, anything else may be mixed with self-serving. Our attitude should be that we are just doing our duty out of love for our Lord.

*Luke 17:7-10: "And which of you, having a servant plowing or tending sheep, will say to him when he has come in from the field, 'Come at once and sit down to eat'? But will he not rather say to him, 'Prepare something for my supper, and gird yourself and serve me till I have eaten and drunk, and afterward you will eat and drink'? Does he thank that servant because he did the things that were commanded him? I think not. So likewise you, when you have done all those things which you are commanded, say 'We are unprofitable servants. We have done what was our duty to do.'"*

## LOVE IS CONTENT

Although love motivates us to serve more by giving more—which means we must acquire more to give—love also causes us to be content with what we have. We know that the Lord is our source and our strength. **Our contentment does not rest in what we have, but in Who we have.**

Before the Lord can give us more, **we must be content** with what we have, where we are right now. As servants of God and soldiers in His army, we must be content with our wages.

*Luke 3:14: Likewise the soldiers asked him, saying, "And what shall we do?" So he said to them, "Do not intimidate anyone or accuse falsely, and be content with your wages."*

*Philippians 4:11: Not that I speak in regard to need, for I have learned in whatever state I am, to be content.*

*Hebrews 13:5: Let your conduct be without covetousness, and be content with such things as you have. For He Himself has said, "I will never leave you nor forsake you."*

**Materialism (covetousness or self-seeking) is the desire for more than I already have; it is reaching for more.**

**Materialism (covetousness or self-seeking) is NOT possessing wealth. It is NOT acquiring wealth. It is NOT making a profit. Money is NOT the root of evil; the LOVE of money is.**

*Matthew 6:33: "But seek first the kingdom of God and His righteousness, and all these things shall be added to you."*

*1 Timothy 6:5-8: ...useless wranglings of men of corrupt minds and destitute of the truth, who suppose that godliness is a means of gain. From such withdraw yourself. But godliness with contentment is great gain. For we brought nothing into this world, and it is certain we can carry nothing out. And having food and clothing, with these we shall be <u>content.</u>*

**Godliness** (God-seeking, God-serving) **is righteous obedience to God** which aligns us with His universal laws and purpose. **Contentment is not desiring more than I already have.**

**Godliness + Contentment = Great Gain . —
G+C=GG**

**The materialist (coveter or self-seeker) can never keep or enjoy wealth.**

*1 Timothy 6:9-11: But those **who desire to be rich** fall into temptation and a snare, and into many foolish and harmful lusts which drown men in destruction and perdition. For the **love of money** is a root of all kinds of evil, for which some have strayed from the faith in their greediness, and pierced themselves through with many sorrows. But you O man of God, flee these things and pursue righteousness, godliness, faith, love, patience, gentleness.*

*James 5:1-3: Come now, you rich, weep and howl for your miseries that are coming upon you! Your riches are corrupted, and your garments are **moth-eaten**. Your gold and silver are **corroded**, and their corrosion will be a witness against you and will eat your flesh like fire. You have heaped up treasure in the last days.*

"Rich" is a relative term. Many of you reading this would probably be considered rich by a brother in one of the third-world nations. If you ask a man with one million dollars, "Are you rich?", he would probably say, "No, I'm not rich," and would point toward the man with more and say, "He's rich." A rich man is one who owns **any amount** of wealth that is not given over to God's control for His use.

Garments that are being worn do not become moth-eaten; gold and silver coins that are being used do not corrode. Riches that are being used to meet the needs of mankind (according to God's direction) will not destroy the one who possesses them. If our lives are wholly given over to God's control, all of our possessions will be His and will be used in His kingdom. In a very real sense, no matter how much God has placed in our possession, we have no riches. They all belong one hundred percent to God.

*Ecclesiastes 5:10,13: He who loves silver **will not be satisfied** with silver; nor he who loves abundance, with increase. This also is vanity. There is a severe evil which*

*I have seen under the sun: **Riches kept for their owner to his hurt.***

*Luke 18:24b: "How hard it is for those who **have riches** to enter the kingdom of God."*

*Psalm 37:7-11,25,35-36: Rest in the Lord, and wait patiently for Him; do not fret because of him who prospers in his way, because of the man who brings wicked schemes to pass. Cease from anger, and forsake wrath: do not fret—it only causes harm.*

*For evildoers shall be cut off; but those who wait on the Lord, they shall inherit the earth. For yet a little while and the wicked shall be no more; indeed, you will look diligently for his place, but it shall be no more. But the meek shall inherit the earth, and shall delight themselves in the abundance of peace. I have been young, and now am old; yet I have not seen the righteous forsaken, nor his descendants begging bread.*

*I have seen the wicked in great power, and spreading himself like a native green tree. Yet he passed away, and behold, he was no more; indeed I sought him, but he could not be found.*

**Only the God-seeking, God-serving person can enjoy wealth.**

**We do not seek wealth. We become wealthy while seeking to serve.** We do not hold back any part for ourselves. But because of our obedience, He will give us a portion as our own just to enjoy. He will give us the power to eat of it and to rejoice. We must seek His direction for His goods at all times.

*Proverbs 10:22: The blessing of the Lord makes one rich, and He adds no sorrow with it.*

*Proverbs 13:22: "A good man leaves an inheritance to his children's children, but the **wealth of the sinner is stored up for the righteous.***

*Ecclesiastes 5:19: As for every man to whom God has given riches and wealth, and given him power to eat of it, to receive his heritage and rejoice in his labor- this is the gift of God.*

*1 Timothy 6:17: Command those who are rich in this present age not to be haughty, nor to trust in uncertain riches but in the living God, who gives us richly all things to **enjoy.***

God desires for His people to possess the earth with all its abundance and rule it for Him. He will give us power to get wealth, to take over the kingdoms of Earth, and He will give us enjoyment as we manage His goods.

## LOVE STEWARDS

**We must be managers of God's goods and not owners.**

*Luke 19:12-13,16-20,22a,24-26: "A certain nobleman went into a far country to receive for himself a kingdom and to return. So he called ten of his servants, delivered to them ten minas, and said to them, 'Do business till I come.'*

*"Then came the first, saying, 'Master, your mina has earned ten minas.' And he said to him, 'Well done, good servant; because you were faithful in a very little, have authority over ten cities.' And the second came, saying, 'Master, your mina has earned five minas.' Likewise he said to him, 'You also be over five cities.'*

*"And another came, saying 'Master, here is your mina, which I have kept put away in a handkerchief.' And the master said to him, 'Out of your own mouth I will judge you, you wicked servant.' And he said to those who stood by 'Take the mina from him, and give it to him who has ten minas' But they said to him, ' Master, he has ten minas.'*

*"For I say to you, that to everyone who has more will be given; and from him who does not have, even what he has will be taken away from him."*

*Matthew 25:14-15,19-21,24a,25-26a,28,30: "For the kingdom of heaven is like a man traveling to a far country, who called his own servants and delivered his goods to them. And to one he gave five talents, to another two, and to another one, to each according to his own ability; and immediately he went on a journey.*

*"After a long time the lord of those servants came and settled accounts with them. So he who had received five talents came and brought five other talents, saying, 'Lord, you delivered to me five talents; look, I have gained five more talents besides them.' His lord said to him, 'Well done, good and faithful servant; you were faithful over a few things, I will make you ruler over many things. Enter into the joy of your lord.'*

*"Then he who had received the one talent came and said, '...and I was afraid, and went and hid your talent in the ground. Look, there you have what is yours.' But his lord answered and said to him, 'You wicked and lazy servant...' Therefore take the talent from him, and give it to him who has ten talents. ...And cast the unprofitable servant into the outer darkness. There will be weeping and gnashing of teeth.'"*

We are given the Master's money to **do business** with until he calls for it. If we manage His money in alignment with kingdom principles, we will have a good report at our accounting time. The most profitable way to do business is according to kingdom principles.

There are many principles to be considered, and there are always balancing principles in God's kingdom. Before we take a giant leap based on a principle, we are well-advised to search out and understand the balancing principles as well. Understanding God's kingdom-principles will help us to hear His direction for our lives more perfectly. **Principles are a "road" for us to hear on. But we must hear God's direction.**

One of the major principles is to **use money to do good.** If we can **put money to work creating activity** (commerce, industry, etc.) **which will put people to work meeting each other's needs,** then we are headed in the direction of prosperity. We will do more long-term good by this type of investing, than we would have done by giving away all the money to meet an immediate need.

**What we do with the money that we have is more important than how much money we make.** How we use what we have today determines what we will have tomorrow. Many of us have not understood that God gave us money to use to do business. We thought it was all for us to use for our own desires and needs. We have thrown away our financial future by increasing our lifestyle just because we had more money. We've used money to make us feel better. Babylon's business pattern is to "get all you can, and can all you get".

*Luke 16: 9-13: "And I say to you, make friends for yourselves by unrighteous mammon (money), that when you fail, they may receive you into everlasting habitations. He who is faithful in what is least (money) is faithful also in much; and he who is unjust in what is least is unjust also in much.*

*"Therefore, if you have not been faithful in the unrighteous mammon, who will commit to your trust the **true riches**? And if you have not been faithful in what is another man's, who will give you what is **your own**?*

*" No servant can serve two masters; for either he will hate the one and love the other, or else he will be loyal to the one and despise the other. **You cannot serve God and mammon.**"*

**Money is the least commodity in the kingdom**. We must be faithful with the least (money) before we can be trusted with true riches (the power and authority of God). We are to make friends of God's people with money. When we are received into the everlasting habitation, we will be welcomed by our friends. Make friends in the kingdom now with money.

**Do a good job with His money and He will give you your own** (that portion for you to use for those nice things God wants you to have). Enter into the joy of the Lord.

**Do not serve money, but serve God with money**. Don't hide it or consume it. Don't give it away when God has not said to; use it to do business. Seek God's direction and further understanding of His principles about how and where to do business.

**If we diligently use all God has given us to serve Him by doing business, we will be given more.** It will be **added** to us. All that we possess should be actively used to meet the needs of mankind, and especially those of the household of faith.

Man has three basic areas of need: those which relate to his spirit, those which relate to his soul (mind, will, and emotions), and those which relate to his body. Anything that we do with the resources God has given us to meet needs in any of these areas is **doing business**. Whether it is preaching the Word, growing potatoes, or teaching physics, if it meets the needs of the brethren, it is doing business in the kingdom of God.

**How am I using what I have to meet the needs of mankind?**

**How diligent am I in using what I have to meet needs?**

**What can I do better to add more value to mankind?**

Start with what you have. Does a warm smile and an encouraging word meet a need in a person's soul? Can a prayer and a thought from the Word meet needs of the spirit of a person? Can doing that **extra** amount on the job with a good attitude meet someone's needs? Does cooperating with the boss and speaking a good word about him meet more needs than complaining and giving a bad report? Consider what you have, what is in your hand, what gifts and talents you have. Then consider and ask God how they may be used to meet the needs of others.

Would investing that extra twenty-five dollars in someone's business or ministry help meet their need for captial so they could meet more needs? Could giving your talents and abilities to help a ministry or kingdom business, help meet needs? Could improving your own skills help you to be able to meet more needs?

In Babylon, people go to school to get more education so that they can get more money, so that they can have the power and things they want. In the kingdom, we sharpen our tools by getting more education and training so that we can meet more and greater needs of others. The more skilled we are, the more we have to give, and the more we will be blessed. The more we are blessed, the more we have to share. Love causes us to make the best we can of ourselves and of what we have.

There is more than one dimension to meeting needs. There is both **quanity** and **quality.** You can meet a little need for a lot of people, or you can meet a great need for a few people. Manufacturing chewing gum can put a good taste in millions of people's mouths; doing brain surgery can greatly impact a few people. The total amount of value added to mankind could be the same. So, if you can't do something big, do a whole lot of the little things that you can do, while seeking to improve your skills so that you can do more.

### LOVE CARES

Not only does love motivate us to serve by doing the business of meeting the needs of others, it also is the **medium** that serves. In **Babylon**, most customers expect to be helped or served by the business person. They do not expect the business person to really care about them. Once people learn that in the **kingdom**, the business person cares about them, and not just about their money, they develop a whole new attitude. If they know that you really care, they will trust you with their business. Whether we are supplying a spiritual need or a physical need, love will cause us to really care about others' interest and well-being. Caring cannot be faked. Eventually, a phony will be spotted.

Love cares about fellow workers, including the boss. Love causes employees to feel a great sense of security and loyalty, because they know the boss has their interest in mind. Love cares about the quality of product or service being provided. Love is the key to increased productivity and efficiency.

## LOVE IS LIFE

We could continue with practical examples of how the love of God causes abundant life. The essence of God's love permeates every aspect of kingdom-life.

First Corinthians, chapter thirteen, gives a picture of what love is and teaches that no matter how great our gifts or works are, they are meaningless without love. Love makes it happen and keeps it in order in the kingdom.

**Love is the greatest secret in the world.** There is no other force or power in the world as great as love. Love will cause us to give up our very lives to the death of all selfishness. Only after love motivates us to die, do we know resurrection life. Just as Jesus gave up His life for others and then was resurrected to a far greater life, we will experience a far greater life now as love motivates us to selflessly serve. Yet the world, for the most part, cannot comprehend the value of the love of God flowing to us and through us.

# NOTES

# CHAPTER 26

## THE SECOND GREATEST MYSTERY
### (THE SEED AND THE EGG )

I just came in from my vegetable garden a moment ago and sat down to write. While in the garden, I picked green beans, dug new potatoes, and pulled some onions. Tomorrow morning I will pull some sweet corn and pick some banana peppers. This spring I planted the seeds for these vegetables in the soil of my garden. Before planting the seed, I spread chicken manure on the soil and tilled the soil. I planted the different kinds of seeds where I wanted them to grow. **I chose the seeds and planted them, but I did not grow them. The <u>soil</u> grew them.** I cannot explain how the seed became a growing, producing plant. Nor can I explain how the soil grew them. But I can go into the garden at harvest time and gather the fruit.

the hard- pressed, wayside soil of the wounded, hardened heart, the stony soil of our fixed preconceived convictions, and the thorny soil of caring for the things of this life. Hopefully we have each dealt with these conditions in each of our own lives. Now, we must receive the greater hidden light: **the revelation of the production of the kingdom of God now on Earth through the good heart-soil.** This is a very great mystery and the focus of this key parable.

If we receive the revelation of this great mystery, we will have the ability to bring forth the fruit (production) of the kingdom of God in our lives and in the world. Nothing will be impossible to us. If, however, we do not understand the mystery of this parable, we may have difficulty receiving revelation from all the parables.

*Mark 4:13: And He said to them, "Do you not understand this parable? How then will you understand all the parables?"*

*Matthew 13:8-13,16-18,23:* **"But others fell on good ground and yielded a crop: some a hundredfold, some sixty, some thirty.** *He who has ears to hear let him hear!"* And the disciples came and said to Him, "Why do You speak to them in parables?" He answered and said to them, **"Because it has been given to you to know the mysteries of the kingdom of heaven,** *but to them it has not been given. For whoever has, to him more will be given, and he will have abundance; but whoever does not have, even what he has will be taken away from him. Therefore I speak to them in parables, because seeing they do not see, and hearing they do*

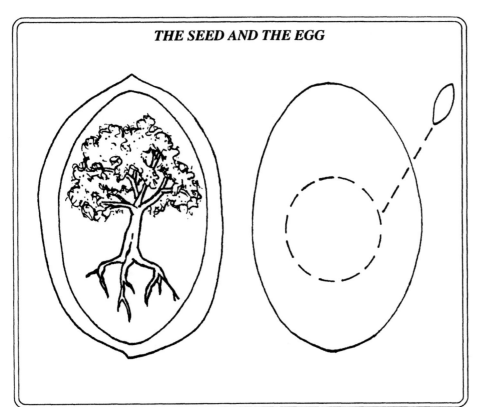

**THE SEED AND THE EGG**

Jesus said the kingdom of God is like my garden. He said the heart of man is the soil that can "grow" the kingdom-of-God seed. We've received a lot of light from the parable of the sower. We've seen the heart-soils that could not grow the kingdom seed to fruition:

*not hear, nor do they understand. But blessed are your eyes for they see, and your ears for they hear; for assuredly, I say to you that many prophets and righteous men desired to see what you see, and did not see it, and to hear what you hear, and did not hear it. Therefore hear the parable of the sower:* **(When anyone hears the word of the kingdom...) But he who received seed on the good ground is he who hears the word (of the kingdom) and understands it, who indeed bears fruit and produces: some a hundredfold, some sixty, some thirty."**

*Mark 4:20:* **"But these are the ones sown on good ground, those who hear the word accept it, and bear fruit: some thirtyfold some sixty, and some a hundred."**

The verses you just read contain one of the greatest hidden mysteries of all life. This great secret is meant to come to light. All hidden mysteries in the Word are to be revealed. Please give great heed to your hearing at this point. Please do not regard these scriptures lightly. Pray for revelation and meditate these verses. Wait upon God, and do not let the powerful truths get by you. You must have an ear to hear. Not everyone will hear the great mystery hidden in these parables. Many great men of God from the past have sought to know and hear these mysteries and could not. The time is now for those who are pure in heart to hear. If there are yet needs and impurities remaining in your heart, the great impact of this revelation will not appear to you. If, however, your once-hardened heart-soil is healed, freed from rocks and thorn bushes, you may hear and continue to hold onto the powerful understanding of the production of the kingdom of heaven on earth. Nothing will be impossible to you.

*Mark 4:21-25: And He said to them, "Is a lamp brought to be put under a basket or under a bed? Is it not to be set on a lampstand? For there is nothing* **hidden** *which will not be* **revealed** *nor has anything been* **kept secret** *but that it should* **come to light.** *If anyone has ears to hear, let him hear."*

*And He said to them,* **"Take heed what you hear.** *With the same measure you use, it will be measured to you; and to you who hear more will be given. For whoever has, to him more will be given; but whoever does not have, even what he has will be taken away from him."*

### The mystery is revealed only to those who are entering the king-dome.

*Luke 8:16-18: "No one, when he has lit a lamp, covers it with a vessel or puts it under a bed, but sets it on a lampstand, that* **those who** <u>**enter**</u> **may see the light.** *For nothing is* **secret** *that will not be* **revealed,** *nor anything* **hidden** *that will not be known and come to* **light.** *Therefore* **take heed how you hear.** *For whoever has, to him more will be given; and whoever does not have, even what he seems to have will be taken from him."*

Prophets and angels desired to hear the great mystery of the kingdom in this parable. **If you are purifying your heart by the revelation (manifestation) of Jesus Christ within you, through the Holy Spirit, to the sincere love** of the brethren, and are receiving the incorruptible **seed,** the **Word** (rhema) of God, you may hear and understand this great mystery.

*Peter 1:10,12,13b,20b: Of this salvation (deliverance)* **the prophets have inquired and searched diligently,** *who prophesied of the grace that would come to you,...To them it was revealed that, not to themselves, but to us they were ministering the things which now have been reported to you through those who have preached the gospel to you by the Holy Spirit sent from heaven—things which* **angels desired to look into.**

*"...rest your hope fully upon the grace that is to be brought to you at the* **revelation** *(or manifestation) of Jesus Christ...* **manifest** *(or revealed) in these last times for you. (***"Christ** <u>**IN YOU**</u> **the hope of glory."** *Eph. 1:28) ("...when He comes (or appears), in that day, to be glorified* <u>**IN**</u> **His saints..."** *2 Thessalonians. 1-10a").*

### Jesus is the Word of God, the Truth, and the Seed of God, sown in our heart-soil, producing the life of Jesus in us, ruling and reigning with us now.

*1 Peter 1:22-23: Since you have* **purified your souls in obeying the truth through the Spirit in the sincere love of the brethren,** *love one another fervently with a* **pure heart,** *having been born again, not of corruptible* **seed** *but incorruptible, through the* **word** *of God which lives and abides forever.*

Jesus Christ is the Word of God, the express image of the Father sent out from God. He was the original mind of creation. It was through Him that all creation was made and by Him all creation continues to exist. Jesus has authority over all creation.

*John 1:1-4,10: In the beginning was the Word, and the Word was with God, and the Word was God. He was in the beginning with God. **All things were made by Him, and without Him nothing was made that was made.** In Him was life, and the life was the light of men. — He was in the world, and the world was made through Him, and the world did not know Him.*

*Colossians 1:16-17: **For by Him (Jesus) all things were created** that are in heaven and that are on earth, visible and invisible, whether thrones or dominions or principalities or powers. **All things were created through Him and for Him. And He is before all things, and in Him all things consist.***

Jesus became the seed, the Word from God, sown into the hearts of men and is reproducing His life in the lives of His people through the Holy Spirit. **Jesus, living in us now, will produce the plan and rule of God on earth. Jesus in us has all authority over creation.** Jesus, planted in the soil of the heart of man, can grow into the abundant, fulfilling, powerful, and peaceful kingdom-of-God life. Jesus, by the Holy Spirit, can enrich our heart-soil with the supernatural, spiritual nutrition of the powers of creation.

The heart soil of man under Jesus' control is the creation center for God on Earth. God can bring forth anything that He desires on Planet Earth through the Jesus-filled child of God. He need only to plant the seed into the yielded, cleansed, and prepared heart of a man or woman, and the natural growth processes will of themselves grow His plan into the earth.

A seed is a living pattern that grows. Only in recent years have scientists begun to learn a little about genetics. It is known that every living organism has something called DNA or genetic coding—an extremely complex series of chemical coding that completely describes and determines the organism. Millions of different genes in different arrangements determine what the organism is, what it will look like, coloring, potential size, intelligence-level potential, and every

characteristic for each individual. A complete living pecan tree is within each pecan. Somehow in the meat of the pecan, which we may choose to crack and eat, is the whole living pecan tree with all its characteristics coded genetically within the seed.

As it is in the natural, so it is in the spiritual. A word from God is a spiritually, genetically-coded seed. It is living and completely defined within the seed or word. As the life within a natural seed is dormant until the seed is planted in the soil, so also a word from God to us is dormant until planted in the soil of our heart. A word from God is a seed (a living pattern that grows). God furnishes the seed; that's His part. Man's part is to plant the seed in good soil. **The seed is a word, a vision, a picture, an idea for changing creation to conform to God's desire.** A seed is a living design from God for changing the earth and things on the earth.

God speaks (sows) His word into the heart of man through the receiver in man's heart (the ear to hear). Thus a word (seed) from the spiritual realm is received into the physical realm, and, if believed, (received and planted) into the heart-soil of man, it can sprout and grow into the physical realm.

## THE EARTH EGG

In addition to growing a garden, I also raise chickens. I gather eggs and select some to put in the incubator. The others are taken to the house and put in the refrigerator to be eaten. When I crack the eggs to put them in a cake or perhaps to scramble some for breakfast, a shapeless glob of clear matter with a round yellow part in the center falls out. The glob has no form and, apparently, no life in it. If, however, that same egg had received a seed from a male chicken and had been placed in my incubator or brooded over by the female chicken, it would have taken on form and identity and become a living, breathing, baby chick, with all kinds of intricate systems for life. It would have eyes to see, a little beak to peck with, dainty feet to walk with, tiny toe nails to scratch with, and even a built in peep-peep.

The chick will grow to be like his father who supplied the seed and his mother who supplied the egg. *("Male and female he created them")*. The egg is a mass of raw material waiting for a seed to define it. If the seed came from a large black rooster, the genetic coding would probably cause the egg to turn into a little black chick, which would grow into a large black chicken. If the rooster had been a small red one, the chick would probably become a small red chicken. The earth and all it contains are like the egg. Without a defining word from God, it is a formless glob. When God speaks a word, multitudes of spiritual, genetic coding is released to bring form and order to the glob of creation. The male part of creation is God's part (the genetically-coded spiritual seed); the female (wife) part is our part (the good soil).

The earth was without form and void. It was like an egg; the raw material was there, but it had no shape, no form, no identification. An egg is just a mass of runny, white stuff and a glob of yellow matter. You may have had one this morning for breakfast—splattered out, and then fried or scrambled. The earth, like an egg, was brooded over by the Holy Spirit, then **GOD SAID.** The word of God (the seed) came, and the earth took on form and intricate systems of life. Multitudes of spiritual, genetic coding came forth as God spoke forth creation.

*Genesis 1:2-3,6,9,11,14,20,24:* **The earth was without form, and void;** *and darkness was on the face of the deep.* **And the Spirit of God was hovering (or brooding) over the face of the waters.** *Then* **GOD SAID,** *"Let there be light", and there was light. Then* **GOD SAID,** *"Let there be a firmament in the midst of the waters, and let it divide the waters from the waters." Then* **GOD SAID,** *"Let the waters under the heavens be gathered together in one place, and let the dry land appear." ...Then* **GOD SAID,** *"Let the earth bring forth grass, the herb that yields seed, and the fruit tree that yields fruit according to its kind, whose seed is in itself, on the earth." ... Then* **GOD SAID,** *"Let there be lights in the firmament of the heavens to divide the day from the night.'" ... Then* **GOD SAID,** *"Let the earth bring forth the living creature according to its kind: cattle and creeping thing and beast of the earth, each according to its kind."*

### Are you hearing the mystery?

Why does one man labor and strive to accomplish things in life, only to end in frustrated failure—while another man, with equal or less ability and opportunity, accomplishes great works in his lifetime. What is the key?

What makes the difference in what our lives become and what we will accomplish in our lifetime?

Why is one man very successful and able to accomplish noble miracles—while another man with equal or greater potential can't seem to accomplish anything of significant value, regardless of how hard he tries?

The answer is not more intelligence, better breaks, noble birth, mere chance, harder work, devious scheming, fate, or any other natural circumstance. Who we are by birth, where we came from, and what breaks we get are not the primary factors that will determine our success in life. The answer will be found in the revelation of the mystery of the natural growth of a thought, (idea, word) in the heart. **It is what we hear.** What we really listen to and believe will shape our life and the world around us. The thoughts that we receive and allow to remain in our hearts will create who we are and what we do, which will determine our destiny in life.

We don't have to know how it works; we don't have to know how it will be done. But we **must** believe what God says. Then the goal He has for our life will grow into being. *"...for it is God who works in you both to will and to do for His good pleasure." Philippians 2:13.*

Who can know how a glob of clear matter in an egg can become a living, breathing being with instincts, intelligence, and personality that can hear, feel, smell, taste, and see. Consider all the tiny organs, nerves, blood vessels, etc., that must be perfectly formed to sustain life. By some miraculous process, the DNA of the seed defines all these things and in only twenty one days, of brooding the transformation is complete. How does the tiny heart begin pumping? What turns it on or starts it up? If you will tell me exactly how all of this happens, I will tell you how a word planted in the heart of man can transform the things of earth.

When we speak of a word, obviously we are not just talking about letters arranged together on a page. A word is a thought, an idea, a vision, or picture. A vision or dream may contain a series of pictures with many thoughts and feelings. When God spoke all growing and living things into being, He had to express an immeasurable amount of minute details. Everything was defined in what he said, the spiritual DNA or genetic coding emanating from Him. A word, thought, idea, or vision is like a seed. It has the power to define life and grow into creation. A word is alive and potentially very powerful if it is received into the heart. The seed must be planted in the soil or in the egg. The Bible calls this process of receiving and planting, **"faith"**.

Every work or accomplishment of man begins with a thought, an idea. Every great building in our vast cities of today began with a thought. Every great church, ministry, business, or any other work of man was, at one time, a seed or word. Without a doubt, every invention, scientific discovery, or work of art began as a thought, an idea, a word.

Jesus, the greatest miracle worker, once said, "The Son can do nothing of Himself, but what He sees the Father do." Where and how did He see the Father doing things? The Father is Spirit. Jesus was in a natural body. He saw by the Spirit within Him. He heard and saw words, visions, and ideas from the Spirit.

# CHAPTER 27

## SUPERNATURAL NATURAL GROWTH

**Well, are you hearing the great mystery yet?** Are you beginning to realize that literally anything you can hear and see in the spirit is possible?. We can do nothing but what is first heard or seen and planted ("faithed"). We cannot build a life. We cannot build a business or a ministry. We must receive good seed in good soil and let the earth grow it. Indeed, this is a great mystery. We will become what we hear, believe, and say. *"As you believe, so be it unto you." "Your faith has made you well." **"If you can believe, all things are possible to him who believes." "With God all things are possible."** "As a man thinks in his heart, so is he."*

*Mark 4:26-32:  And He said, **"The kingdom of God is as if a man should scatter seed on the ground, and should sleep by night and rise by day, and the seed should sprout and grow, he himself does not know how. For the earth yields crops by itself: first the blade, then the head, after that the full grain in the head.** But when the grain ripens, immediately he puts in the sickle, because the harvest has come."*

*And He said, "To what shall we liken the kingdom of God? Or with what parable shall we picture it? It is like a mustard seed which, when it is sown on the ground, is smaller than all the seeds on earth; but when*

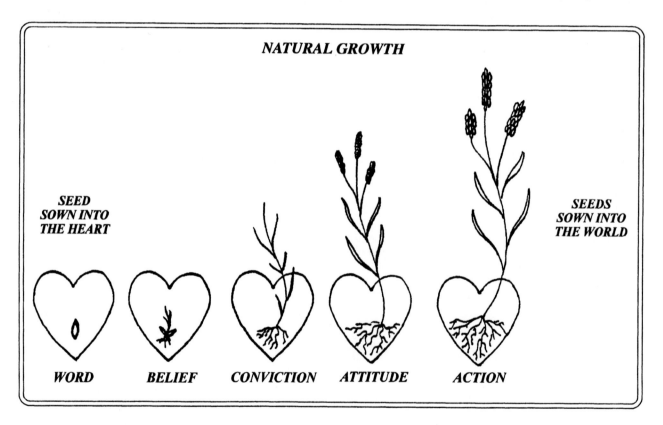

A **word** (seed) planted in our heart-soil becomes a **belief** as it sprouts; the belief becomes a **conviction** as it grows a blade; a conviction becomes our **attitude** as it grows a head; and finally our attitudes become our **actions** as the full grain in the head, seeds (words) sown into the world.

*it is sown,  it grows up and becomes greater than all herbs, and shoots out large branches, so that the birds of the air can nest under its shade."*

*1 Corinthians 3:6:  I planted, Apollos watered, but **God gave the increase.***

*Psalm 127:1-2: Unless **the Lord builds the house,** they labor in vain who build it; unless the Lord guards the city, the watchman stays awake in vain. It is vain for you to rise up early, to sit up late, to eat the bread of sorrows; for so He gives His beloved sleep.*

The heart of man is the **spiritual/physical interface.** Spirit God, and physical earth meet in the heart of man. The pure heart of man is like a fruitful garden; it receives the seed from God, and it grows by a natural process of God. *("The earth yields crops by itself.")* The soil must be moistened and protected by the life-giving brooding of the Holy Spirit.

The pure heart of man is God's production center on earth that fills the world with God's plan and rule. Only the pure heart of man is the wife of God, capable of **intimately relating** to Him, receiving seed from Him and giving birth to God's plan and rule into the earth. If we love God, we will intimately relate to Him and will receive His seed. We will be pregnant with God's plan. If, however, we love the world, <u>its</u> seeds will be planted in us.

Things in the world are changed by the process of the seed and natural growth. We cannot change our character and actions by trying. Trying to stop doing something we want to do, or trying to start doing something we do not want to do, will not make permanent changes. We must change what we hear, what we think, and believe. We must receive new seed!

*Luke 8:15: But the ones that fell on the good ground are those who, having heard the word with **a noble and good heart,** keep it and bear fruit with **patience** (endurance).*

Patience is required to reap a harvest. There is a space of time between the planting and the production. Our part is to wait patiently for the harvest and to care for the soil and the growing seedling or plant. There is nothing we can do to make the seed have life. The life is put into the seed by God, and He causes it to sprout and grow. We can and must however, provide the proper atmosphere, nutrients, and care for the seed to grow to fruition.

This means holding on to the idea or vision— even when we cannot see anything with our natural eye that indicates the idea is growing. The larger the idea or vision, the longer the gestation period. A large

work like a large animal or plant takes much longer. A chicken is birthed in only three weeks and is fully grown in about twelve weeks. A human baby is birthed in nine months and takes about twenty years to be fully grown. You can grow a radish in the garden in a few weeks; an oak tree will take many years. The vision may die if we abandon it. Many worthy works planted in man's heart by God may have failed to come to fruition because they were prematurely abandoned. If a brood hen sitting on eggs leaves the nest even one day too soon, the chicks in the eggs will all die.

Just as a natural gardener works to care for the soil, keeping it loosened so it will not become too hard for the seed to grow, we must keep our heart-soil tender by forgiving and receiving healing for all offenses that could press down and harden our heart. The soil must be kept moist and the temperature in the proper range by the presence of the Holy Spirit. We must keep the weeds of useless words (bad seeds) out of our soil. Useless negative words or thoughts will grow weeds that will rob the nutrients from the good seed and keep them from growing as they should.

We must not only allow time for growth, we must also allow space. Seeds that are going to produce a large plant will require more space in the soil of our heart. Planting too many seeds in too small a space will cause them to grow improperly and bear little or no fruit. After the plants are up and growing, it may be necessary to pull up some of them so that there will be adequate space for growth. With some plants, it will be necessary to prune or trim the limbs to provide space on the plant for good fruit to grow.

Keeping the weeds out means taking every thought captive. We must remove the thoughts that would hinder the growth of the vision. Negative thoughts of doubt, worry, and fear will choke the vision. The enemy of the vision will always try to plant the seed that "you cannot do it", that "you are just not capable enough to do whatever God has said". And he is exactly right. We cannot do it. We are not supposed to be able to do it. **God does it!** We must hear, believe, and obey what God tells us to do next. **The earth brings forth the crop by itself.**

Thinning the plants means that we may need to lay down some really good ideas in order to concentrate on the more important vision. Our heart-soil just is not big enough and enriched enough to bring forth all the good ideas in the world at one time. If there are too many ideas or visions in one heart, none of them will grow well.

Trimming and pruning branches means cutting off excessive or wild growth of the vision. Too many branches on a fruit tree may cause the fruit to be small, and may cause disease because sunlight cannot enter. Branches that are too long or improperly shaped may break when the fruit nears maturity. We may need to limit some of the parts of the idea or vision.

**We are the manager of our garden.** What we decide to hear, what we believe, what and how we think, are the seeds that will produce our life. Poor thinking will always produce poor life. Quality thinking will always produce quality life. The difference in the man who tries hard but always accomplishes little and the man who can do great things is what they each hear and believe—in other words, how they manage their gardens. All of those seemingly unrelated negative events that consistently happen to the poor man are all the product of seeds growing to fruition. All of those seemingly unrelated doors of opportunity and bless-

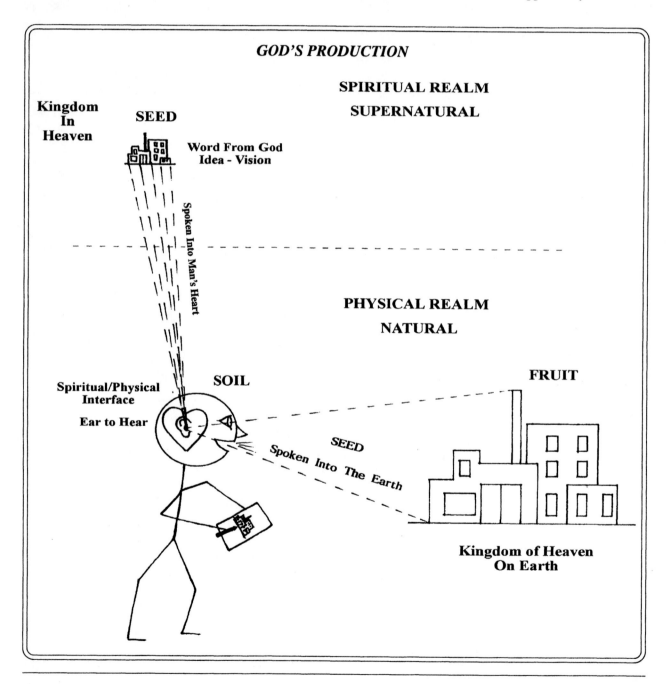

ings that consistently come to the prospering man are also the results of seeds. Nothing happens until somebody believes something.

Remember, **"the earth yields crops by itself". We cannot make growth,** but we must care for the soil, thin and trim the plants, protect the seedling from a hostile environment, pull the weeds, and above all, keep the soil moist with the presence of the Holy Spirit through prayer. **Communing with God in prayer, and meditating the word (vision, seed) in the Holy Spirit, is the process by which the natural growth and eventual harvest will come.**

Prayer and meditation is speaking to and hearing God. Speaking to and hearing God does not involve audible words, only. Communing with God involves speaking and hearing pictures and feelings. It is seeing what God is saying, experiencing in the spiritual realm what God desires to bring into the natural realm. One must come to a quiet place where the thoughts and distractions of the world can be closed out. Close your eyes, quiet your soul, and seek to enter into the presence of the Father. Ask God what He wants to do with your life and wait before Him quietly. When you have a word, a vision from God, meditate it in your spiritual mind. Look at it, understand it, get to know it. See it happening. Feel how it feels. Then pray the vision back to God. With the vision in your spirit, go to Him and ask Him to give you the vision He has shown you. Daily continue this praying. You will find that the vision will change some; it will become more detailed with a little more of this and a little less of that, as God continues to clarify the vision in you.

You are now pregnant with the word from God. The vision is now alive within you. Allow yourself to become excited as you feel the first movements of the living vision within you. Original creation is now beginning to be reshaped as the vision in the spiritual realm begins to impact the physical realm. All over the world things may begin to move or adjust in order to set the stage to bring about the vision from God that is in your heart.

Next begin to speak the vision out loud into the earth. Share it with those who can hear. Let your enthusiasm for the vision come forth as you speak it to others. You may need to begin writing it down or sketching it out on paper. Don't be alarmed if the vision is a thousand times greater than you think possible. Remember it is God's baby; He will bring it to birth.

Be faithful to pray the vision and be ready to take whatever next step the Lord will show you. Wait and watch for the opportunities and circumstances that in time will appear before you to birth the vision.

## GOD'S PRODUCTION

Man is made in the image of God to rule the earth. God blessed man to be fruitful, to fill the earth and subdue it, to have dominion. It is God's desire that the earth be ruled according to His plan. Man has the potential to grow the seed of God, or the seed of the enemy. Only man has the God-given position to rule the earth. Only man has the potent heart-soil that is the interface between the spiritual realm and the physical realm.

*Genesis 1:27-28: So God created man in His own image; in the image of God He created him; male and female He created them. Then God blessed them, and God said to them, "Be fruitful and multiply; fill the earth and subdue it; have dominion over the fish of the sea, over the birds of the air, and over every living thing that moves on the earth."*

After our hearts are seeded with the plan of God, then **we become seeds sown into the world** to bear fruit, to bring forth the plan of God on Earth. We are at the end of the age. The good news of the kingdom is being preached; the rule of God is coming forth on Earth; pure-hearted sons of God are bringing forth the plan of God on our planet now. The sons of the wicked are being removed now from the kingdom of God and cast into fire. They will repent and be purified or continue in the fiery judgment of God. Then the pure-hearted sons of God, bearing His plan, will shine forth on Planet Earth.

*Matthew 13:24-30,37-43: Another parable He put forth to them, saying, "The kingdom of heaven is like a man who sowed good seed in his field; but while men slept, his enemy came and sowed tares among the wheat and went his way. But when the grain had sprouted and produced a crop, then the tares also appeared. So the servants of the owner came and said to him, 'Sir, did you not sow good seed in your field? How then does it have tares?'*

*"He said to them, 'An enemy has done this.' The servants said to him, 'Do you want us then to go gather them up?' But he said, 'No, lest while you gather up*

*the tares, you also uproot the wheat with them. Let both grow together until the harvest, and at the time of harvest I will say to the reapers, "First gather together the tares and bind them in bundles to burn them, but gather the wheat into my barn."'"*

*He (Jesus) answered and said to them: "He who sows the good seed is the Son of Man. **The field is the world, the good seeds are the sons of the kingdom, but the tares are the sons of the wicked one.** The enemy who sowed them is the devil, the harvest is the end of the age, and the reapers are the angels.*

*"Therefore as the **tares are gathered and burned in the fire,** so it will be at the end of this age. The Son of Man will send out His angels, and **they will gather out of His kingdom all things that offend, and those who practice lawlessness,** and will cast them into the furnace of fire. There will be wailing and gnashing of teeth. Then the righteous will shine forth as the sun in the **kingdom of their Father.** He who has ears to hear, let him hear!"*

The first soil is the heart of man in which the seed of God's plan is sown. The second soil is the field of the world into which we are sown to produce God's plan which was sown into our heart. The field of the world is also sown with those who have had their heart sown with a different conflicting seed.

We are to keep the tares (weeds) from growing in our own heart-soil, but the scene has changed in this parable. We are no longer looking at the soil of our heart, but at the soil of the world. God, by his angels will remove the tares from the world. They are allowed to grow together for a season. The tare is a plant in the kingdom that does not produce good fruit.

Thank God for the purifying fire we are coming through. We are being cleansed and healed in our heart to become good soil, receive good seed, and become fruitful producers in the kingdom of God. **We cannot change our life by changing our actions.** We must clear the land of our heart and plant the word (plan) of God. **We must change what we hear and what we think,** which will change our attitudes and actions, which will change our destiny. We are not controlled by our circumstances; we are in control of our circumstances.

Someone once said, "The man with an experience is never at the mercy of a man with an argument." My own experience parallels that of every other man who has heard and employed this mystery. It is not possible to share with you the miraculous, overcoming experiences of my sixty-plus years, with over forty years seeking to serve the Lord. They would become other books of many pages. I have sought in this work to give to you the foundational core of truth and wisdom resulting from experiencing God and His word. For illustration's sake, let us take a few brief peeks into some small windows of experience. We will by no means set the stage or give the background or complete story, but just some window peeks.

In the late sixties, after beginning to hear the mystery of "as you believe, so be it unto you", I began to prosper and to be used in giving. Through a series of changes, I had left my first miraculously, prosperous job experience to manage a very small industrial-instrument sales company. Everything about the small company was minimal and poor. There were two employees. One was a middle-aged Indian lady who wore the same pillow-tick dress most everyday, ate a whole onion for lunch each day, and had a teenage son who slept in a coffin. The other employee was a young alcoholic man who had the top of his left ear bitten off in a bar fight. The previous owner/manager smoked cigars and spit on the floor. Total sales for the first month were about eleven thousand dollars at about twenty percent gross profit. That is about twenty two hundred dollars before wages and overhead, which left nothing for me.

There was no doubt, however, that God had put me there for a purpose. My life was to be dedicated at this time to giving money to the work of God in the world. God made it clear to me that this was what He wanted to do with this business endeavor. As I prayed, God began to give me visions of how the place and the business could be cleaned up and rearranged. I would see the changes in my heart and later look back upon what I had seen in the spirit which had come to pass and was functioning in the business.

I would ask God, "What do you want to do in sales this year?" I was usually shocked at first, as He revealed to me an amount that seemed, to my mind, far too great for the business to accomplish. Yet I had come to believe that God could do what He said. So I would get a piece of paper and draw a graph representing the increase that God had said. I had no idea at this point how this tremendous increase could occur. As I prayed, I would take that line on the graph to God and ask Him to give me that. I would meditate before Him the vision of that increase coming to pass. I let myself feel what it was like to actually experience the increase happening.

After only a few months, the Lord gave me the little company. I purchased it without any money and suddenly found myself for the first time totally responsible for a business. God began to reveal the vast unlimited potential of the situation. The whole world was a potential market place. All the products of the world were potential goods to be marketed. There was no one over me to say it could not be done. The only limitation was what God said, and what I believed.

I am convinced that most men have never really touched the potential of their lives. Most of us experience only the smallest fraction of what God would like to do with us. We have been so planted and trained with the limitations of natural thinking and dependency upon our natural selves that we have rarely touched the vast, unlimited, spiritual realm of ruling and reigning with God. God will do anything in our lives that He says and we believe.

As I continued to pray and meditate the vision before Him, God would give me creative ideas and specific instructions for the next step. One example of these ideas was the printing of a catalog. No distributor of industrial temperature and pressure instruments had ever printed their own catalog. All the distributors used the manufacturers' printed material. We printed our own stock catalog, listing and describing all of the particular items that we carried in local inventory. We did all the photography, type-setting, and layout ourselves in our own office. It was a new experience; none of us had any experience in such procedures. Some who worked on the little blue catalog were so proud of it that they didn't want to give them away to customers!

The idea worked and grew. The next catalog was the size of a telephone book and brought together a product mix that could not be had anywhere else.

Soon the Lord directed other divisions of the corporation and expansion into branch operations over the southwest United States market area that we served. We were among the first in our field to use WATTS telephone service for incoming sales calls across the nation. In only three years, God's little company had become a multi-million dollar corporation. We sought to employ only maturing Christians. Some actually got saved in the employment interview and went on to spend much of their working life serving the Lord in the company. Not only were significant amounts of money flowing through me personally into the work of God, but many of the employees tithed into churches and other ministries. Many were thankful to have a place to work where Christian values and morals were the norm.

I was never qualified to do this work. I had only a high school and some Bible college education. My work experience had been mostly in route sales, selling milk or bread on a commission basis. I worked exceptionally hard to earn commissions to provide for my five children. There was nothing in my background that said I could do this thing. But God said it and I believed it.

It takes courage to hear God and obey what He says. I can recall occasions when God would tell me something to do. Sometimes it didn't seem to make much sense according to the facts as we knew them at the time. It was even more difficult for some of my business associates to accept some of the actions. Later, some of them came to me and said something like, "How did you know these things were going to happen?" The seemingly unreasonable actions we had taken earlier all made perfect sense as new developments occurred, and we were sitting in exactly the right place at the right time to benefit. I would simply reply, "I didn't know. I was just obeying God."

# CHAPTER 28

## THE BANK OF HEAVEN
### (UNIVERSAL RECIPROCITY)

The Bank of Heaven is the only completely secure bank. All other banks could fail, but our deposits are secure in God's bank. Just as a natural bank is a place where we deposit our money or treasures until we call for them, so the bank of heaven is a depository for our treasures until we call for them. "Someone" would like for us to believe that we cannot make withdrawals from the bank of heaven now—that we must wait until we die and go to heaven to have any use of our account in heaven. That someone wants us to believe that everything about heaven pertains to later, and not now. But this would be just like the bank forbidding us the use of our checking account. Yes, we are to lay up our treasures in heaven, and not on earth. But where does Scripture say that we must die and go to heaven to receive from them.?

*Matthew 6:19-20: "Do not lay up for yourselves treasures on earth, where moth and rust destroy and where thieves break in and steal; but lay up for yourselves treasures in heaven, where neither moth nor rust destroy and where thieves do not break in and steal."*

God's **"storehouse"** is the "Bank of Heaven", and when we make the proper deposits, He opens the **"bank window"** of heaven and pours out a blessing. God oversees the **book of remembrance** (our bank book). Our bank account will be kept accurately.

*Malachi 3:10,16: "Bring all the tithes into the storehouse, that there may be food in My house, and prove Me now in this", says the Lord of hosts, "if I will not open for you the windows of heaven and pour out for you such blessing that there will not be room enough to receive it." So a book of remembrance was written before Him for those who fear the Lord and who meditate on His name.*

*Philippians. 4:17: Not that I seek the gift, but I seek the fruit that abounds to your account.*

*Matthew 19:21: Jesus said to him, "If you want to be perfect, go sell what you have and give to the poor, and you will have treasure in heaven; and come, follow Me."*

*1 Peter 1:4: ...to an inheritance incorruptible and undefiled and that does not fade away, reserved in heaven for you.*

## SOWING AND REAPING

One of the major banking laws governing the business activities of the "Universal Bank of Heaven" is the universal law of **Sowing** and **Reaping.** In the realm of physics, this law may be expressed by man as the law of "cause and effect". Isaac Newton said, "For every action, there is an equal and opposite reaction." In the realm of finance, one might refer to it as the law of "investment and return". The preacher might express it as "giving and receiving". The farmer would speak of "planting and harvesting". In any case, the law always involves a costly sowing process. We must take what we have and plant it. We may really desire to eat it and meet our immediate need, but we know there will be no harvest if we do not plant.

*Psalm 126:5-6: Those who sow in tears shall reap in joy. He who continually goes forth weeping, bearing seed for sowing, shall doubtless come again with rejoicing, bringing his sheaves with him.*

*Galatians 6:7-10: Do not be deceived, God is not mocked; for whatever a man sows, that he will also reap. For he who sows to his flesh will of the flesh reap corruption, but he who sows to the Spirit will of the Spirit reap everlasting life. And let us not grow weary while doing good, for in due season we shall reap if we do not lose heart. Therefore, as we have opportunity, let us do good to all, especially to those who are of the household of faith.*

We will reap what we sow, if we don't faint. We must remain until harvest time. All sowing requires a period of natural growth before harvest. If we, for any reason, lose patience and leave or quit before the harvest time, we will miss the harvest. Man does not decide when it is harvest time; the crop does. But we must be available to put in the sickle immediately when the harvest time comes.

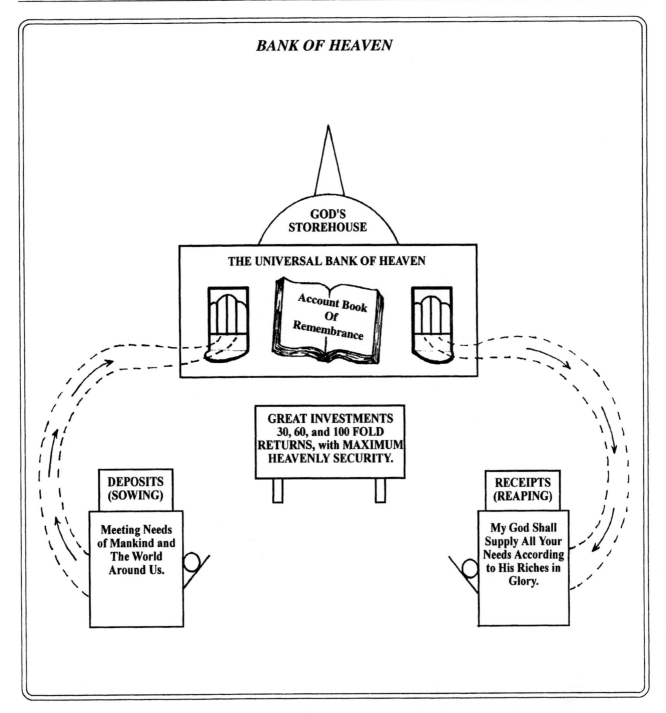

**GOD'S STOREHOUSE**

**THE UNIVERSAL BANK OF HEAVEN**

Account Book Of Remembrance

**GREAT INVESTMENTS 30, 60, and 100 FOLD RETURNS, with MAXIMUM HEAVENLY SECURITY.**

**DEPOSITS (SOWING)**

Meeting Needs of Mankind and The World Around Us.

**RECEIPTS (REAPING)**

My God Shall Supply All Your Needs According to His Riches in Glory.

No one can reap until someone has sown. To look for a harvest without sowing means we are looking to eat from what someone else has sown. This is borrowing and must be paid back at some time; the books will be balanced. To continue to borrow (seeking to reap without sowing) will put us further and further in debt and into the bondage of poverty. It's much the same as if we continued to borrow money from a natural bank, but made no payments.

We are to sow ("doing good") to all, but especially to those of the household of faith. The more we can do to really meet the needs of God's people and all men, the more we will reap. Helping to provide food for people by farming, processing, or distributing, is sowing. Using what we have to clean clothes, furnish clean water, furnish good housing, furnish transportation, medical services, and so on, are forms of meeting needs. The greatest need that mankind has is to be rightly related to God. Preaching and teaching the Word of God, bringing forth the ministry of Jesus by the Holy Spirit to save, heal and deliver is one area of meeting human needs. The more we can do to establish systems or provide resources to accomplish these things, the more we will reap.

*2 Corinthians 9:6-12: But this I say: "He who sows sparingly will also reap sparingly, and he **who sows bountifully will also reap bountifully**. So let each one give as he purposes in his heart, not grudgingly or of necessity; for God loves a cheerful giver. And God is able to make all grace abound toward you, that you, always having all sufficiency in all things, have an **abundance for every good** <u>**work**</u>. As it is written: 'He has dispersed abroad, He has given to the poor; His righteousness remains forever.'" Now may He who supplies **seed** to the sower, and **bread** for food, **supply and multiply** the seed you have sown and **increase** the fruits of your righteousness, while you are enriched in everything for all liberality, which causes thanksgiving through us to God. For the administration of this service not only supplies the needs of the saints, but also is abounding through many thanksgivings to God.*

*Hebrews 6:10: For God is not unjust to forget your **work and labor of love** which you have shown toward His name, in that you have **ministered to the saints, and do minister.***

Who can meet more needs for mankind, the skilled or the unskilled, the diligent or the slothful, those with Godly wisdom or the unwise, the one who cares for others or the one who cares only for himself, the one who receives wise counsel or the one who hears only himself, the one who labors or the one who talks idly? The one who meets more needs is making more deposits and subsequently will reap more from the Bank of Heaven.

It is not necessary that men know of the good that we do to benefit others. The reward does not depend on men. It depends on God and His accounting and reward system in Heaven. We will be rewarded openly for using what we have to meet the needs of others in secret. Prayer and fasting also make a deposit in the Bank of Heaven. Anything that meets human need, especially the needs of the brethren, makes a deposit.

*Matthew 6:1-4,6,17-18: "Take heed that you do not do your charitable deeds before men, to be seen by them. Otherwise you have no reward from your Father in Heaven. Therefore, when you do a charitable deed, do not sound a trumpet before you as the hypocrites do in the synagogues and in the streets, that they may have glory from men. Assuredly, I say to you, they have their reward. But when you do a **charitable deed,** do not let your left hand know what you right hand is doing, that your charitable deed may be in secret; and your **Father who sees in secret will Himself reward you openly.**" "But you when you **pray,** go into your room, and when you have shut your door, pray to your Father who is in the secret place; and your **Father who sees in secret will reward you openly.**" "But you, when you **fast,** anoint your head and wash your face, so that you do not appear to men to be fasting, but to your **Father who is in the secret place; and your Father who sees in secret will reward you openly.**"*

Giving to a church or other organizations **that are meeting human needs** makes a deposit. Investing in a company that is **meeting human needs** makes a deposit.

The amount of return is based on the net value produced. It costs something to maintain our life and any system of endeavor. The net product is what is left of the value we added, after we subtract the value that we consumed or used.

There is positive and negative sowing. If we do good to one person, but take away from another person, the value added to mankind is lessened by the amount of negative we sowed. If we go out to help the world, but offend our own children, we may take away as much or more than we deposited. The net value added to mankind is our deposit in the Bank of Heaven. If we have not been giving to God by adding value to mankind, but consuming all God has given us, we may be robbing God; robbing the bank of heaven.

*Malachi 3:8-9: "Will a man rob God? Yet you have robbed Me! But you say, 'In what way have we robbed You?'" "In tithes and offerings. You are cursed with a curse, **for you have robbed Me, even this whole nation.**"*

Jesus said that when we give to the brethren, we give to Him. We give to God by giving to others. Our gift to a church or organization is a gift to God only if the organization or church is meeting people's needs.

# CHAPTER 29

## THE THIRD GREATEST MYSTERY
### (GOD IS GOOD)

Everything God is doing, has ever done, or ever will do, is good. God never has done anything bad and never will do anything bad. Because God is good, there is hope. **Hope is the essence of positive believing**, the light for the future, and the beginning of joy.

If, for any reason, we think we have seen God do something bad, we are wrong. Our perspective is not in order. Our goals are not God's goals. Our purpose is not God's purpose. All things are good if we are in line with His purposes.

*Romans 8:28: And we know that all things work together for **good** to those who love God, to those who are the called **according to His purpose**.*

Our extremely limited view from our human position in life gives us a false perspective of good and bad. What may appear to us as a very bad happening would be seen as good if understood in the full scope of God's plan and the total situation and circumstances.

As an example, the Bible records many incidents of entire nations of people, including women and children, being destroyed by God or at His direction. Some may see this as a very bad act of God. But if they understood the full impact that sparing them would have upon the plan of God and His children in the future, they could see the love and goodness of God in the act. The continued multiplication of an evil tribe could have had a devastating effect upon millions in the future. Only God could know how sparing them would have a future tragic impact upon the world.

One error often made by Christians today is to ascribe every act that looks bad to them to the devil, and every act that looks good to them to God. To blame the devil for every act that we consider to be bad is foolishness. To do so, one must esteem the devil equal with God. The devil can do nothing that is not allowed by God. And everything God allows is good. Only God can see the astronomical myriad of all events and their impact upon one another and the entire plan of God for the world. Therefore, only God can accurately determine what is good and what is bad in the full scope of

considering all things now, in the future, and in eternity.

*Job 2:10: But he said to her, "You speak as one of the foolish women speaks. **Shall we indeed accept good from God, and shall we not accept adversity?"** In all this Job did not sin with his lips.*

*2 Corinthians 1:18-20: But as God is faithful, our word to you was not "Yes" and "No". For the son of God, Jesus Christ, who was preached among you by us-by me, Silvanus, and Timothy-was **not "Yes and No"**, but in Him was "Yes". **For all the promises of God in Him are "Yes"**, and in Him Amen, to the glory of God through us.*

God is only positive. There is nothing negative in God at all. If God did not provide judgment or chastening for man's evil actions, but instead rewarded man with health, prosperity, and good fortune for his evil deeds, He would not be a good God. Everything God does is positive in that it all moves toward the ultimate plan of God. All systems of creation are designed by God to arrive at the ultimate goal that He has in mind.

Man is given dominion on the earth, but he will not prosper in his journey until he moves into the plan of God. But, even the lack of prospering is good, because it brings the out-of-order person toward order with God's plan.

**God has only good in mind for mankind.** God's plan is the beautiful New Jerusalem lifestyle of peace and prosperity. God has no negative plan for man. His idea is one hundred percent perfect for man. He planned no sickness nor disorder of any kind for man.

**Man is the one who decides to come up with another plan.** It is man who decides to disobey God and eat from the tree of knowledge of good and evil, (seeking to know what is good and bad from our perspective), rather than the tree of life, (seeking to hear from God, from His perspective). Man's alternate plans lead to chastening from God. The result is built into the system of universal law from God, and leads toward death, (separation from God and His benefits). Even the chastening of the Lord is positive and gives us hope of attaining God's plan.

*Ezekiel 18:20a: "The soul who sins shall die."*

*Romans 6:23:* ***For the wages of sin is death,*** *but the gift of God is eternal life in Christ Jesus our Lord.*

*Hebrews 12 5b-6: My son, do not despise the chastening of the Lord; nor be discouraged when you are rebuked by Him; for whom the Lord loves He chastens, and scourges every son whom He receives.*

*1 Corinthians 11:31-32: For if we would judge ourselves, we would not be judged. But when we are judged,* ***we are chastened by the Lord,*** *that we may not be condemned with the world.*

*Hebrews 12:11: Now no chastening seems to be joyful for the present, but grievous; nevertheless, afterward it yields the peaceable fruit of righteousness to those who have been trained by it.*

God is able to deliver the righteous and protect them from judgment, as He did with Lot in Sodom and Gomorrah. But even Lot was affected by the evil of the land. He, at the very least, endured serious inconvenience because of the corporate living apart from God's plan.

*2 Peter 2:4-10: For if God did not spare the angels who sinned, but cast them down to hell and delivered them into chains of darkness, to be reserved for judgment; and did not spare the ancient world, but saved Noah, one of eight people, a preacher of righteousness, bringing in the flood on the world of the ungodly; and* ***turning the cities of Sodom and Gomorrah into ashes, condemned them to destruction,*** *making them an example to those who afterward would live ungodly; and* ***delivered righteous Lot, who was oppressed*** *with the filthy conduct of the wicked (for the righteous man, dwelling among them,* ***vexed [tormented] his righteous soul*** *from day to day by seeing and hearing their lawless deeds)-then* ***the Lord knows how to deliver the godly*** *out of temptations and to reserve the unjust under punishment for judgment, and especially those who walk according to the flesh in the lust of uncleanness and despise authority. They are presumptuous, self-willed; they are not afraid to speak evil of glories (dignitaries).*

Though the righteous are delivered, they may yet endure oppression because of the evil around them. Collectively man is tied together in families, communities, nations, and the world. Each individual will bear, to some degree, the responsibility for the life decisions of the whole. Everyone in the U.S.A. will be affected by the cost of major diseases such as aids. Some less guilty persons may contract the disease and die, simply because we are tied together. We are foremost affected by our own life decisions; and secondly, we are greatly affected by our family; and, decreasingly, less affected by our community, nation, and world. Even the whole world is in some way affected by every person's decision not to live according to God's plan.

Conversely, the entire world is in some way affected by our decision to live according to God's plan. We first have the most effect upon our own life; secondly, we have a great effect upon our family; and decreasingly have less effect upon our community, nation, and the world. But we do have an effect on every person in the world.

The violent destruction of all the little girls and boys along with their parents in Sodom and Gomorrah was good and not bad. God was responsible for the actual act of raining fire and brimstone, not the devil. Man caused it to happen by accepting the devil's alternate plan and leaving God's plan. The **bad part was man's leaving God's plan.** God, however, was good in destroying those who did. If God had rewarded them with prosperity, posterity, and longevity, He would not be a good God.

*Psalm 106: l: Praise the Lord! Oh give thanks to the Lord, for He is good! For his mercy endures forever.*

God is good and His mercies endure forever. The mercy of God is available to all, and the chastening of the Lord will cause us to turn to His mercy. His grace can then empower us from within to live in God's pattern and plan. We can then participate in His beautiful holiness and peace. The kingdom of God is righteousness, peace, and joy in the Holy Spirit.

Thank you, God, for your goodness! And thank you, God, for loving us enough to cause us to change! Thank you for our great hope for the future and our great joy for today!

## GOD IS HAPPY

Even the darkest night can be endured by hope. **Because God is good, hope continues** until morning. Hope gives peace in the dark night and joy in the bright morning.

*Psalm 30:5b: Weeping may endure for a night, but joy comes in the morning.*

*Psalm 34:19: Many are the afflictions of the righteous, but God delivers him out of them all.*

If God were not good, hope would not exist in the darkness of trials and difficulties. Rejection, persecution, and affliction would overwhelm and defeat even the righteous in the dark night.

Happiness is a pleasurable state of mind. The World seeks to produce happiness through an arrangement of external circumstances to stimulate pleasurable feelings and emotions. Real happiness is from within the believer, from God, who is happy.

**To seek to be happy apart from love, faith, and hope is futile.** The one who knows God's love personally is not at all dependent upon circumstances for peace and joy. Rather than being overcome by circumstances, he will impact and overcome the circumstances with his inner peace and joy.

**Praise is the embodiment and expression of love, faith, hope, peace and joy.** As we praise God, we reflect and express positive, affirming, gratifying life to God. As we praise His children, our brothers and sisters, we praise God Himself, and "flow" life-edification to the person.

*Matthew 25:40: "And the King will answer and say to them, 'Assuredly, I say to you, inasmuch as you did it to one of the least of these My brethren, you did it to Me.'"*

God inhabits His praises. God is in praise. Praise comes from God within our heart as He produces love, faith, hope, peace, and joy. Where there is no reality of God within, there is no real praise. There is nothing negative in God. There is nothing negative in praise. And there is no praise in negativity or criticism. WE CANNOT PRAISE GOD AND CRITICIZE HIS CHILDREN! Criticism and negativity destroys hope. It is not ever of God and will always defer hope, which leads to sickness and death, not well-being and life.

*Proverbs 13:12a: Hope deferred makes the heart sick.*

*Proverbs 17:29a: A merry heart does good, like a medicine.*

The positive force of praise cannot be faked. It must come from a pure, sincere heart. Only after love, faith, and hope has done its work, can sincere praise come forth. One may speak and act words of praise with a negative, critical heart, but the words will come out only as phony, cheap flattery. The words will still carry the sting of death and will not edify. It is futile for a person or group to seek to enter into high praises to God without first experiencing true repentance, cleansing, and healing.

There is nothing on earth more beautiful, more gratifying, and fulfilling than to enter into true praise and worship with an assembly of pure-hearted children of God. God does inhabit His praises.

---

*1 Corinthians 13:13: And now abide faith, hope, love, these three; but the greatest of these is love.*

**LOVE**, "The Greatest Mystery", produces righteousness.

**FAITH,** "The Second Greatest Mystery", produces power.

**HOPE**, "The Third Greatest Mystery", produces **peace, joy, and PRAISE.**

---

*Psalm 150: Praise the Lord! Praise God in His sanctuary. Praise Him in His mighty firmament (expanse of heaven)! Praise Him for His mighty acts. Praise Him according to His excellent greatness! Praise Him with the sound of the trumpet. Praise Him with the lute and harp! Praise Him with the timbrel and dance. Praise Him with stringed instruments and flutes! Praise Him with loud cymbals. Praise Him with high sounding cymbals! Let everything that has breath praise the Lord. Praise the Lord!*

Happiness is praising and worshipping God with our whole heart, our whole life, in all we do or say, every hour of every day.

161

# CHAPTER 30

## WHAT NOW?

### *(EPILOGUE)*

If the Spirit of God has worked in your life while you studied this material, as He worked in my life during the sixty-plus years of living, preparation and writing it, then you are being formed into His jewel.

*Malachi 3:17-18:* *"They shall be Mine,"* says the Lord of hosts, *"on the day that I make them **My jewels**. And I will spare them as a man spares his own son who serves him. **Then you shall again discern between the righteous and the wicked,** between one who serves God and one who does not serve Him."*

Your heart has been further purified; your motives are more pure and more holy. You will find a new level of real discernment, an ability to discern between the righteous and the wicked. Follow that discernment. Keep moving toward the light. Do not look to the right or the left, but follow that pure discernment within you. Do not compromise, and you will not loose your spiritual sensitivity.

Continue to seek further purification of your inner motives. Continue in forgiveness and healing within your heart. Continue to grow in faith and love. Live continuously in thanksgiving and praise. Let your life be a living sacrifice to God by giving up whatever is necessary to remain in intimacy with God continuosly. Seek Him in prayer, meditation, and His Word. Feed on the word of God; ask God to reveal it to your heart and wait on Him. Continue with those of like precious faith and do not become unequally yoked.

Above all, be careful not to judge. You will now be able to discern between those who serve only God and those who partially serve Him. **DO NOT JUDGE** those who are not yet purified. Continue to submit where God has planted you. Pray for those in authority over you and respect them greatly.

If God desires for you to make changes, He can tell you. You must not partake of the tree of knowledge and reason it out for yourself. Love one another with a pure heart.

Seek to build the principles you've learned into your life. It's not just what we know that brings Godly prosperity; it's what we do with it that really counts. When we are living the things God has given us, He will give us more. Review and meditate the truths and principles you have read in this work. You may find as much or more the second and third time you review this material. Your heart may be more receptive than the first time you read it.

Let the love of Jesus rise up within you greatly to love those who persecute you. Buffeting will come to you because of the revelation you've received. The greater the revelation is, the greater the buffeting will be. **(R = B.)** The messengers of Satan will come to test you and, if possible, to steal the revelation, but **it will only serve to increase your love and strengthen your faith.**

*2 Corinthians 12:7:* *"And lest I should be exalted above measure by the **abundance of the revelations**....a messenger of Satan to buffet me, lest I be exalted above measure.*

Every kick on the shin, every rejection, every time your pure motives are misunderstood, there is another opportunity for the love of Jesus to manifest within you and flow out as the joy of the Lord fills your heart and life. Let that love flow to everyone around you. The flow of love will cause an unreasonable joy and peace to fill your life. Your health and happiness will be improved by the abundance of peace.

*Matthew 5:44:* *"But I say unto you **love your enemies,** bless those who curse you, do good to those who hate you, and pray for those who spitefully use you and persecute you."*

You have not yet arrived; but are on a marvelous adventurous journey. You are a part of the generation actually experiencing the kingdom of heaven on Planet Earth. You will see marvelous and severe events take place as the will of God from Heaven comes forth on Earth.

One of the results of increased purification in the heart is an increase in spiritual insight and discernment of the times. You will be able to see in more spiritual depth; able to understand what is below the surface or behind what is happening. Your expanded understanding will allow you to be more effective in being the part of the kingdom God has designed you to be. Continue to seek the kingdom of God and his righteous ways of doing and being. Wisdom will continue to grow within you as you seek His righteous ways.

The things written in this work have had a very great impact upon my own life. Yet they, all taken together, are only the smallest beginning of the principles, understanding, and wisdom of the kingdom of God. Much Bible truth has been veiled to us in the past because of a lack of revelation of the kingdom, and therefore subject to misinterpretation. We will now be able to gain more understanding of the Bible as we allow the Holy Spirit to teach us more perfectly the meaning of the Scriptures. Particularly as we go back to the original Greek and Hebrew words and hear their meaning in light of kingdom revelation. We believe God will cause various men to bring forth many works to further proclaim the "gospel of the kingdom" and teach the Scriptures without the veils of the past.

We also believe God is directing us personally to write and publish additional volumes of specific studies of the Bible. Therefore our intention at this time is to make available as soon as possible studies of the Scripture with an emphasis on examining the original language in the light of the revelation of the kingdom. Our preparation for this new work to this point has been very exciting and revealing.

# NOTES